# Business Guide to Western Europe

## Volume 3

*Business Guides to the World*™

The Internationalist Publishing Company
96 Walter Street, Suite 200
Boston, MA 02131

The Internationalist Business Guide to Western Europe
Volume 3 of 6 volume Business Guides to the World™

Edited by Patrick W. Nee

The Internationalist Publishing Company
96 Walter Street, Suite 200
Boston, MA 02131
(617) 570-0810

ISBN 0-9633905-3-8

A  B  C  D  E  F  G  H  I  J

# *The Internationalist*

## Table of Contents

## Introduction

The *Internationalist® Business Guides* for executives and investors contain the essential, core information about countries around the world. They include information about the economics of a country, its infrastructure, people, government and geography. The data has been compiled from the most authoritative government sources.

The Guides have been designed for ease of use by the busy executive or investor. The Guides are divided into six economic/geographic regions. Information is simply and precisely presented. The compact size permits use when traveling on international business. Important telephone numbers are included.

Fast moving political or economic events may affect certain elements of a country's situation, however, the basic underlying facts about a country remain constant. Those basic facts are what are covered by the guides.

# COUNTRIES

# AUSTRIA

150 km

## Economy

**Overview:** Austria boasts a prosperous and stable socialist market economy with a sizable but falling proportion of nationalized industry and extensive welfare benefits. Thanks to its raw material endowment, a technically skilled labor force, and strong links to German industrial firms, Austria occupies specialized niches in European industry and services (tourism, banking) and produces almost enough food to feed itself with only 8% of the labor force in agriculture. Increased export sales resulting from German unification, boosted Austria's economy through 1991, but Austria's GDP growth slowed to 2% in 1992 and -0.5% in 1993 due to the weak international economy, particularly in Germany—its largest trading partner. GDP growth will resume slowly in 1994, with estimates ranging from a 0.5% to a 1% increase. Unemployment has risen to 7% as a result of the slowdown and will continue to rise in 1994. Problems for the 1990s include an aging population, the high level of subsidies, and the struggle to keep welfare benefits within budgetary capabilities. Austria's government has taken measures to make the economy more liberal and open by introducing a major tax reform, privatizing state-owned firms, and liberalizing cross-border capital movements. Although it will face increased competition, Austria should benefit from the continued opening of eastern European markets, as well as the 1 January 1994 start of the European Economic Area which extends the European Union rules on the free movement of people, capital, and goods and services to four members (including Austria) of the European Free Trade Association (EFTA). Austria has concluded membership negotiations with the European Union and is expected to join in early 1995, thus broadening European economic unity. The government, however, plans to hold a national referendum on the matter on 12 June 1994; support for and opposition to membership appears about equal.

**National product:** GDP—purchasing power equivalent—$134.4 billion (1993)

**National product real growth rate:** -0.5% (1993)

**National product per capita:** $17,000 (1993)

**Inflation rate (consumer prices):** 3.7% (1993 est.)

**Unemployment rate:** 7% (1993 est.)

**Budget:**

*revenues:* $52.2 billion

*expenditures:* $60.3 billion, including capital expenditures of $NA (1993 est.)

**Exports:** $39.9 billion (f.o.b., 1993)

*commodities:* machinery and equipment, iron and steel, lumber, textiles, paper products, chemicals

*partners:* EC 63.5% (Germany 38.9%), EFTA 9.0%, Eastern Europe/FSU 12.3%, Japan 1.5%, US 3.35% (1993)

**Imports:** $48.5 billion (f.o.b., 1993)

*commodities:* petroleum, foodstuffs, machinery and equipment, vehicles, chemicals, textiles and clothing, pharmaceuticals

*partners:* EC 66.8% (Germany 41.3%), EFTA 6.7%, Eastern Europe/FSU 7.5%, Japan 4.4%, US 4.4% (1993)
**External debt:** $16.2 billion (1993 est.)
**Industrial production:** growth rate -4.5% (1993 est.)
**Electricity:**
*capacity:* 17,600,000 kW
*production:* 49.5 billion kWh
*consumption per capita:* 6,300 kWh (1992)
**Industries:** foods, iron and steel, machines, textiles, chemicals, electrical, paper and pulp, tourism, mining, motor vehicles
**Agriculture:** accounts for 3.2% of GDP (including forestry); principal crops and animals—grains, fruit, potatoes, sugar beets, sawn wood, cattle, pigs, poultry; 80-90% self-sufficient in food
**Illicit drugs:** transshipment point for Southwest Asian heroin transiting the Balkan route and Eastern Europe
**Economic aid:**
*donor:* ODA and OOF commitments (1970-89), $2.4 billion
**Currency:** 1 Austrian schilling (S) = 100 groschen
**Exchange rates:** Austrian schillings (S) per US$1—12.255 (January 1994), 11.632 (1993), 10.989 (1992), 11.676 (1991), 11.370 (1990), 13.231 (1989)

**Fiscal year:** calendar year

---

**Communications**

**Railroads:** 5,749 km total; 5,652 km government owned and 97 km privately owned (0.760-, 1.435- and 1.000-meter gauge); 5,394 km 1.435-meter standard gauge of which 3,154 km is electrified and 1,520 km is double tracked; 339 km 0.760-meter narrow gauge of which 84 km is electrified
**Highways:**
*total:* 95,412 km
*paved:* 21,812 km (including 1,012 km of autobahn)
*unpaved:* mostly gravel and earth 73,600 km
**Inland waterways:** 446 km
**Pipelines:** crude oil 554 km; natural gas 2,611 km; petroleum products 171 km

**Ports:** Vienna, Linz (Danube river ports)
**Merchant marine:** 29 ships (1,000 GRT or over) totaling 158,724 GRT/259,594 DWT, cargo 23, refrigerated cargo 2, oil tanker 1, bulk 3
**Airports:**
*total:* 55
*usable:* 55
*with permanent-surface runways:* 20
*with runways over 3,659 m:* 0
*with runways 2,440-3,659 m:* 6
*with runways 1,220-2,439 m:* 4
**Telecommunications:** highly developed and efficient; 4,014,000 telephones; broadcast stations—6 AM, 21 (545 repeaters) FM, 47 (870 repeaters) TV; satellite ground stations for Atlantic Ocean INTELSAT, Indian Ocean INTELSAT, and EUTELSAT systems

---

**Defense Forces**

**Branches:** Army (including Flying Division)
**Manpower availability:** males age 15-49 2,018,954; fit for military service 1,693,341; reach military age (19) annually 48,710 (1994 est.)
**Defense expenditures:** exchange rate conversion—$1.7 billion, 0.9% of GDP (1993 est.)

---

**Geography**

**Location:** Central Europe, between Germany and Hungary
**Map references:** Africa, Arctic Region, Europe, Standard Time Zones of the World
**Area:**
*total area:* 83,850 sq km
*land area:* 82,730 sq km
*comparative area:* slightly smaller than Maine
**Land boundaries:** total 2,496 km, Czech Republic 362 km, Germany 784 km, Hungary 366 km, Italy 430 km, Liechtenstein 37 km, Slovakia 91 km, Slovenia 262 km, Switzerland 164 km
**Coastline:** 0 km (landlocked)
**Maritime claims:** none; landlocked
**International disputes:** none
**Climate:** temperate; continental, cloudy; cold winters with frequent rain in lowlands and

snow in mountains; cool summers with occasional showers
**Terrain:** in the west and south mostly mountains (Alps); along the eastern and northern margins mostly flat or gently sloping
**Natural resources:** iron ore, petroleum, timber, magnesite, aluminum, lead, coal, lignite, copper, hydropower
**Land use:**
*arable land:* 17%
*permanent crops:* 1%
*meadows and pastures:* 24%
*forest and woodland:* 39%
*other:* 19%
**Irrigated land:** 40 sq km (1989)
**Environment:**
*current issues:* some forest degradation caused by air and soil pollution; soil pollution results from the use of agricultural chemicals; air pollution results from emissions by coal- and oil-fired power stations and industrial plants
*natural hazards:* NA
*international agreements:* party to—Air Pollution, Air Pollution-Nitrogen Oxides, Air Pollution-Sulphur, Antarctic Treaty, Climate Change, Endangered Species, Environmental Modification, Hazardous Wastes, Nuclear Test Ban, Ozone Layer Protection, Ship Pollution, Tropical Timber, Wetlands; signed, but not ratified—Air Pollution-Volatile Organic Compounds, Antarctic-Environmental Protocol, Biodiversity, Law of the Sea
**Note:** landlocked; strategic location at the crossroads of central Europe with many easily traversable Alpine passes and valleys; major river is the Danube; population is concentrated on eastern lowlands because of steep slopes, poor soils, and low temperatures elsewhere

---

### People

**Population:** 7,954,974 (July 1994 est.)
**Population growth rate:** 0.45% (1994 est.)
**Birth rate:** 11.38 births/1,000 population (1994 est.)
**Death rate:** 10.34 deaths/1,000 population (1994 est.)
**Net migration rate:** 3.46 migrant(s)/1,000 population (1994 est.)

**Infant mortality rate:** 7.1 deaths/1,000 live births (1994 est.)
**Life expectancy at birth:**
*total population:* 76.65 years
*male:* 73.44 years
*female:* 80.03 years (1994 est.)
**Total fertility rate:** 1.48 children born/woman (1994 est.)
**Nationality:**
*noun:* Austrian(s)
*adjective:* Austrian
**Ethnic divisions:** German 99.4%, Croatian 0.3%, Slovene 0.2%, other 0.1%
**Religions:** Roman Catholic 85%, Protestant 6%, other 9%
**Languages:** German
**Literacy:** age 15 and over can read and write (1974 est.)
*total population:* 99%
*male:* NA%
*female:* NA%
**Labor force:** 3.47 million (1989)
*by occupation:* services 56.4%, industry and crafts 35.4%, agriculture and forestry 8.1%
*note:* an estimated 200,000 Austrians are employed in other European countries; foreign laborers in Austria number 177,840, about 6% of labor force (1988)

---

### Government

**Names:**
*conventional long form:* Republic of Austria
*conventional short form:* Austria
*local long form:* Republik Oesterreich
*local short form:* Oesterreich
**Digraph:** AU
**Type:** federal republic
**Capital:** Vienna
**Administrative divisions:** 9 states (bundeslander, singular—bundesland); Burgenland, Karnten, Niederoesterreich, Oberoesterreich, Salzburg, Steiermark, Tirol, Vorarlberg, Wien
**Independence:** 12 November 1918 (from Austro-Hungarian Empire)
**National holiday:** National Day, 26 October (1955)
**Constitution:** 1920; revised 1929 (reinstated

1 May 1945)
**Legal system:** civil law system with Roman law origin; judicial review of legislative acts by a Constitutional Court; separate administrative and civil/penal supreme courts; has not accepted compulsory ICJ jurisdiction
**Suffrage:** 19 years of age, universal; compulsory for presidential elections
**Executive branch:**
*chief of state:* President Thomas KLESTIL (since 8 July 1992); election last held 24 May 1992 (next to be held 1996); results of second ballot—Thomas KLESTIL 57%, Rudolf STREICHER 43%
*head of government:* Chancellor Franz VRANITZKY (since 16 June 1986); Vice Chancellor Erhard BUSEK (since 2 July 1991)
*cabinet:* Council of Ministers; chosen by the president on the advice of the chancellor
**Legislative branch:** bicameral Federal Assembly (Bundesversammlung)
*Federal Council (Bundesrat):* consists of 63 members representing each of the provinces on the basis of population, but with each province having at least 3 representatives
*National Council (Nationalrat):* elections last held 7 October 1990 (next to be held October 1994); results—SPOE 43%, OEVP 32.1%, FPOE 16.6%, GAL 4.5%, KPOE 0.7%, other 3.1%; seats—(183 total) SPOE 80, OEVP 60, FPOE 33, GAL 10
**Judicial branch:** Supreme Judicial Court (Oberster Gerichtshof) for civil and criminal cases, Administrative Court (Verwaltungsgerichtshof) for bureaucratic cases, Constitutional Court (Verfassungsgerichtshof) for constitutional cases
**Political parties and leaders:** Social Democratic Party of Austria (SPOE), Franz VRANITZKY, chairman; Austrian People's Party (OEVP), Erhard BUSEK, chairman; Freedom Party of Austria (FPOE), Joerg HAIDER, chairman; Communist Party (KPOE), Walter SILBERMAYER, chairman; Green Alternative List (GAL), Peter PILZ, chairman; Liberal Forum (LF), Heidi SCHMIDT
**Other political or pressure groups:** Federal Chamber of Commerce and Industry; Austrian Trade Union Federation (primarily Socialist); three composite leagues of the Austrian People's Party (OEVP) representing business, labor, and farmers; OEVP-oriented League of Austrian Industrialists; Roman Catholic Church, including its chief lay organization, Catholic Action
**Member of:** AfDB, AG (observer), AsDB, Australia Group, BIS, CCC, CE, CEI, CERN, COCOM (cooperating), CSCE, EBRD, ECE, EFTA, ESA, FAO, G-9, GATT, IADB, IAEA, IBRD, ICAO, ICC, ICFTU, IDA, IEA, IFAD, IFC, ILO, IMF, IMO, INTELSAT, INTERPOL, IOC, IOM, ISO, ITU, LORCS, MINURSO, MTCR, NAM (guest), NEA, NSG, OAS (observer), OECD, ONUSAL, PCA, UN, UNCTAD, UNESCO, UNDOF, UNFICYP, UNHCR, UNIDO, UNIKOM, UNOMIG, UNTAC, UNTSO, UPU, WCL, WFTU, WHO, WIPO, WMO, WTO, ZC
**Diplomatic representation in US:**
*chief of mission:* Ambassador Helmut TUERK
*chancery:* 3524 International Court NW, Washington, DC 20008-3035
*telephone:* (202) 895-6700
*FAX:* (202) 895-6750
*consulate(s) general:* Chicago, Los Angeles, and New York
**US diplomatic representation:**
*chief of mission:* Ambassador Swanee G. HUNT
*chancery:* Boltzmanngasse 16, A-1091, Vienna
*mailing address:* Unit 27937, Vienna
*telephone:* [43] (1) 313-39
*FAX:* [43] (1) 513-43-51
*consulate(s) general:* Salzburg
**Flag:** three equal horizontal bands of red (top), white, and red

---

**U.S. Government Contacts:**

**U.S. Trade Desk**: (202) 482-2920

**American Embassy Commercial Section**
Boltzmanngasse 16
A-1091, Vienna, Austria
APO AE 09108-0001
Tel: 43-222-31-55-11
Fax: 43-222-34-12-61

**Chambers of Commerce &
Organizations:**

**American Chamber of Commerce in Austria**
Porzellangasse 35
1090 Vienna, Austria
Tel: 43-1-319-5751
Fax: 43-1-319-5151

**Travel:**

**International Hotels in Country:**
Vienna
Bristol, Tel: 431-0222/515160, Fax: 431-0222/515-16550
InterContinental, Tel: 431-0222/711220, Fax: 431-0222/713-4489
Marriott, Tel: 431-0222/51580, Fax: 431-0222/515-186722.

# BELGIUM

50 km

North Sea

Oostende • Antwerp •
Kortrijk • BRUSSELS ★
Mons • Liège •
Charleroi •
Bastogne •

## Economy

**Overview:** This small private enterprise economy has capitalized on its central geographic location, highly developed transport network, and diversified industrial and commercial base. Industry is concentrated mainly in the populous Flemish area in the north, although the government is encouraging reinvestment in the southern region of Walloon. With few natural resources Belgium must import substantial quantities of raw materials and export a large volume of manufactures, making its economy unusually dependent on the state of world markets. Three fourths of its trade is with other EC countries. The economy grew at a strong 4% pace during the period 1988-90, but economic growth slowed to a 1% pace in 1991-92 and dropped by 1.5% in 1993. Belgium's public debt has risen to 140% of GDP, and the government is trying to control its expenditures to bring the figure more into line with other industrialized countries.

**National product:** GDP—purchasing power equivalent—$177.5 billion (1993)

**National product real growth rate:** -1.5% (1993)

**National product per capita:** $17,700 (1993)

**Inflation rate (consumer prices):** 2.8% (1993 est.)

**Unemployment rate:** 13.5% (March 1994)

**Budget:**
*revenues:* $97.8 billion
*expenditures:* $109.3 billion, including capital expenditures of $NA (1989)

**Exports:** $117 billion (f.o.b., 1992) Belgium-Luxembourg Economic Union
*commodities:* iron and steel, transportation equipment, tractors, diamonds, petroleum products
*partners:* EC 75.5%, US 3.7%, former Communist countries 1.4% (1991)

**Imports:** $120 billion (c.i.f., 1992) Belgium-Luxembourg Economic Union
*commodities:* fuels, grains, chemicals, foodstuffs
*partners:* EC 73%, US 4.8%, oil-exporting less developed countries 4%, former Communist countries 1.8% (1991)

**External debt:** $31.3 billion (1992 est.)

**Industrial production:** growth rate -0.1% (1993 est.); accounts for 25% of GDP

**Electricity:**
*capacity:* 17,500,000 kW
*production:* 68 billion kWh
*consumption per capita:* 6,790 kWh (1992)

**Industries:** engineering and metal products, motor vehicle assembly, processed food and beverages, chemicals, basic metals, textiles, glass, petroleum, coal

**Agriculture:** accounts for 2.0% of GDP; emphasis on livestock production—beef, veal, pork, milk; major crops are sugar beets, fresh vegetables, fruits, grain, tobacco; net importer of farm products

**Illicit drugs:** source of precursor chemicals for South American cocaine processors; important gateway country for cocaine entering the European market

**Economic aid:**
*donor:* ODA and OOF commitments (1970-89), $5.8 billion
**Currency:** 1 Belgian franc (BF) = 100 centimes
**Exchange rates:** Belgian francs (BF) per US$1—36.242 (January 1994), 34.597 (1993), 32.150 (1992), 34.148 (1991), 33.418 (1990), 39.404 (1989)
**Fiscal year:** calendar year

## Communications

**Railroads:** Belgian National Railways (SNCB) operates 3,568 km 1.435-meter standard gauge, government owned; 2,563 km double track; 2,207 km electrified
**Highways:**
*total:* 137,876 km
*paved:* 129,603 km (including 1,631 km of limited access divided highway)
*unpaved:* 8,273 km (1989)
**Inland waterways:** 2,043 km (1,528 km in regular commercial use)
**Pipelines:** petroleum products 1,167 km; crude oil 161 km; natural gas 3,300 km
**Ports:** Antwerp, Brugge, Gent, Oostende, Zeebrugge
**Merchant marine:** 21 ships (1,000 GRT or over) totaling 36,200 GRT/52,039 DWT, cargo 9, oil tanker 5, liquefied gas 1, chemical tanker 5, bulk 1
**Airports:**
*total:* 42
*usable:* 42
*with permanent-surface runways:* 24
*with runways over 3,659 m:* 0
*with runways 2,440-3,659 m:* 15
*with runways 1,220-2,439 m:* 3
**Telecommunications:** highly developed, technologically advanced, and completely automated domestic and international telephone and telegraph facilities; extensive cable network; limited microwave radio relay network; 4,720,000 telephones; broadcast stations—3 AM, 39 FM, 32 TV; 5 submarine cables; 2 satellite earth stations—Atlantic Ocean INTELSAT and EUTELSAT systems; nationwide mobile phone system

## Defense Forces

**Branches:** Army, Navy, Air Force, National Gendarmerie
**Manpower availability:** males age 15-49 2,558,109; fit for military service 2,130,172; reach military age (19) annually 61,710 (1994 est.)
**Defense expenditures:** exchange rate conversion—$4 billion, 2% of GDP (1992)

## Geography

**Location:** Western Europe, bordering on the North Sea, between France and the Netherlands
**Map references:** Arctic Region, Europe, Standard Time Zones of the World
**Area:**
*total area:* 30,510 sq km
*land area:* 30,230 sq km
*comparative area:* slightly larger than Maryland
**Land boundaries:** total 1,385 km, France 620 km, Germany 167 km, Luxembourg 148 km, Netherlands 450 km
**Coastline:** 64 km
**Maritime claims:**
*continental shelf:* equidistant line with neighbors
*exclusive fishing zone:* equidistant line with neighbors (extends about 68 km from coast)
*territorial sea:* 12 nm
**International disputes:** none
**Climate:** temperate; mild winters, cool summers; rainy, humid, cloudy
**Terrain:** flat coastal plains in northwest, central rolling hills, rugged mountains of Ardennes Forest in southeast
**Natural resources:** coal, natural gas
**Land use:**
*arable land:* 24%
*permanent crops:* 1%
*meadows and pastures:* 20%
*forest and woodland:* 21%
*other:* 34%
**Irrigated land:** 10 sq km (1989 est.)
**Environment:**
*current issues:* Meuse River, a major source of drinking water, polluted from steel production

wastes; other rivers polluted by animal wastes and fertilizers; industrial air pollution contributes to acid rain in neighboring countries
*natural hazards:* NA
*international agreements:* party to—Air Pollution, Air Pollution-Sulphur, Antarctic Treaty, Endangered Species, Environmental Modification, Hazardous Wastes, Marine Dumping, Marine Life Conservation, Nuclear Test Ban, Ozone Layer Protection, Ship Pollution, Tropical Timber, Wetlands; signed, but not ratified—Air Pollution-Nitrogen Oxides, Air Pollution-Volatile Organic Compounds, Antarctic-Environmental Protocol, Biodiversity, Climate Change, Law of the Sea
**Note:** crossroads of Western Europe; majority of West European capitals within 1,000 km of Brussels which is the seat of the EC

## People

**Population:** 10,062,836 (July 1994 est.)
**Population growth rate:** 0.2% (1994 est.)
**Birth rate:** 11.71 births/1,000 population (1994 est.)
**Death rate:** 10.26 deaths/1,000 population (1994 est.)
**Net migration rate:** 0.6 migrant(s)/1,000 population (1994 est.)
**Infant mortality rate:** 7.2 deaths/1,000 live births (1994 est.)
**Life expectancy at birth:**
*total population:* 76.96 years
*male:* 73.67 years
*female:* 80.44 years (1994 est.)
**Total fertility rate:** 1.62 children born/woman (1994 est.)
**Nationality:**
*noun:* Belgian(s)
*adjective:* Belgian
**Ethnic divisions:** Fleming 55%, Walloon 33%, mixed or other 12%
**Religions:** Roman Catholic 75%, Protestant or other 25%
**Languages:** Dutch 56%, French 32%, German 1%, legally bilingual 11% divided along ethnic lines

**Literacy:** age 15 and over can read and write (1980 est.)
*total population:* 99%
*male:* NA%
*female:* NA%
**Labor force:** 4.126 million
*by occupation:* services 63.6%, industry 28%, construction 6.1%, agriculture 2.3% (1988)

## Government

**Names:**
*conventional long form:* Kingdom of Belgium
*conventional short form:* Belgium
*local long form:* Royaume de Belgique
*local short form:* Belgique
**Digraph:** BE
**Type:** constitutional monarchy
**Capital:** Brussels
**Administrative divisions:** 9 provinces (French: provinces, singular—province; Flemish: provincien, singular—provincie); Antwerpen, Brabant, Hainaut, Liege, Limburg, Luxembourg, Namur, Oost-Vlaanderen, West-Vlaanderen

**Independence:** 4 October 1830 (from the Netherlands)
**National holiday:** National Day, 21 July (ascension of King Leopold to the throne in 1831)
**Constitution:** 7 February 1831, last revised 14 July 1993; parliament approved a constitutional package creating a federal state
**Legal system:** civil law system influenced by English constitutional theory; judicial review of legislative acts; accepts compulsory ICJ jurisdiction, with reservations
**Suffrage:** 18 years of age, universal and compulsory
**Executive branch:**
*chief of state:* King ALBERT II (since NA August 1993)
*head of government:* Prime Minister Jean-Luc DEHAENE (since 6 March 1992)
*cabinet:* Cabinet; the king appoints the ministers who are chosen by the legislature
**Legislative branch:** bicameral Parliament
*Senate:* (Flemish—Senaat, French—Senat); elections last held 24 November 1991 (next to

be held by November 1996); results—percent of vote by party NA; seats—(184 total; of which 106 are directly elected) CVP 20, SP 14, PVV (now VLD) 13, VU 5, AGALEV 5, VB 5, ROSSEN 1, PS 18, PRL 9, PSC 9, ECOLO 6, FDF 1

*Chamber of Representatives:* (Flemish—Kamer van Volksvertegenwoordigers, French—Chambre des Representants); elections last held 24 November 1991 (next to be held by November 1996); results—CVP 16.7%, PS 13.6%, SP 12.0%, PVV (now VLD) 11.9%, PRL 8.2%, PSC 7.8%, VB 6.6%, VU 5.9%, ECOLO 5.1%, AGALEV 4.9%, FDF 2.6%, ROSSEM 3.2%, FN 1.5%; seats—(212 total) CVP 39, PS 35, SP 28, PVV (now VLD) 26, PRL 20, PSC 18, FB 12, VU 10, ECOLO 10, AGALEV 7, FDF 3, ROSSEM 3, FN 1

**Judicial branch:** Supreme Court of Justice (Flemish—Hof van Cassatie, French—Cour de Cassation)

**Political parties and leaders:** Flemish Social Christian (CVP), Johan van HECKE, president; Francophone Social Christian (PSC), Melchior WATHELET, president; Flemish Socialist (SP), Frank VANDENBROUCKE, president; Francophone Socialist (PS), Philippe BUSQUIN; Flemish Liberals and Democrats (VLD), Guy VERHOFSTADT, president; Francophone Liberal (PRL), Jean GOL, president; Francophone Democratic Front (FDF), Georges CLERFAYT, president; Volksunie (VU), Bert ANCIAUX, president; Communist Party (PCB), Louis VAN GEYT, president; Vlaams Blok (VB), Karel DILLEN, chairman; ROSSEM, Jean Pierre VAN ROSSEM; National Front (FN), Werner van STEEN; AGALEV (Flemish Greens), no president; ECOLO (Francophone Ecologists), no president; other minor parties

**Other political or pressure groups:**

Christian and Socialist Trade Unions; Federation of Belgian Industries; numerous other associations representing bankers, manufacturers, middle-class artisans, and the legal and medical professions; various organizations represent the cultural interests of Flanders and Wallonia; various peace groups such as the Flemish Action Committee Against

Nuclear Weapons and Pax Christi

**Member of:** AG (observer), ACCT, AfDB, AsDB, Australian Group, Benelux, BIS, CCC, CE, CERN, COCOM, CSCE, EBRD, EC, ECE, EIB, ESA, FAO, G-9, G-10, GATT, IADB, IAEA, IBRD, ICAO, ICC, ICFTU, IDA, IEA, IFAD, IFC, ILO, IMF, IMO, INMARSAT, INTELSAT, INTERPOL, IOC, IOM, ISO, ITU, LORCS, MINURSO, MTCR, NACC, NATO, NEA, NSG, OAS (observer), OECD, PCA, UN, UNCTAD, UNESCO, UNHCR, UNIDO, UNMOGIP, UNOSOM, UNPROFOR, UNRWA, UNTAC, UNTSO, UPU, WCL, WEU, WHO, WIPO, WMO, WTO, ZC

**Diplomatic representation in US:**
*chief of mission:* Ambassador Juan CASSIERS
*chancery:* 3330 Garfield Street NW, Washington, DC 20008
*telephone:* (202) 333-6900
*FAX:* (202) 333-3079
*consulate(s) general:* Atlanta, Chicago, Los Angeles, and New York

**US diplomatic representation:**
*chief of mission:* Ambassador Alan J. BLINKEN
*embassy:* 27 Boulevard du Regent, Brussels
*mailing address:* B-1000 Brussels, APO AE 09724
*telephone:* [32] (2) 513-3830
*FAX:* [32] (2) 511-2725

**Flag:** three equal vertical bands of black (hoist side), yellow, and red; the design was based on the flag of France

---

**U.S. Government Contacts:**

**U.S. Trade Desk:** (202) 482-5401

**American Embassy Commercial Section**
27 Boulevard du Regent
B-1000 Brussels
APO AE 09724
Tel: 32-2-513-3830
Fax: 32-2-512-6653

---

**Belgian Government Contacts**

**Embassy of Belgium Commercial Section**
3330 Garfield Street, N.W.

Washington, DC 20008
Tel: 202-333-6900

**Belgian Department of Foreign Trade**
Marc Servotte: Director-General
162, Boulevard Emile Jacqmain
1210 Brussels
Tel: 02/209.35.11
Fax: 02/217.61.23

**Service for Foreign Investors Ministry of Economic Affairs**
J. De Buck, Coordinator
de Meeussquare 23,
1040 Brussels
Tel: 02.506.54.14
Fax: 02/514.03.89

**Chambers of Commerce & Organizations:**

**American Chamber of Commerce in Belgium**
Rue de la Fusse 100
1130 Brussels, Belgium
Tel: 02-720-9130

**Legal Services:**

**De Wolf, De Boel & Brugmans**
Jozef de Somstraat 67
2018 Antwerp, Belgium
Tel: 010-32-3-248-49-47
Fax: 010-32-3-248-49-47
*Engaged in Belgian, European and International Law Practice. European Community Law, International Business Law, Transport and Maritime Law.*

**Charles A. Dilley**
Avenue Legrand, 62
1050 Brussels, Belgium
Tel: 322-646-8800
Fax: 322-646-9405
*General and International Law Practice. Firm authorized to appear before the Belgian Courts.*

**Advokatfirman Vinge**
Avenue Louise 465-B12
B-1050 Brussels, Belgium

Tel: 322-646-36-20
Fax: 322-646-41-46
*EC-Law, Sweidsh and International Law Practice, Contracts, Corporate, Transport, Foreign Investments in Scandinavia, Arbitration.*

**Ernst & Young Tax Consultants**
Avenue Marcel Thiry 204
1200 Bruxelles
Tel: 011-32-2-774 91 11
Fax: 011-32-2-774 9090

**Travel:**

**International Airlines to Country:**
American, United

**International Hotels in Country:**
Brussels:
Conrad, Tel: 322-02/542-42-42, Fax: 322-02/542-43-42
Hilton International, Tel: 322-02/504-11-11-11, Fax: 322-02/504-21-11
SAS Royal Hotel, Tel: 322-02/219-28-28, Fax: 322-02/504-21-11.

# BOSNIA AND HERZEGOVINA

**Note:** Bosnia and Herzegovina is suffering from interethnic civil strife which began in March 1992 after the Government of Bosnia and Herzegovina held a referendum on independence. Bosnia's Serbs—supported by neighboring Serbia—responded with armed resistance aimed at partitioning the republic along ethnic lines and joining Serb-held areas to a "greater Serbia." Since the onset of the conflict, which has driven approximately half of the pre-war population of 4.4 million from their homes, both the Bosnian Serbs and the Bosnian Croats have asserted control of more than three-quarters of the territory formerly under the control of the Government of Bosnia and Herzegovina. The UN and the EU are continuing to try to mediate a plan for peace. In March 1994 Bosnian Muslims and Bosnian Croats signed an agreement in Washington, DC, creating a Federation of Bosnia and Herzegovina, which is to include territories in which Muslims or Croats predominated, according to the 1991 census. Bosnian Serbs refused to become a part of this Federation.

## Economy

**Overview:** Bosnia and Herzegovina ranked next to The Former Yugoslav Republic of Macedonia as the poorest republic in the old Yugoslav federation. Although agriculture has been almost all in private hands, farms have been small and inefficient, and the republic traditionally has been a net importer of food. Industry has been greatly overstaffed, one reflection of the rigidities of Communist central planning and management. Tito had pushed the development of military industries in the republic with the result that Bosnia hosted a large share of Yugoslavia's defense plants. As of April 1994, Bosnia and Herzegovina was being torn apart by the continued bitter interethnic warfare that has caused production to plummet, unemployment and inflation to soar, and human misery to multiply. No reliable economic statistics for 1992-93 are available, although output clearly has fallen substantially below the levels of earlier years.

**National product:** GDP—purchasing power equivalent—$NA
**National product real growth rate:** NA%
**National product per capita:** $NA
**Inflation rate (consumer prices):** NA%
**Unemployment rate:** NA%
**Budget:**
*revenues:* $NA
*expenditures:* $NA, including capital expenditures of $NA
**Exports:** $NA
*commodities:* NA
*partners:* NA
**Imports:** $NA

*commodities:* NA
*partners:* NA
**External debt:** $NA
**Industrial production:** growth rate NA%, but production is sharply down because of interethnic and interrepublic warfare (1991-93)
**Electricity:**

*capacity:* NA kW
*production:* NA kWh
*consumption per capita:* NA kWh
**Industries:** steel production, mining (coal, iron ore, lead, zinc, manganese, and bauxite), manufacturing (vehicle assembly, textiles, tobacco products, wooden furniture, 40% of former Yugoslavia's armaments including tank and aircraft assembly, domestic appliances), oil refining (1991)
**Agriculture:** accounted for 9.0% of GDP in 1989; regularly produces less than 50% of food needs; the foothills of northern Bosnia support orchards, vineyards, livestock, and some wheat and corn; long winters and heavy precipitation leach soil fertility reducing agricultural output in the mountains; farms are mostly privately held, small, and not very productive (1991)
**Illicit drugs:** NA
**Economic aid:** $NA
**Currency:** 1 dinar = 100 para; Croatian dinar used in Croat-held area, presumably to be replaced by new Croatian kuna; old and new Serbian dinars used in Serb-held area; hard currencies probably supplanting local currencies in areas held by Bosnian government
**Exchange rates:** NA
**Fiscal year:** calendar year

---

**Communications**

**Railroads:** NA km
**Highways:**
*total:* 21,168 km
*paved:* 11,436 km
*unpaved:* gravel 8,146 km; earth 1,586 km (1991)
**Inland waterways:** NA km
**Pipelines:** crude oil 174 km, natural gas 90 km (1992); note—pipelines now disrupted
**Ports:** coastal—none; inland—Bosanski Brod on the Sava River
**Airports:**
*total:* 28
*usable:* 24
*with permanent-surface runways:* 5
*with runways over 3659:* 0
*with runways 2440-3659 m:* 3

*with runways 1220-2439 m:* 6
**Telecommunications:** telephone and telegraph network is in need of modernization and expansion, many urban areas being below average compared with services in other former Yugoslav republics; 727,000 telephones; broadcast stations—9 AM, 2 FM, 6 TV; 840,000 radios; 1,012,094 TVs; satellite ground stations—none

---

**Defense Forces**

**Branches:** Army
**Manpower availability:** males age 15-49 1,298,102; fit for military service 1,054,068; reach military age (19) annually 38,283 (1994 est.)
**Defense expenditures:** $NA, NA% of GDP

---

**Geography**

**Location:** Balkan State, Southeastern Europe, on the Balkan Peninsula, between Croatia and Serbia and Montenegro
**Map references:** Africa, Arctic Region, Ethnic Groups in Eastern Europe, Europe, Standard Time Zones of the World
**Area:**
*total area:* 51,233 sq km
*land area:* 51,233 sq km
*comparative area:* slightly larger than Tennessee
**Land boundaries:** total 1,459 km, Croatia 932 km, Serbia and Montenegro 527 km (312 km with Serbia; 215 km with Montenegro)
**Coastline:** 20 km
**Maritime claims:**
*continental shelf:* 200-m depth
*exclusive economic zone:* 12 nm
*exclusive fishing zone:* 12 nm
*territorial sea:* 12 nm

**Nationality:**
*noun:* Bosnian(s), Herzegovinian(s)
*adjective:* Bosnian, Herzegovinian
**Ethnic divisions:** Muslim 44%, Serb 31%, Croat 17%, other 8%
**Religions:** Muslim 40%, Orthodox 31%, Catholic 15%, Protestant 4%, other 10%
**Languages:** Serbo-Croatian 99%
**Literacy:**

*total population:* NA%
*male:* NA%
*female:* NA%
**Labor force:** 1,026,254
*by occupation:* agriculture 2%, industry,
mining 45% (1991 est.)

## Government

**Names:**
*conventional long form:* Republic of Bosnia
and Herzegovina
*conventional short form:* Bosnia and
Herzegovina
*local long form:* Republika Bosna i
Hercegovina
*local short form:* Bosna i Hercegovina
**Digraph:** BK
**Type:** emerging democracy
**Capital:** Sarajevo
**Administrative divisions:** 109 districts
(opstinas, singular—opstina) Banovici, Banja
Luka, Bihac, Bijeljina, Bileca, Bosanska
Dubica, Bosanska Gradiska, Bosanska Krupa,
Bosanski Brod, Bosanski Novi, Bosanski
Petrovac, Bosanski Samac, Bosansko
Grahovo, Bratunac, Brcko, Breza, Bugojno,
Busovaca, Cazin, Cajnice, Capljina, Celinac,
Citluk, Derventa, Doboj, Donji Vakuf, Foca,
Fojnica, Gacko, Glamoc, Gorazde, Gornji
Vakuf, Gracanica, Gradacac, Grude, Han
Pijesak, Jablanica, Jajce, Kakanj, Kalesija,
Kalinovik, Kiseljak, Kladanj, Kljuc, Konjic,
Kotor Varos, Kresevo, Kupres, Laktasi,
Listica, Livno, Lopare, Lukavac, Ljubinje,
Ljubuski, Maglaj, Modrica, Mostar, Mrkonjic-
Grad, Neum, Nevesinje, Odzak, Olovo, Orasje,
Posusje, Prijedor, Prnjavor, Prozor, (Pucarevo)
Novi Travnik, Rogatica, Rudo, Sanski Most,
Sarajevo-Centar, Sarajevo-Hadzici, Sarajevo-
Ilidza, Sarajevo-Ilijas, Sarajevo-Novi Grad,
Sarajevo-Novo, Sarajevo-Pale, Sarajevo-Stari
Grad, Sarajevo-Trnovo, Sarajevo-Vogosca,
Skender Vakuf, Sokolac, Srbac, Srebrenica,
Srebrenik, Stolac, Sekovici, Sipovo, Teslic,
Tesanj, Drvar, Duvno, Travnik, Trebinje,
Tuzla, Ugljevik, Vares, Velika Kladusa,
Visoko, Visegrad, Vitez, Vlasenica,
Zavidovici, Zenica, Zvornik, Zepce, Zivinice
*note:* currently under negotiation with the

assistance of international mediators
**Independence:** NA April 1992 (from
Yugoslavia)
**National holiday:** NA
**Constitution:** promulgated in 1974 (under the
Communists), amended 1989, 1990, and 1991;
**International disputes:** as of May 1994,
members of the Bosnian Serb armed factions,
desirous of establishing a separate state linked
with neighboring Serbia, occupied 70% of
Bosnia after having killed or driven out non-
Serb inhabitants; the Bosnian Croats, occupied
and declared an independent state in an
additional 10% of Bosnia in 1993, but in March
1994, this faction and the Bosnian Government
settled their dispute and entered into a
bicommunal Federation; a Bosnian
Government army commander who opposes
the leadership of Bosnian President
IZETBEGOVIC is leading an insurrection in
the government-held enclave of Bihac
**Climate:** hot summers and cold winters; areas
of high elevation have short, cool summers and
long, severe winters; mild, rainy winters along
coast
**Terrain:** mountains and valleys
**Natural resources:** coal, iron, bauxite,
manganese, timber, wood products, copper,
chromium, lead, zinc
**Land use:**
*arable land:* 20%
*permanent crops:* 2%
*meadows and pastures:* 25%
*forest and woodland:* 36%
*other:* 17%
**Irrigated land:** NA sq km
**Environment:**
*current issues:* air pollution from metallurgical
plants; water scarce; sites for disposing of
urban waste are limited; widespread casualties
and destruction of infrastructure because of
civil strife
*natural hazards:* subject to frequent and
destructive earthquakes
*international agreements:* party to—Air
Pollution, Marine Life Conservation, Ozone
Layer Protection

## People

**Population:** 4,651,485 (July 1994 est.)
*note:* all data dealing with population is subject to considerable error because of the dislocations caused by military action and ethnic cleansing
**Population growth rate:** 0.69% (1994 est.)
**Birth rate:** 13.33 births/1,000 population (1994 est.)
**Death rate:** 6.39 deaths/1,000 population (1994 est.)
**Net migration rate:** 0 migrant(s)/1,000 population (1994 est.)
**Infant mortality rate:** 12.7 deaths/1,000 live births (1994 est.)
**Life expectancy at birth:**
*total population:* 75.13 years
*male:* 72.43 years
*female:* 78.02 years (1994 est.)
**Total fertility rate:** 1.61 children born/woman (1994 est.)
the Assembly planned to draft a new constitution in 1991, before conditions deteriorated; constitution of Federation of Bosnia and Herzegovina (including Muslim and Croatian controlled parts of Republic) ratified April 1994
**Legal system:** based on civil law system
**Suffrage:** 16 years of age, if employed; 18 years of age, universal
**Executive branch:**
*chief of state:* President Alija IZETBEGOVIC (since 20 December 1990), other members of the collective presidency: Ejup GANIC (since NA November 1990), Nijaz DURAKOVIC (since NA October 1993), Stjepan KLJUJIC (since NA October 1993), Ivo KOMSIC (since NA October 1993), Mirko PEJANOVIC (since NA June 1992), Tatjana LJUJIC-MIJATOVIC (since NA December 1992)
*head of government:* Prime Minister Haris SILAJDZIC (since NA October 1993); Deputy Prime Minister Edib BUKVIC (since NA October 1993)
*cabinet:* executive body of ministers; members of, and responsible to, the National Assembly
**Legislative branch:** bicameral National Assembly

*Chamber of Municipalities (Vijece Opeina):* elections last held November-December 1990 (next to be held NA); seats—(110 total) SDA 43, SDS BiH 38, HDZ BiH 23, Party of Democratic Changes 4, DSS 1, SPO 1
*Chamber of Citizens (Vijece Gradanstvo):* elections last held November-December 1990 (next to be held NA); seats—(130 total) SDA 43, SDS BiH 34, HDZ BiH 21, Party of Democratic Changes 15, SRSJ BiH 12, MBO 2, DSS 1, DSZ 1, LS 1
*note:* legislative elections for the Federation of Bosnia and Herzegovina are slated for late 1994
**Judicial branch:** Supreme Court, Constitutional Court
**Political parties and leaders:** Party of Democratic Action (SDA), Alija IZETBEGOVIC; Croatian Democratic Union of Bosnia and Herzegovina (HDZ BiH), KresimirZUBAK; Serbian Democratic Party of Bosnia and Herzegovina (SDS BiH), Radovan KARADZIC, president; Muslim-Bosnian Organization (MBO), Adil ZULFIKARPASIC, president; Democratic Party of Socialists (DSS), Nijaz DURAKOVIC, president; Party of Democratic Changes, leader NA; Serbian Movement for Renewal (SPO), Milan TRIVUNCIC; Alliance of Reform Forces of Yugoslavia for Bosnia and Herzegovina (SRSJ BiH), Dr. Nenad KECMANOVIC, president; Democratic League of Greens (DSZ), Drazen PETROVIC; Liberal Party (LS), Rasim KADIC, president
**Other political or pressure groups:** NA
**Member of:** CEI, CSCE, ECE, ICAO, ILO, IMO, INTELSAT (nonsignatory user), INTERPOL, IOC, ITU, NAM (guest), UN, UNCTAD, UNESCO, UNIDO, UPU, WHO
**Diplomatic representation in US:**
*chief of mission:* (vacant); Minister-Counselor, Charge d'Affaires ad interim Seven ALKALAJ
*chancery:* Suite 760, 1707 L Street NW, Washington, DC 10036
*telephone:* (202) 833-3612, 3613, and 3615
*FAX:* (202) 833-2061
*consulate(s) general:* New York
**US diplomatic representation:**
*chief of mission:* (vacant); Charge d'Affaires Victor JACKOVICH

# CROATIA

100 km

ZAGREB

Rijeka · Osijek

Pula

Zadar

Adriatic
Sea

Split

Kardeljevo
(Ploče)

Dubrovnik

## Economy

**Overview:** Before the dissolution of
Yugoslavia, the republic of Croatia, after
Slovenia, was the most prosperous and
industrialized area, with a per capita output
roughly comparable to that of Portugal and
perhaps one-third above the Yugoslav average.
At present, Croatian Serb Nationalists control
approximately one third of the Croatian
territory, and one of the overriding
determinants of Croatia's long-term political
and economic prospects will be the resolution
of this territorial dispute. Croatia faces
monumental economic problems stemming
from: the legacy of longtime Communist
mismanagement of the economy; large foreign
debt; damage during the fighting to bridges,
factories, power lines, buildings, and houses;
the large refugee population, both Croatian and
Bosnian; and the disruption of economic ties to
Serbia and the other former Yugoslav
republics, as well as within its own territory. At
the minimum, extensive Western aid and
investment, especially in the tourist and oil
industries, would seem necessary to salvage a
desperate economic situation. However, peace

and political stability must come first; only
then will recent government moves toward a
"market-friendly" economy reverse the sharp
drop in output. As of May 1994, fighting
continues among Croats, Serbs, and Muslims,
and national boundaries and final political
arrangements are still in doubt.
**National product:** GDP—purchasing power
equivalent—$21.8 billion (1992 est.)
**National product real growth rate:** -19%
(1992 est.)
**National product per capita:** $4,500 (1992
est.)
**Inflation rate (consumer prices):** 26%
monthly average (1993 est.)
**Unemployment rate:** 21% (December 1993)
**Budget:**
*revenues:* $NA
*expenditures:* $NA, including capital
expenditures of $NA
**Exports:** $3.9 billion (f.o.b., 1993)
*commodities:* machinery and transport
equipment 30%, other manufacturers 37%,
chemicals 11%, food and live animals 9%, raw
materials 6.5%, fuels and lubricants 5% (1990)
*partners:* EC countries, Slovenia
**Imports:** $4.7 billion (c.i.f., 1993)
*commodities:* machinery and transport
equipment 21%, fuels and lubricants 19%,
food and live animals 16%, chemicals 14%,
manufactured goods 13%, miscellaneous
manufactured articles 9%, raw materials 6.5%,
beverages and tobacco 1% (1990)
*partners:* EC countries, Slovenia, FSU
countries
**External debt:** $2.6 billion (December 1993)
**Industrial production:** growth rate -5.9%
(1993 est.)
**Electricity:**
*capacity:* 3,570,000 kW
*production:* 11.5 billion kWh
*consumption per capita:* 2,400 kWh (1992)
**Industries:** chemicals and plastics, machine
tools, fabricated metal, electronics, pig iron
and rolled steel products, aluminum reduction,
paper, wood products (including furniture),

building materials (including cement), textiles, shipbuilding, petroleum and petroleum refining, food processing and beverages
**Agriculture:** Croatia normally produces a food surplus; most agricultural land in private hands and concentrated in Croat-majority districts in Slavonia and Istria; much of Slavonia's land has been put out of production by fighting; wheat, corn, sugar beets, sunflowers, alfalfa, and clover are main crops in Slavonia; central Croatian highlands are less fertile but support cereal production, orchards, vineyards, livestock breeding, and dairy farming; coastal areas and offshore islands grow olives, citrus fruits, and vegetables
**Economic aid:** $NA
**Currency:** 1 Croatian dinar (CD) = 100 paras; a new currency, the kuna, replaced the dinar on 30 May 1994
**Exchange rates:** Croatian dinar per US $1— 6,544 (January 1994), 3,637 (15 July 1993), 60.00 (April 1992)
**Fiscal year:** calendar year

## Communications

**Railroads:** 2,592 km of standard guage (1.435 m) of which 864 km are electrified (1992); note—disrupted by territorial dispute
**Highways:**
*total:* 32,071 km
*paved:* 23,305 km
*unpaved:* gravel 8,439 km; earth 327 km (1990)
**Inland waterways:** 785 km perennially navigable
**Pipelines:** crude oil 670 km, petroleum products 20 km, natural gas 310 km (1992); note—now disrupted because of territorial dispute
**Ports:** coastal—Omisalj (oil), Ploce, Rijeka, Split; inland—Osijek, Slavonski Samac, Vukovar, Zupanja
**Merchant marine:** 28 ships (1,000 GRT or over) totaling 108,194 GRT/131,880 DWT, cargo 18, roll-on/roll-off cargo 2, short-sea passenger 3, passenger 2, refrigerated cargo 1, container 1, oil tanker 1
*note:* also controlled by Croatian shipowners are 151 ships (1,000 GRT or over) under flags

of convenience—primarily Malta and St. Vincent—totaling 2,221,931 GRT/3,488,263 DWT; includes cargo 60, roll-on/ roll-off 8, refrigerated cargo 4, container 12, multifunction large load carriers 3, bulk 45, oil tanker 9, liquified gas 1, chemical tanker 4, service vessel 5
**Airports:**
*total:* 75
*usable:* 70
*with permanent-surface runways:* 16
*with runways over 3,659 m:* 0
*with runways 2,440-3,659 m:* 7
*with runways 1,220-2,439 m:* 5
**Telecommunications:** 350,000 telephones; broadcast stations—14 AM, 8 FM, 12 (2 repeaters) TV; 1,100,000 radios; 1,027,000 TVs; satellite ground stations—none

## Defense Forces

**Branches:** Ground Forces, Naval Forces, Air and Air Defense Forces
**Manpower availability:** males age 15-49 1,182,767; fit for military service 946,010; reach military age (19) annually 33,166 (1994 est.)
**Defense expenditures:** 337-393 billion Croatian dinars, NA% of GDP (1993 est.); note—conversion of defense expenditures into US dollars using the current exchange rate could produce misleading results

## Geography

**Location:** Balkan State, Southeastern Europe, on the Balkan Peninsula, bordering the Adriatic Sea, between Slovenia and Bosnia and Herzegovina
**Map references:** Africa, Ethnic Groups in Eastern Europe, Europe, Standard Time Zones of the World
**Area:**
*total area:* 56,538 sq km
*land area:* 56,410 sq km
*comparative area:* slightly smaller than West Virginia
**Land boundaries:** total 2,028 km, Bosnia and Herzegovina 932 km, Hungary 329 km,

Serbia and Montenegro 266 km (241 km with Serbia; 25 km with Montenego), Slovenia 501 km
**Coastline:** 5,790 km (mainland 1,778 km, islands 4,012 km)
**Maritime claims:**
*continental shelf:* 200-m depth or to depth of exploitation
*exclusive economic zone:* 12 nm
*exclusive fishing zone:* 12 nm
*territorial sea:* 12 nm
**International disputes:** Serbs have occupied UN protected areas in eastern Croatia and along the western Bosnia and Herzegovinian border; dispute with Slovenia over fishing rights in Adriatic
**Climate:** Mediterranean and continental; continental climate predominant with hot summers and cold winters; mild winters, dry summers along coast
**Terrain:** geographically diverse; flat plains along Hungarian border, low mountains and highlands near Adriatic coast, coastline, and islands
**Natural resources:** oil, some coal, bauxite, low-grade iron ore, calcium, natural asphalt, silica, mica, clays, salt
**Land use:**
*arable land:* 32%
*permanent crops:* 20%
*meadows and pastures:* 18%
*forest and woodland:* 15%
*other:* 15%
**Irrigated land:** NA sq km
**Environment:**
*current issues:* air pollution from metallurgical plants is damaging the forests; coastal pollution from industrial and domestic waste; widespread casualties and destruction of infrastructure in border areas affected by civil strife
*natural hazards:* subject to frequent and destructive earthquakes
*international agreements:* party to—Air Pollution, Marine Dumping, Nuclear Test Ban, Ozone Layer Protection, Ship Pollution; signed, but not ratified—Biodiversity, Climate Change
**Note:** controls most land routes from Western Europe to Aegean Sea and Turkish Straits

## People

**Population:** 4,697,614 (July 1994 est.)
**Population growth rate:** 0.07% (1994 est.)
**Birth rate:** 11.27 births/1,000 population (1994 est.)
**Death rate:** 10.54 deaths/1,000 population (1994 est.)
**Net migration rate:** 0 migrant(s)/1,000 population (1994 est.)
**Infant mortality rate:** 8.7 deaths/1,000 live births (1994 est.)
**Life expectancy at birth:**
*total population:* 73.6 years
*male:* 70.14 years
*female:* 77.26 years (1994 est.)
**Total fertility rate:** 1.65 children born/woman (1994 est.)
**Nationality:**
*noun:* Croat(s)
*adjective:* Croatian
**Ethnic divisions:** Croat 78%, Serb 12%, Muslim 0.9%, Hungarian 0.5%, Slovenian 0.5%, others 8.1%
**Religions:** Catholic 76.5%, Orthodox 11.1%, Slavic Muslim 1.2%, Protestant 0.4%, others and unknown 10.8%
**Languages:** Serbo-Croatian 96%, other 4%
**Literacy:**
*total population:* NA%
*male:* NA%
*female:* NA%
**Labor force:** 1,509,489
*by occupation:* industry and mining 37%, agriculture 16% (1981 est.), government NA%, other

## Government

**Names:**
*conventional long form:* Republic of Croatia
*conventional short form:* Croatia
*local long form:* Republika Hrvatska
*local short form:* Hrvatska
**Digraph:** HR
**Type:** parliamentary democracy
**Capital:** Zagreb
**Administrative divisions:** 21 counties (zupanijas, zupanija—singular): Bjelovar-

Bilogora, City of Zagreb, Dubrovnik-Neretva, Istra, Karlovac, Koprivnica-Krizevci, Krapina-Zagorje, Lika-Senj, Medimurje, Osijek-Baranja, Pozega-Slavonija, Primorje-Gorski Kotar, Sibenik, Sisak-Moslavina, Slavonski Brod-Posavina, Split-Dalmatia, Varazdin, Virovitica-Podravina, Vukovar-Srijem, Zadar-Knin, Zagreb

**Independence:** NA June 1991 (from Yugoslavia)

**National holiday:** Statehood Day, 30 May (1990)

**Constitution:** adopted on 2 December 1990

**Legal system:** based on civil law system

**Suffrage:** 16 years of age, if employed; 18 years of age, universal

**Executive branch:**

*chief of state:* President Franjo TUDJMAN (since 30 May 1990); election last held 4 August 1992 (next to be held NA 1995); Franjo TUDJMAN reelected with about 56% of the vote; his opponent Dobroslav PARAGA got 5% of the vote

*head of government:* Prime Minister Nikica VALENTIC (since 3 April 1993); Deputy Prime Ministers Mato GRANIC (since 8 September 1992), Ivica KOSTOVIC (since NA), Vladimir SEKS (since September 1992), Borislav SKEGRO (since NA)

*cabinet:* Council of Ministers; appointed by the president

**Legislative branch:** bicameral Assembly (Sabor)

*House of Districts (Zupanije Dom):* elections last held 7 and 21 February 1993 (next to be held NA February 1997); seats—(68 total; 63 elected, 5 presidentially appointed) HDZ 37, HSLS 16, HSS 5, Istrian Democratic Assembly 3, SPH-SDP 1, HNS 1

*House of Representatives (Predstavnicke Dom):* elections last held 2 August 1992 (next to be held NA August 1996); seats—(138 total) HDZ 85, HSLS 14, SPH-SDP 11, HNS 6, Dalmatian Action/Istrian Democratic Assembly/ Rijeka Democratic Alliance coalition 6, HSP 5, HSS 3, SNS 3, independents 5

**Judicial branch:** Supreme Court, Constitutional Court

**Political parties and leaders:** Croatian Democratic Union (HDZ), Stjepan MESIC, chairman of the executive council; Croatian People's Party (HNS), Savka DABCEVIC-KUCAR, president; Serbian People's Party (SNS), Milan DUKIC; Croatian Party of Rights (HSP), leader NA; Croatian Social Liberal Party (HSLS), Drazen BUDISA, president; Croatian Peasant Party (HSS), leader NA; Dalmatian Action/Istrian Democratic Assembly/Rijecka Democratic Alliance coalition; Social Democratic Party of Croatia-Party of Democratic Changes (SPH-SDP), Ivica RACAN

**Other political or pressure groups:** NA

**Member of:** CE (guest), CEI, CSCE, ECE, IAEA, IBRD, ICAO, IDA, IFC, ILO, IMF, IMO, INMARSAT, INTELSAT, INTERPOL, IOC, IOM (observer), ITU, NAM (observer), UN, UNCTAD, UNESCO, UNIDO, UPU, WHO, WIPO, WMO

**Diplomatic representation in US:**

*chief of mission:* Ambassador Petr A. SARCEVIC

*chancery:* (temporary) 236 Massachusetts Avenue NE, Washington, DC 20002

*telephone:* (202) 543-5580

**US diplomatic representation:**

*chief of mission:* Ambassador Peter W. GALBRAITH

*embassy:* Andrije Hebranga 2, Zagreb

*mailing address:* Unit 25402, Zagreb; American Embassy APO AE 09213

*telephone:* [38] (41) 444-800

*FAX:* [38] (41) 440-235

**Flag:** red, white, and blue horizontal bands with Croatian coat of arms (red and white checkered)

# CYPRUS

Mediterranean Sea

50 km

Rizokarpaso

Kyrenia

buffer zone

Turkish Cypriot-administered area

NICOSIA

Famagusta

Polis

Area controlled by Cyprus Government (Greek area)

Larnaca

Paphos

Vasilikos

Episkopi  Limassol

Mediterranean Sea

## Economy

**Overview:** The Greek Cypriot economy is small, diversified, and prosperous. Industry contributes 16% to GDP and employs 29% of the labor force, while the service sector contributes 60% to GDP and employs 57% of the labor force. An average 6.8% rise in real GDP between 1986 and 1990 was temporarily checked in 1991, because of the adverse effects of the Gulf War on tourism. Economic growth surged again in 1992, bolstered by strong foreign and domestic demand. As the economy gained momentum, however, it began to overheat; inflation reached 6.5%. The economy has likely recorded a sharp drop in growth in 1993, due to the recession in Western Europe, Cyprus' main trading partner, but probably will pick up again in 1994. The Turkish Cypriot economy has less than one-third the per capita GDP in the south. Because it is recognized only by Turkey, it has had much difficulty arranging foreign financing, and foreign firms have hesitated to invest there. The economy remains heavily dependent on agriculture, which employs more than one-quarter of the workforce. Moreover, because the Turkish lira is legal tender, the Turkish Cypriot economy has suffered the same high inflation as mainland Turkey. To compensate for the economy's weakness, Turkey provides direct and indirect aid to nearly every sector; financial support has reached about one-third of Turkish Cypriot GDP.

**National product:**
*Greek area:* GDP—purchasing power equivalent—$6.7 billion (1992)
*Turkish area:* GDP—purchasing power equivalent—$550 million (1992)

**National product real growth rate:**
*Greek area:* 8.2% (1992)
*Turkish area:* 7.3% (1992)

**National product per capita:**
*Greek area:* $11,390 (1992)
*Turkish area:* $3,130 (1992)

**Inflation rate (consumer prices):**
*Greek area:* 6.5% (1992)
*Turkish area:* 63.4% (1992)

**Unemployment rate:**
*Greek area:* 1.8% (1992)
*Turkish area:* 1.2% (1992)

**Budget:**
*revenues:* Greek area—$1.7 billion
Turkish area—$273 million
*expenditures:* Greek area—$2.2 billion, including capital expenditures of $350 million
Turkish area—$360 million, including capital expenditures of $78 million (1994)

**Exports:** $1.1 billion (f.o.b., 1993 est.)
*commodities:* citrus, potatoes, grapes, wine, cement, clothing and shoes
*partners:* UK 19%, Greece 8%, Lebanon 2%, Egypt 7%

**Imports:** $3.3 billion (f.o.b., 1993 est.)
*commodities:* consumer goods, petroleum and lubricants, food and feed grains, machinery
*partners:* UK 11%, Japan 11%, Italy 10%, Germany 9%, US 8%

**External debt:** $1.6 billion (1992)

**Industrial production:** growth rate 4.0% (1993 est.); accounts for 16.0% of GDP

**Electricity:**

*capacity:* 620,000 kW
*production:* 1.77 billion kWh
*consumption per capita:* 2,530 kWh (1991)
**Industries:** food, beverages, textiles, chemicals, metal products, tourism, wood products
**Agriculture:** contributes 7% to GDP and employs 26% of labor force in the south; major crops—potatoes, vegetables, barley, grapes, olives, citrus fruits; vegetables and fruit provide 25% of export revenues
**Illicit drugs:** transit point for heroin via air routes and container traffic to Europe, especially from Lebanon and Turkey
**Economic aid:**
*recipient:* US commitments, including Ex-Im (FY70-89), $292 million; Western (non-US) countries, ODA and OOF bilateral commitments (1970-89), $250 million; OPEC bilateral aid (1979-89), $62 million; Communist countries (1970-89), $24 million
**Currency:** 1 Cypriot pound (£C) = 100 cents; 1 Turkish lira (TL) = 100 kurus
**Exchange rates:** Cypriot pounds (£C) per $US1—0.5148 (December 1993), 0.4970 (1993), 0.4502 (1992), 0.4615 (1991), 0.4572 (1990), 0.4933 (1989); Turkish liras (TL) per US$1—15,196.1 (January 1994), 10,983.3 (1993), 6,872.4 (1992), 4,171.8 (1991), 2,608.6 (1990), 2,121.7 (1989)
**Fiscal year:** calendar year

---

## Communications

**Highways:**
*total:* 10,780 km
*paved:* 5,170 km
*unpaved:* gravel, crushed stone, earth 5,610 km
**Ports:** Famagusta, Kyrenia, Larnaca, Limassol, Paphos
**Merchant marine:** 1,399 ships (1,000 GRT or over) totaling 22,743,484 GRT/39,874,985 DWT, short-sea passenger 12, passenger-cargo 2, cargo 496, refrigerated cargo 67, roll-on/roll-off cargo 24, container 82, multifunction large load carrier 4, oil tanker 122, specialized tanker 3, liquefied gas 3, chemical tanker 27, combination ore/oil 32, bulk 469, vehicle carrier 3, combination bulk 48, railcar carrier 1, passenger 4

*note:* a flag of convenience registry; Cuba owns 26 of these ships, Russia owns 61, Latvia owns 7, Croatia owns 2, and Romania owns 4
**Airports:**
*total:* 14
*usable:* 14
*with permanent-surface runways:* 11
*with runways over 3,659 m:* 0
*with runways 2,440-3,659 m:* 7
*with runways 1,220-2,439 m:* 2
**Telecommunications:** excellent in both the area controlled by the Cypriot Government (Greek area), and in the Turkish-Cypriot administered area; 210,000 telephones; largely open-wire and microwave radio relay; broadcast stations—11 AM, 8 FM, 1 (34 repeaters) TV in Greek sector and 2 AM, 6 FM and 1 TV in Turkish sector; international service by tropospheric scatter, 3 submarine cables, and satellite earth stations—1 Atlantic Ocean INTELSAT, 1 Indian Ocean INTELSAT and EUTELSAT earth stations

---

## Defense Forces

**Branches:**
*Greek area:* Greek Cypriot National Guard (GCNG; including air and naval elements), Greek Cypriot Police
*Turkish area:* Turkish Cypriot Security Force
**Manpower availability:** males age 15-49 186,807; fit for military service 128,444; reach military age (18) annually 5,233 (1994 est.)
**Defense expenditures:** exchange rate conversion—$407 million, 6.5% of GDP (1993)

---

## Geography

**Location:** Middle East, in the eastern Mediterrenean Sea, 97 km west of Syria and 64 km west of Turkey
**Map references:** Africa, Middle East, Standard Time Zones of the World
**Area:**
*total area:* 9,250 sq km
*land area:* 9,240 sq km
*comparative area:* about 0.7 times the size of Connecticut
**Land boundaries:** 0 km

**Coastline:** 648 km
**Maritime claims:**
*continental shelf:* 200-m depth or to depth of exploitation
*territorial sea:* 12 nm
**International disputes:** 1974 hostilities divided the island into two de facto autonomous areas, a Greek area controlled by the Cypriot Government (60% of the island's land area) and a Turkish-Cypriot area (35% of the island), that are separated by a narrow UN buffer zone; in addition, there are two UK sovereign base areas (about 5% of the island's land area)
**Climate:** temperate, Mediterranean with hot, dry summers and cool, wet winters
**Terrain:** central plain with mountains to north and south
**Natural resources:** copper, pyrites, asbestos, gypsum, timber, salt, marble, clay earth pigment
**Land use:**
*arable land:* 40%
*permanent crops:* 7%
*meadows and pastures:* 10%
*forest and woodland:* 18%
*other:* 25%
**Irrigated land:** 350 sq km (1989)
**Environment:**
*current issues:* water resource problems (no natural reservoir catchments seasonal disparity in rainfall, and most potable resources concentrated in the Turkish Cypriot area); water pollution from sewage and industrial wastes; coastal degradation; loss of wildlife habitats from urbanization
*natural hazards:* moderate earthquake activity
*international agreements:* party to—Air Pollution, Endangered Species, Environmental Modification, Hazardous Wastes, Law of the Sea, Marine Dumping, Nuclear Test Ban, Ozone Layer Protection, Ship Pollution; signed, but not ratified—Biodiversity, Climate Change

---

## People

**Population:** 730,084 (July 1994 est.)
**Population growth rate:** 0.91% (1994 est.)
**Birth rate:** 16.69 births/1,000 population (1994 est.)

**Death rate:** 7.61 deaths/1,000 population (1994 est.)
**Net migration rate:** 0 migrant(s)/1,000 population (1994 est.)
**Infant mortality rate:** 9 deaths/1,000 live births (1994 est.)
**Life expectancy at birth:**
*total population:* 76.22 years
*male:* 73.97 years
*female:* 78.58 years (1994 est.)
**Total fertility rate:** 2.32 children born/woman (1994 est.)
**Nationality:**
*noun:* Cypriot(s)
*adjective:* Cypriot
**Ethnic divisions:** Greek 78%, Turkish 18%, other 4%
**Religions:** Greek Orthodox 78%, Muslim 18%, Maronite, Armenian, Apostolic, and other 4%
**Languages:** Greek, Turkish, English
**Literacy:** age 15 and over can read and write (1987 est.)
*total population:* 94%
*male:* 98%
*female:* 91%
**Labor force:**
*Greek area:* 285,500
*by occupation:* services 57%, industry 29%, agriculture 14% (1992)
*Turkish area:* 75,000
*by occupation:* services 52%, industry 22%, agriculture 26% (1992)

---

## Government

**Names:**
*conventional long form:* Republic of Cyprus
*conventional short form:* Cyprus
**Digraph:** CY
**Type:** republic
*note:* a disaggregation of the two ethnic communities inhabiting the island began after the outbreak of communal strife in 1963; this separation was further solidified following the Turkish invasion of the island in July 1974, which gave the Turkish Cypriots de facto control in the north; Greek Cypriots control the only internationally recognized government; on 15 November 1983 Turkish Cypriot President Rauf DENKTASH declared

independence and the formation of a "Turkish Republic of Northern Cyprus" (TRNC), which has been recognized only by Turkey; both sides publicly call for the resolution of intercommunal differences and creation of a new federal system of government

**Capital:** Nicosia

**Administrative divisions:** 6 districts; Famagusta, Kyrenia, Larnaca, Limassol, Nicosia, Paphos

**Independence:** 16 August 1960 (from UK)

**National holiday:** Independence Day, 1 October (15 November (1983) is celebrated as Independence Day in the Turkish area)

**Constitution:** 16 August 1960; negotiations to create the basis for a new or revised constitution to govern the island and to better relations between Greek and Turkish Cypriots have been held intermittently; in 1975 Turkish Cypriots created their own Constitution and governing bodies within the "Turkish Federated State of Cyprus," which was renamed the "Turkish Republic of Northern Cyprus" in 1983; a new Constitution for the Turkish area passed by referendum in 5 May 1985

**Legal system:** based on common law, with civil law modifications

**Suffrage:** 18 years of age; universal

**Executive branch:**
*chief of state and head of government:* President Glafkos CLERIDES (since 28 February 1993); election last held 14 February 1993 (next to be held February 1998); results—Glafkos CLERIDES 50.3%, George VASSILIOU 49.7%
*cabinet:* Council of Ministers; appointed jointly by the president and vice-president
*note:* Rauf R. DENKTASH has been president of the Turkish area since 13 February 1975; Hakki ATUN has been prime minister of the Turkish area since 1 January 1994; there is a Council of Ministers (cabinet) in the Turkish area

**Legislative branch:** unicameral
*House of Representatives (Vouli Antiprosopon):* elections last held 19 May 1991 (next to be held NA); results—DISY 35.8%, AKEL (Communist) 30.6%, DIKO 19.5%, EDEK 10.9%; others 3.2%; seats—(56 total) DISY 20, AKEL (Communist) 18, DIKO 11, EDEK 7

*Turkish Area: Assembly of the Republic (Cumhuriyet Meclisi):* elections last held 12 December 1993 (next to be held NA); results—percent of vote by party NA; seats—(50 total) UBP (conservative) 17, DP 15, CTP 13, TKP 5

**Judicial branch:** Supreme Court; note—there is also a Supreme Court in the Turkish area

**Political parties and leaders:**
*Greek Cypriot:* Progressive Party of the Working People (AKEL, Communist Party), Dimitrios CHRISTOFIAS; Democratic Rally (DISY), John MATSIS; Democratic Party (DIKO), Spyros KYPRIANOU; United Democratic Union of the Center (EDEK), Vassos LYSSARIDIS; Socialist Democratic Renewal Movement (ADISOK), Mikhalis PAPAPETROU; Liberal Party, Nikos ROLANDIS; Free Democrats, George VASSILIOU
*Turkish area:* National Unity Party (UBP), Dervis EROGLU; Communal Liberation Party (TKP), Mustafa AKINCI; Republican Turkish Party (CTP), Ozker OZGUR; New Cyprus Party (YKP), Alpay DURDURAN; Social Democratic Party (SDP), Ergun VEHBI; New Birth Party (YDP), Ali Ozkan ALTINISHIK; Free Democratic Party (HDP), Ismet KOTAK; National Struggle Party (MSP), Zorlu TORE; Unity and Sovereignty Party (USP), Arif Salih KIRDAG; Democratic Party (DP), Hakki ATUN; Fatherland Party (VP), Orhan UCOK; *note:* CTP, TKP, and YDP joined in the coalition Democratic Struggle Party (DMP) for the 22 April 1990 legislative election; the CTP and TKP boycotted the by-election of 13 October 1991, in which 12 seats were at stake; the DMP was dissolved after the 1990 election

**Other political or pressure groups:** United Democratic Youth Organization (EDON; Communist controlled); Union of Cyprus Farmers (EKA, Communist controlled); Cyprus Farmers Union (PEK, pro-West); Pan-Cyprian Labor Federation (PEO, Communist controlled); Confederation of Cypriot Workers (SEK, pro-West); Federation of Turkish Cypriot Labor Unions (Turk-Sen); Confederation of Revolutionary Labor Unions (Dev-Is)

**Member of:** C, CCC, CE, CSCE, EBRD,
ECE, FAO, G-77, GATT, IAEA, IBRD,
ICAO, ICC, ICFTU, IDA, IFAD, IFC, ILO,
IMF, IMO, INMARSAT, INTELSAT,
INTERPOL, IOC, IOM, ISO, ITU, NAM,
OAS (observer), UN, UNCTAD, UNESCO,
UNIDO, UPU, WCL, WFTU, WHO, WIPO,
WMO, WTO

**Diplomatic representation in US:**
*chief of mission:* Ambassador Andreas
JACOVIDES
*chancery:* 2211 R Street NW, Washington, DC
20008
*telephone:* (202) 462-5772
*consulate(s) general:* New York
*note:* Representative of the Turkish area in the
US is Namik KORMAN, office at 1667 K
Street NW, Washington, DC, telephone (202)
887-6198

**US diplomatic representation:**
*chief of mission:* Ambassador Richard
BOUCHER
*embassy:* corner of Metochiou and
Ploutarchou Streets, Nicosia
*mailing address:* APO AE 09836
*telephone:* [357] (2) 476100
*FAX:* [357] (2) 465944

**Flag:** white with a copper-colored silhouette
of the island (the name Cyprus is derived from
the Greek word for copper) above two green
crossed olive branches in the center of the flag;
the branches symbolize the hope for peace and
reconciliation between the Greek and Turkish
communities
*note:* the Turkish Cypriot flag has a horizontal
red stripe at the top and bottom with a red
crescent and red star on a white field

**U.S. Government Contacts:**

**U.S. Trade Desk:** (202) 482-3945

**Travel:**

**International Hotels in Country:**
Nicosia:
Cyprus Hilton, Tel: 3572/377777, Fax:
3572/377788
Kennedy Holiday Inn, Tel: 3572/475131, Fax:
3572/473337.

# CZECH REPUBLIC

150 km

## Economy

**Overview:** The dissolution of Czechoslovakia into two independent nation states—the Czech Republic and Slovakia—on 1 January 1993 has complicated the task of moving toward a more open and decentralized economy. The old Czechoslovakia, even though highly industrialized by East European standards, suffered from an aging capital plant, lagging technology, and a deficiency in energy and many raw materials. In January 1991, approximately one year after the end of communist control of Eastern Europe, the Czech and Slovak Federal Republic launched a sweeping program to convert its almost entirely state-owned and controlled economy to a market system. In 1991-92 these measures resulted in privatization of some medium- and small-scale economic activity and the setting of more than 90% of prices by the market—but at a cost in inflation, unemployment, and lower output. For Czechoslovakia as a whole inflation in 1991 was roughly 50% and output fell 15%. In 1992, in the Czech lands, inflation dropped to an estimated 12.5% and GDP was down a more moderate 5%. In 1993, Czech aggregate output remained unchanged, prices rose about 19%, and unemployment hovered above 3%; exports to Slovakia fell roughly 30%. An estimated 40% of the economy was privately owned. In 1994, Prague expects 2% to 3% growth in GDP, roughly 9% inflation, and 5% unemployment. Economic growth in 1994 is less important than continued economic restructuring; a mere 1% growth would be noteworthy if restructuring is accompanied by rising unemployment and enterprise bankruptcies.

**National product:** GDP—purchasing power equivalent—$75 billion (1993 est.)

**National product real growth rate:** 0% (1993 est.)

**National product per capita:** $7,200 (1993 est.)

**Inflation rate (consumer prices):** 19% (1993 est.)

**Unemployment rate:** 3.3% (1993 est.)

**Budget:**
*revenues:* $11.9 billion
*expenditures:* $11.9 billion, including capital expenditures of $NA (1993 est.)

**Exports:** $12.6 billion (f.o.b., 1993 est.)
*commodities:* manufactured goods, machinery and transport equipment, chemicals, fuels, minerals, and metals
*partners:* Germany, Slovakia, Poland, Austria, Hungary, Italy, France, US, UK, CIS republics

**Imports:** $12.4 billion (f.o.b., 1993 est.)
*commodities:* machinery and transport equipment, fuels and lubricants, manfactured goods, raw materials, chemicals, agricultural products
*partners:* Slovakia, CIS republics, Germany, Austria, Poland, Switzerland, Hungary, UK, Italy

**External debt:** $8.6 billion (October 1993)

**Industrial production:** growth rate -5.5% (December 1993 over December 1992)

**Electricity:**
*capacity:* 16,500,000 kW
*production:* 62.2 billion kWh

*consumption per capita:* 6,030 kWh (1992)
**Industries:** fuels, ferrous metallurgy, machinery and equipment, coal, motor vehicles, glass, armaments
**Agriculture:** largely self-sufficient in food production; diversified crop and livestock production, including grains, potatoes, sugar beets, hops, fruit, hogs, cattle, and poultry; exporter of forest products
**Illicit drugs:** transshipment point for Southwest Asian heroin and Latin American cocaine to Western Europe
**Economic aid:**
*donor:* the former Czechoslovakia was a donor—$4.2 billion in bilateral aid to non-Communist less developed countries (1954-89)
**Currency:** 1 koruna (Kc) = 100 haleru
**Exchange rates:** koruny (Kcs) per US$1—30.122 (January 1994), 29.153 (1993), 28.26 (1992), 29.53 (1991), 17.95 (1990), 15.05 (1989)
*note:* values before 1993 reflect Czechoslovak exchange rates
**Fiscal year:** calendar year

## Communications

**Railroads:** 9,434 km total (1988)
**Highways:**
*total:* 55,890 km (1988)
*paved:* NA
*unpaved:* NA
**Inland waterways:** NA km; the Elbe (Labe) is the principal river
**Pipelines:** natural gas 5,400 km
**Ports:** coastal outlets are in Poland (Gdynia, Gdansk, Szczecin), Croatia (Rijeka), Slovenia (Koper), Germany (Hamburg, Rostock); principal river ports are Prague on the Vltava, Decin on the Elbe (Labe)
**Merchant marine:** 18 ships (1,000 GRT or over) totaling 225,934 GRT/350,330 DWT, cargo 11, bulk 7
**Airports:**
*total:* 155
*usable:* 123
*with permanent-surface runways:* 27
*with runways over 3,659 m:* 1
*with runways 2,440-3,659 m:* 17

*with runways 1,060-2,439 m:* 52
*note:* a C-130 can land on a 1,060-m airstrip
**Telecommunications:** NA

## Defense Forces

**Branches:** Army, Air and Air Defense Forces, Civil Defense, Railroad Units
**Manpower availability:** males age 15-49 2,747,126; fit for military service 2,091,532; reach military age (18) annually 93,342 (1994 est.)
**Defense expenditures:** 23 billion koruny, NA% of GNP (1993 est.); note—conversion of defense expenditures into US dollars using the current exchange rate could produce misleading results

## Geography

**Location:** Central Europe, between Germany and Slovakia
**Map references:** Ethnic Groups in Eastern Europe, Europe, Standard Time Zones of the World
**Area:**
*total area:* 78,703 sq km
*land area:* 78,645 sq km
*comparative area:* slightly smaller than South Carolina
**Land boundaries:** total 1,880 km, Austria 362 km, Germany 646 km, Poland 658 km, Slovakia 214 km
**Coastline:** 0 km (landlocked)
**Maritime claims:** none; landlocked
**International disputes:** Liechtenstein claims 1,606 sq km of Czech territory confiscated from its royal family in 1918; Sudeten German claims for restitution of property confiscated in connection with their expulsion after World War II versus the Czech Republic claims that restitution does not proceed before February 1948 when the Communists seized power; unresolved property issues with Slovakia over redistribution of property of the former Czechoslovak federal government
**Climate:** temperate; cool summers; cold, cloudy, humid winters
**Terrain:** two main regions: Bohemia in the

west, consisting of rolling plains, hills, and plateaus surrounded by low mountains; and Moravia in the east, consisting of very hilly country

**Natural resources:** hard coal, soft coal, kaolin, clay, graphite

**Land use:**
*arable land:* NA%
*permanent crops:* NA%
*meadows and pastures:* NA%
*forest and woodland:* NA%
*other:* NA%
**Irrigated land:** NA sq km
**Environment:**
*current issues:* air and water pollution in areas of northwest Bohemia centered around Zeplica and in northern Moravia around Ostrava presents health hazards; acid rain damaging forests
*natural hazards:* NA
*international agreements:* party to—Air Pollution, Air Pollution-Nitrogen Oxides, Air Pollution-Sulphur, Antarctic Treaty, Biodiversity, Climate Change, Environmental Modification, Hazardous Wastes, Law of the Sea, Ozone Layer Protection, Ship Pollution, Wetlands; signed, but not ratified—Antarctic-Environmental Protocol
**Note:** landlocked; strategically located astride some of oldest and most significant land routes in Europe; Moravian Gate is a traditional military corridor between the North European Plain and the Danube in central Europe

---

## People

**Population:** 10,408,280 (July 1994 est.)
**Population growth rate:** 0.21% (1994 est.)
**Birth rate:** 13.23 births/1,000 population (1994 est.)
**Death rate:** 11.14 deaths/1,000 population (1994 est.)
**Net migration rate:** 0 migrant(s)/1,000 population (1994 est.)
**Infant mortality rate:** 9.3 deaths/1,000 live births (1994 est.)
**Life expectancy at birth:**
*total population:* 73.08 years
*male:* 69.38 years
*female:* 76.99 years (1994 est.)

**Total fertility rate:** 1.84 children born/ woman (1994 est.)
**Nationality:**
*noun:* Czech(s)
*adjective:* Czech
**Ethnic divisions:** Czech 94.4%, Slovak 3%, Polish 0.6%, German 0.5%, Gypsy 0.3%, Hungarian 0.2%, other 1%
**Religions:** atheist 39.8%, Roman Catholic 39.2%, Protestant 4.6%, Orthodox 3%, other 13.4%
**Languages:** Czech, Slovak
**Literacy:**
*total population:* NA%
*male:* NA%
*female:* NA%
**Labor force:** 5.389 million
*by occupation:* industry 37.9%, agriculture 8.1%, construction 8.8%, communications and other 45.2% (1990)

---

## Government

**Names:**
*conventional long form:* Czech Republic
*conventional short form:* Czech Republic
*local long form:* Ceska Republika
*local short form:* Cechy
**Digraph:** EZ
**Type:** parliamentary democracy
**Capital:** Prague
**Administrative divisions:** 8 regions (kraje, kraj—singular); Jihocesky, Jihomoravsky, Praha, Severocesky, Severomoravsky, Stredocesky, Vychodocesky, Zapadocesky
**Independence:** 1 January 1993 (from Czechoslovakia)
**National holiday:** National Liberation Day, 9 May; Founding of the Republic, 28 October
**Constitution:** ratified 16 December 1992; effective 1 January 1993
**Legal system:** civil law system based on Austro-Hungarian codes; has not accepted compulsory ICJ jurisdiction; legal code modified to bring it in line with Conference on Security and Cooperation in Europe (CSCE) obligations and to expunge Marxist-Leninist legal theory
**Suffrage:** 18 years of age; universal

**Executive branch:**
*chief of state:* President Vaclav HAVEL (since 26 January 1993); election last held 26 January 1993 (next to be held NA January 1998); results—Vaclav HAVEL elected by the National Council
*head of government:* Prime Minister Vaclav KLAUS (since NA June 1992); Deputy Prime Ministers Ivan KOCARNIK, Josef LUX, Jan KALVODA (since NA June 1992)
*cabinet:* Cabinet; appointed by the president on recommendation of the prime minister
**Legislative branch:** bicameral National Council (Narodni rada)
*Senate:* elections not yet held; seats (81 total)
*Chamber of Deputies:* elections last held 5-6 June 1992 (next to be held NA 1996); results - percent of vote by party NA; seats—(200 total) Civic Democratic Party/Christian Democratic Party 76, Left Bloc 35, Czech Social Democratic Party 16, Liberal Social Union 16, Christian Democratic Union/Czech People's Party 15, Assembly for the Republic/Republican Party 14, Civic Democratic Alliance 14, Movement for Self-Governing Democracy for Moravia and Silesia 14
**Judicial branch:** Supreme Court, Constitutional Court
**Political parties and leaders:** Civic Democratic Party (ODS), Vaclav KLAUS, chairman; Christian Democratic Union-Czech People's Party (KDU-CSL), Josef LUX, chairman; Civic Democratic Alliance (ODA), Jan KALVODA, chairman; Christian Democratic Party (KDS), Ivan PILIP, chairman; Czech Social Democratic Party, Milos ZEMAN, chairman; Czech-Moravian Center Party, Jan KYCER, chairman; Liberal Social Union (LSU), Frantisek TRNKA; Communist Party of Bohemia/Moravia (KSCM), Miroslav GREBENICEK, chairman; Association for the Republic—Republican Party, Miroslav SLADEK, chairman; Left Bloc, Marie STIBOROVA, chairman
**Other political or pressure groups:** Left Bloc; Liberal Party; Czech-Moravian Chamber of Trade Unions
**Member of:** BIS, CCC, CE (guest), CEI, CERN, COCOM (cooperating), CSCE, EBRD, ECE, FAO, GATT, IAEA, IBRD, ICAO, IDA, IFC, IFCTU, ILO, IMF, IMO, INMARSAT, INTELSAT, INTERPOL, IOC, IOM (observer), ISO, ITU, LORCS, NACC, NSG, PCA, UN (as of 8 January 1993), UNAVEM II, UNCTAD, UNESCO, UNIDO, UNOMIG, UNOMOZ, UNPROFOR, UPU, WFTU, WHO, WIPO, WMO, WTO, ZC

**Diplomatic representation in US:**
*chief of mission:* Ambassador Michael ZANTOVSKY
*chancery:* 3900 Spring of Freedom Street NW, Washington, DC 20008
*telephone:* (202) 363-6315 or 6316
*FAX:* (202) 966-8540

**US diplomatic representation:**
*chief of mission:* Ambassador Adrian A. BASORA
*embassy:* Trziste 15, 11801, Prague 1
*mailing address:* Unit 25402; APO AE 09213
*telephone:* [42] (2) 251-0847
*FAX:* [42] (2) 531-193

**Flag:** two equal horizontal bands of white (top) and red with a blue isosceles triangle based on the hoist side (almost identical to the flag of the former Czechoslovakia)

---

**U.S. Government Contacts:**

**U.S. Trade Desk:** (202) 482-4915

---

**Chambers of Commerce & Organizations:**

**American Chamber of Commerce in the Czech Republic**
Karlovo namesti 24
110 00 Prague 1, Czech Republic
Tel: (42) 2 299-887, 296-778
Fax: (42) 2 291-481

---

**Travel:**

**International Hotels in Country:**
Prague:
Diplomat, Tel: 4202/24394111, Fax: 4202/341731
Palace Praha (Interhotel), Tel: 4202/24093111, Fax: 4202/24221240.

# DENMARK

*Skagerrak*

100 km

Skagen

Faroe Islands and Greenland are separate entries.

Ålborg

*Kattegat*

Århus

Esbjerg

COPENHAGEN

Sjælland

Fyn

Odense

Bornholm

Åbenrå

Møn

Lolland

Falster

*Baltic Sea*

## Economy

**Overview:** This modern economy features high-tech agriculture, up-to-date small-scale and corporate industry, extensive government welfare measures, comfortable living standards, and high dependence on foreign trade. Denmark's new center-left coalition government will concentrate on reducing the persistent high unemployment rate and the budget deficit as well as following the previous government's policies of maintaining low inflation and a current account surplus. In the face of recent international market pressure on the Danish krone, the coalition has also vowed to maintain a stable currency. The coalition hopes to lower marginal income taxes while maintaining overall tax revenues; boost industrial competitiveness through labor market and tax reforms and increased research and development funds; and improve welfare services for the neediest while cutting paperwork and delays. Prime Minister RASMUSSEN's reforms will focus on adapting Denmark to the criteria for European integration by 1999; although Copenhagen has won from the European Union (EU) the right to opt out of the European Monetary Union (EMU) if a national referendum rejects it. Denmark is, in fact, one of the few EU countries likely to fit into the EMU on time. Denmark is weathering the current worldwide slump better than many West European countries. As the EU's single market (formally established on 1 January 1993) gets underway, Danish economic growth is expected to pickup to around 2% in 1994. Danish approval of the Maastricht treaty on EU political and economic union in May 1993 has reversed the drop in investment, further boosting growth. The current account surplus remains strong as limitations on wage increases and low inflation—expected to be around 2% in 1994—improve export competitiveness. Although unemployment is high, it remains stable compared to most European countries.

**National product:** GDP—purchasing power equivalent—$95.6 billion (1993)

**National product real growth rate:** 0.5% (1993)

**National product per capita:** $18,500 (1993)

**Inflation rate (consumer prices):** 1.8% (1993 est.)

**Unemployment rate:** 11.8% (1993 est.)

**Budget:**
*revenues:* $48 billion
*expenditures:* $55.7 billion, including capital expenditures of $NA (1993)

**Exports:** $36.7 billion (f.o.b., 1993)
*commodities:* meat and meat products, dairy products, transport equipment (shipbuilding), fish, chemicals, industrial machinery
*partners:* EC 54.3% (Germany 23.6%, UK 10.1%, France 5.7%), Sweden 10.5%, Norway 5.8%, US 4.9%, Japan 3.6% (1992)

**Imports:** $29.7 billion (c.i.f., 1993 est.)
*commodities:* petroleum, machinery and equipment, chemicals, grain and foodstuffs, textiles, paper
*partners:* EC 53.4% (Germany 23.1%, UK 8.2%, France 5.6%), Sweden 10.8%, Norway 5.4%, US 5.7%, Japan 4.1% (1992)

**External debt:** $40 billion (1992 est.)
**Industrial production:** growth rate -2.5% (1993 est.)
**Electricity:**
*capacity:* 11,215,000 kW
*production:* 34.17 billion kWh
*consumption per capita:* 6,610 kWh (1992)
**Industries:** food processing, machinery and equipment, textiles and clothing, chemical products, electronics, construction, furniture, and other wood products, shipbuilding
**Agriculture:** accounts for 4% of GDP and employs 5.6% of labor force (includes fishing and forestry); farm products account for nearly 15% of export revenues; principal products— meat, dairy, grain, potatoes, rape, sugar beets, fish; self-sufficient in food production
**Economic aid:**
*donor:* ODA and OOF commitments (1970-89), $5.9 billion
**Currency:** 1 Danish krone (DKr) = 100 oere
**Exchange rates:** Danish kroner (DKr) per US$1—6.771 (January 1994), 6.484 (1993), 6.036 (1992), 6.396 (1991), 6.189 (1990), 7.310 (1989)
**Fiscal year:** calendar year

## Communications

**Railroads:** 2,770 km; Danish State Railways (DSB) operate 2,120 km (1,999 km rail line and 121 km rail ferry services); 188 km electrified, 730 km double tracked; 650 km of standard-gauge lines are privately owned and operated
**Highways:**
*total:* 66,482 km
*paved:* concrete, asphalt, stone block 64,551 km
*unpaved:* gravel, crushed stone, improved earth 1,931 km
**Inland waterways:** 417 km
**Pipelines:** crude oil 110 km; petroleum products 578 km; natural gas 700 km
**Ports:** Alborg, Arhus, Copenhagen, Esbjerg, Fredericia; numerous secondary and minor ports
**Merchant marine:** 347 ships (1,000 GRT or over) totaling 4,974,494 GRT/6,820,067 DWT, short-sea passenger 12, cargo 110, refrigerated cargo 21, container 51, roll-on/roll-off cargo 39, railcar carrier 1, oil tanker 33, chemical tanker 24, liquefied gas 36, livestock carrier 4, bulk 15, combination bulk 1
*note:* Denmark has created its own internal register, called the Danish International Ship register (DIS); DIS ships do not have to meet Danish manning regulations, and they amount to a flag of convenience within the Danish register; by the end of 1990, 308 of the Danish-flag ships belonged to the DIS
**Airports:**
*total:* 118
*usable:* 109
*with permanent-surface runways:* 28
*with runways over 3,659 m:* 0
*with runways 2,440-3,659 m:* 9
*with runways 1,220-2,439 m:* 7
**Telecommunications:** excellent telephone, telegraph, and broadcast services; 4,509,000 telephones; buried and submarine cables and microwave radio relay support trunk network; broadcast stations—3 AM, 2 FM, 50 TV; 19 submarine coaxial cables; 7 earth stations operating in INTELSAT, EUTELSAT, and INMARSAT

## Defense Forces

**Branches:** Royal Danish Army, Royal Danish Navy, Royal Danish Air Force, Home Guard
**Manpower availability:** males age 15-49 1,360,050; fit for military service 1,168,940; reach military age (20) annually 36,800 (1994 est.)
**Defense expenditures:** exchange rate conversion—$2.8 billion, 2% of GDP (1992)

## Geography

**Location:** Nordic State, Northern Europe, bordering the North Sea on a peninsula north of Germany
**Map references:** Arctic Region, Europe, Standard Time Zones of the World
**Area:**
*total area:* 43,070 sq km
*land area:* 42,370 sq km
*comparative area:* slightly more than twice the size of Massachusetts

*note:* includes the island of Bornholm in the Baltic Sea and the rest of metropolitan Denmark, but excludes the Faroe Islands and Greenland

**Land boundaries:** total 68 km, Germany 68 km

**Coastline:** 3,379 km

**Maritime claims:**

*contiguous zone:* 4 nm

*continental shelf:* 200-m depth or to depth of exploitation

*exclusive fishing zone:* 200 nm

*territorial sea:* 3 nm

**International disputes:** Rockall continental shelf dispute involving Iceland, Ireland, and the UK (Ireland and the UK have signed a boundary agreement in the Rockall area); dispute between Denmark and Norway over maritime boundary in Arctic Ocean between Greenland and Jan Mayen has been settled by the International Court of Justice

**Climate:** temperate; humid and overcast; mild, windy winters and cool summers

**Terrain:** low and flat to gently rolling plains

**Natural resources:** petroleum, natural gas, fish, salt, limestone

**Land use:**

*arable land:* 61%

*permanent crops:* 0%

*meadows and pastures:* 6%

*forest and woodland:* 12%

*other:* 21%

**Irrigated land:** 4,300 sq km (1989 est.)

**Environment:**

*current issues:* air pollution; nitrogen and phosphorus pollution of the North Sea; drinking and surface water becoming polluted from animal wastes

*natural hazards:* NA

*international agreements:* party to—Air Pollution, Air Pollution-Nitrogen Oxides, Air Pollution-Sulphur, Antarctic Treaty, Biodiversity, Climate Change, Endangered Species, Environmental Modification, Hazardous Wastes, Marine Dumping, Marine Life Conservation, Nuclear Test Ban, Ozone Layer Protection, Ship Pollution, Tropical Timber, Wetlands, Whaling; signed, but not ratified—Air Pollution-Volatile Organic Compounds, Antarctic-Environmental Protocol, Law of the Sea

**Note:** controls Danish Straits linking Baltic and North Seas; about one-quarter of the population lives in Copenhagen

## People

**Population:** 5,187,821 (July 1994 est.)

**Population growth rate:** 0.23% (1994 est.)

**Birth rate:** 12.45 births/1,000 population (1994 est.)

**Death rate:** 11.28 deaths/1,000 population (1994 est.)

**Net migration rate:** 1.1 migrant(s)/1,000 population (1994 est.)

**Infant mortality rate:** 6.9 deaths/1,000 live births (1994 est.)

**Life expectancy at birth:**

*total population:* 75.81 years

*male:* 72.93 years

*female:* 78.86 years (1994 est.)

**Total fertility rate:** 1.68 children born/woman (1994 est.)

**Nationality:**

*noun:* Dane(s)

*adjective:* Danish

**Ethnic divisions:** Scandinavian, Eskimo, Faroese, German

**Religions:** Evangelical Lutheran 91%, other Protestant and Roman Catholic 2%, other 7% (1988)

**Languages:** Danish, Faroese, Greenlandic (an Eskimo dialect), German (small minority)

**Literacy:** age 15 and over can read and write (1980 est.)

*total population:* 99%

*male:* NA%

*female:* NA%

**Labor force:** 2,553,900

*by occupation:* private services 37.1%, government services 30.4%, manufacturing and mining 20%, construction 6.3%, agriculture, forestry, and fishing 5.6%, electricity/gas/water 0.6% (1991)

## Government

**Names:**

*conventional long form:* Kingdom of Denmark

*conventional short form:* Denmark

*local long form:* Kongeriget Danmark

*local short form:* Danmark

**Digraph:** DA
**Type:** constitutional monarchy
**Capital:** Copenhagen
**Administrative divisions:** metropolitan Denmark—14 counties (amter, singular—amt) and 1 city* (stad); Arhus, Bornholm, Frederiksborg, Fyn, Kbenhavn, Nordjylland, Ribe, Ringkbing, Roskilde, Snderjylland, Staden Kbenhavn*, Storstrm, Vejle, Vestsjaelland, Viborg
*note:* see separate entries for the Faroe Islands and Greenland, which are part of the Danish realm and self-governing administrative divisions
**Independence:** 1849 (became a constitutional monarchy)
**National holiday:** Birthday of the Queen, 16 April (1940)
**Constitution:** 5 June 1953
**Legal system:** civil law system; judicial review of legislative acts; accepts compulsory ICJ jurisdiction, with reservations
**Suffrage:** 21 years of age; universal
**Executive branch:**
*chief of state:* Queen MARGRETHE II (since NA January 1972); Heir Apparent Crown Prince FREDERIK, elder son of the Queen (born 26 May 1968)
*head of government:* Prime Minister Poul Nyrup RASMUSSEN (since NA January 1993)
*cabinet:* Cabinet; appointed by the monarch
**Legislative branch:** unicameral
*Parliament (Folketing):* elections last held 12 December 1990 (next to be held by December 1994); results—Social Democratic Party 37.4%, Conservative Party 16.0%, Liberal 15.8%, Socialist People's Party 8.3%, Progress Party 6.4%, Center Democratic Party 5.1%, Radical Liberal Party 3.5%, Christian People's Party 2.3%, other 5.2%; seats—(179 total; includes 2 from Greenland and 2 from the Faroe Islands) Social Democratic 69, Conservative 30, Liberal 29, Socialist People's 15, Progress Party 12, Center Democratic 9, Radical Liberal 7, Christian People's 4
**Judicial branch:** Supreme Court
**Political parties and leaders:** Social Democratic Party, Poul Nyrup RASMUSSEN; Conservative Party, Torben RECHENDORFF; Liberal Party, Uffe ELLEMANN-JENSEN; Socialist People's Party, Holger K. NIELSEN; Progress Party, Johannes SORENSEN; Center Democratic Party, Mimi Stilling JAKOBSEN; Radical Liberal Party, Marianne JELVED; Christian People's Party, Jann SJURSEN; Common Course, Preben Moller HANSEN; Danish Workers' Party
**Member of:** AfDB, AG (observer), AsDB, Australia Group, BIS, CBSS, CCC, CE, CERN, COCOM, CSCE, EBRD, EC, ECE, EIB, ESA, FAO, G-9, GATT, IADB, IAEA, IBRD, ICAO, ICC, ICFTU, IDA, IEA, IFAD, IFC, ILO, IMF, IMO, INMARSAT, INTELSAT, INTERPOL, IOC, IOM, ISO, ITU, LORCS, MTCR, NACC, NATO, NC, NEA, NIB, NSG, OECD, PCA, UN, UNCTAD, UNESCO, UNFICYP, UNHCR, UNIDO, UNIKOM, UNOMIG, UNMOGIP, UNPROFOR, UNTSO, UPU, WEU, WFTU, WHO, WIPO, WMO, ZC
**Diplomatic representation in US:**
*chief of mission:* Ambassador Peter Pedersen DYVIG
*chancery:* 3200 Whitehaven Street NW, Washington, DC 20008
*telephone:* (202) 234-4300
*FAX:* (202) 328-1470
*consulate(s) general:* Chicago, Los Angeles, and New York
**US diplomatic representation:**
*chief of mission:* Ambassador Edward E. ELSON
*embassy:* Dag Hammarskjolds Alle 24, 2100 Copenhagen O
*mailing address:* APO AE 09716
*telephone:* [45] (31) 42-31-44
*FAX:* [45] (35) 43-0223
**Flag:** red with a white cross that extends to the edges of the flag; the vertical part of the cross is shifted to the hoist side, and that design element of the DANNEBROG (Danish flag) was subsequently adopted by the other Nordic countries of Finland, Iceland, Norway, and Sweden

---

**U.S. Government Contacts:**

**U.S. Trade Desk:** (202) 482-3254

**American Embassy Commercial Section**
Dag Hammarskjold Alie 24
2100 Cpenhagen, Denmark
APO AE 09716
Tel: 45-31-42-31-44
Fax: 45-1-42-01-75

---

**Denmark Government Contacts:**

**Embassy of Denmark Commercial Section**
3200 Whitehaven Street, N.W.
Washington, DC 20008
Tel: (202) 234-4300

---

**Legal Services:**

**Kierkegaard & Malby**
Amaliegade 4
P.O. Box 3004
DK-1201 Copenhagen K, Denmark
Tel: 45-33-14-35-15
Fax: 45-33-13-19-25
*Megers and Acquistions, Corporate and Commercial Law, Tax Law, Monopolies and Restrictive Trade Practices, Patent Law, Bankruptcy and Insolvency Law.*

---

**Travel:**

**International Airlines to Country:**
Continental

**International Hotels in Country:**
Copenhagen:
DAngleterre, Tel: 4533/12-00-95, Fax: 4533/12-11-18
Nyhavn 71, Tel: 4533/11-85-85, Fax: 4533/93-15-85
SAS Scandinavia, Tel: 4533/11-23-24, Fax: 4531/57-01-93.

# ESTONIA

### Economy

**Overview:** Bolstered by a widespread national desire to reintegrate into Western Europe, the Estonian government has pursued a program of market reforms and rough stabilization measures, which is rapidly transforming the economy. Two years after independence—and one year after the introduction of the kroon—Estonians are beginning to reap tangible benefits; inflation is low; production declines appear to have bottomed out; and living standards are rising. Economic restructuring is clearly underway with the once-dominant energy-intensive heavy industrial sectors giving way to labor-intensive light industry and the underdeveloped service sector. The private sector is growing rapidly; the share of the state enterprises in retail trade has steadily declined and by June 1993 accounted for only 12.5% of total turnover, and 70,000 new jobs have reportedly been created as a result of new business start-ups. Estonia's foreign trade has shifted rapidly from East to West with the Western industrialized countries now accounting for two-thirds of foreign trade.

**National product:** GDP—purchasing power equivalent—$8.8 billion (1993 estimate from the UN International Comparison Program, as extended to 1991 and published in the World Bank's World Development Report 1993; and as extrapolated to 1993 using official Estonian statistics, which are very uncertain because of major economic changes since 1990)

**National product real growth rate:** -5% (1993 est.)

**National product per capita:** $5.480 (1993 est.)

**Inflation rate (consumer prices):** 2.6% per month (1993 average)

**Unemployment rate:** 3.5% (May 1993); but large number of underemployed workers

**Budget:**
*revenues:* $223 million
*expenditures:* $142 million, including capital expenditures of $NA (1992)

**Exports:** $765 million (f.o.b., 1993)
*commodities:* textile 14%, food products 11%, vehicles 11%, metals 11% (1993)
*partners:* Russia, Finland, Latvia, Germany, Ukraine

**Imports:** $865 million (c.i.f., 1993)
*commodities:* machinery 18%, fuels 15%, vehicles 14%, textiles 10% (1993)
*partners:* Finland, Russia, Sweden, Germany, Netherlands

**External debt:** $650 million (end of 1991)

**Industrial production:** growth rate -27% (1993)

**Electricity:**
*capacity:* 3,700,000 kW
*production:* 22.9 billion kWh
*consumption per capita:* 14,245 kWh (1992)

**Industries:** accounts for 42% of labor force; oil shale, shipbuilding, phosphates, electric motors, excavators, cement, furniture, clothing, textiles, paper, shoes, apparel

**Agriculture:** employs 20% of work force; very efficient by Soviet standards; net exports of meat, fish, dairy products, and potatoes; imports of feedgrains for livestock; fruits and vegetables

**Illicit drugs:** transshipment point for illicit drugs from Central and Southwest Asia and Latin America to Western Europe; limited illicit opium producer; mostly for domestic consumption

**Economic aid:**

*recipient:* US commitments, including Ex-Im (1992), $10 million

**Currency:** 1 Estonian kroon (EEK) = 100 cents (introduced in August 1992)

**Exchange rates:** kroons (EEK) per US$1— 13.9 (January 1994), 13.2 (1993); note— kroons are tied to the German Deutschmark at a fixed rate of 8 to 1

**Fiscal year:** calendar year

---

## Communications

**Railroads:** 1,030 km; does not include industrial lines (1990)

**Highways:**

*total:* 30,300 km

*paved or gravelled:* 29,200 km

*unpaved:* earth 1,100 km (1990)

**Inland waterways:** 500 km perennially navigable

**Pipelines:** natural gas 420 km (1992)

**Ports:** coastal—Tallinn, Novotallin, Parnu; inland—Narva

**Merchant marine:** 69 ships (1,000 GRT or over) totaling 406,405 GRT/537,016 DWT, cargo 50, roll-on/roll-off cargo 6, short-sea passenger 4, bulk 6, container 2, oil tanker 1

**Airports:**

*total:* 29

*usable:* 18

*with permanent-surface runways:* 11

*with runways over 3,659 m:* 0

*with runways 2,440-3,659 m:* 10

*with runways 1,060-2,439 m:* 8

*note:* a C-130 can land on a 1,060-m airstrip

**Telecommunications:** Estonia's telephone system is antiquated and supports about 400,000 domestic telephone circuits, i.e. 25 telephones for each 100 persons; improvements are being made piecemeal, with emphasis on business needs and international connections; there are still about 150,000 unfulfilled requests for telephone service; broadcast stations—3 TV (provide Estonian programs as well Moscow Ostenkino's first and second programs); international traffic is carried to the other former USSR republics by land line or microwave and to other countries partly by leased connection to the Moscow international gateway switch, and partly by a new Tallinn-Helsinki fiber optic submarine cable which gives Estonia access to international circuits everywhere; substantial investment has been made in cellular systems which are operational throughout Estonia and also Latvia and which have access to the international packet switched digital network via Helsinki

---

## Defense Forces

**Branches:** Ground Forces, Maritime Border Guard, National Guard (Kaitseliit), Security Forces (internal and border troops), Coast Guard

**Manpower availability:** males age 15-49 392,135; fit for military service 308,951; reach military age (18) annually 11,789 (1994 est.)

**Defense expenditures:** 124.4 million kroons, NA% of GDP (forecast for 1993); note— conversion of the military budget into US dollars using the current exchange rate could produce misleading results

---

## Geography

**Location:** Eastern Europe, bordering the Baltic Sea, between Sweden and Russia

**Map references:** Arctic Region, Asia, Europe, Standard Time Zones of the World

**Area:**

*total area:* 45,100 sq km

*land area:* 43,200 sq km

*comparative area:* slightly larger than New Hampshire and Vermont combined

*note:* includes 1,520 islands in the Baltic Sea

**Land boundaries:** total 557 km, Latvia 267 km, Russia 290 km

**Coastline:** 1,393 km

**Maritime claims:**

*territorial sea:* 12 nm

**International disputes:** none

**Climate:** maritime, wet, moderate winters, cool summers
**Terrain:** marshy, lowlands
**Natural resources:** shale oil, peat, phosphorite, amber
**Land use:**
*arable land:* 22%
*permanent crops:* 0%
*meadows and pastures:* 11%
*forest and woodland:* 31%
*other:* 36%
**Irrigated land:** 110 sq km (1990)
**Environment:**
*current issues:* air heavily polluted with sulfur dioxide from oil-shale burning power plants in northeast; contamination of soil and ground water with petroleum products, chemicals at military bases
*natural hazards:* NA
*international agreements:* party to—Hazardous Wastes, Ship Pollution; signed, but not ratified—Biodiversity, Climate Change

---

## People

**Population:** 1,616,882 (July 1994 est.)
**Population growth rate:** 0.52% (1994 est.)
**Birth rate:** 13.98 births/1,000 population (1994 est.)
**Death rate:** 12.04 deaths/1,000 population (1994 est.)
**Net migration rate:** 3.29 migrant(s)/1,000 population (1994 est.)
**Infant mortality rate:** 19.1 deaths/1,000 live births (1994 est.)
**Life expectancy at birth:**
*total population:* 69.96 years
*male:* 64.98 years
*female:* 75.19 years (1994 est.)
**Total fertility rate:** 2 children born/woman (1994 est.)
**Nationality:**
*noun:* Estonian(s)
*adjective:* Estonian
**Ethnic divisions:** Estonian 61.5%, Russian 30.3%, Ukrainian 3.17%, Byelorussian 1.8%, Finn 1.1%, other 2.13% (1989)
**Religions:** Lutheran
**Languages:** Estonian (official), Latvian, Lithuanian, Russian, other

**Literacy:** age 9-49 can read and write (1989)
*total population:* 100%
*male:* 100%
*female:* 100%
**Labor force:** 750,000 (1992)
*by occupation:* industry and construction 42%, agriculture and forestry 20%, other 38% (1990)

---

## Government

**Names:**
*conventional long form:* Republic of Estonia
*conventional short form:* Estonia
*local long form:* Eesti Vabariik
*local short form:* Eesti
*former:* Estonian Soviet Socialist Republic
**Digraph:** EN
**Type:** republic
**Capital:** Tallinn
**Administrative divisions:** 15 counties (maakonnad, singular—maakond) and 6 municipalities*: Harju maakond (Tallinn), Hiiu maakond (Kardla), Ida-Viru maakond (Johvi), Jarva maakond (Paide), Jogeva maakond (Jogeva), Kohtla-Jarve*, Laane maakond (Haapsalu), Laane-Viru maakond (Rakvere), Narva*, Parnu*, Parnu maakond (Parnu), Polva maakond (Polva), Rapla maakond (Rapla), Saare maakond (Kuessaare), Sillamae*, Tallinn*, Tartu*, Tartu maakond (Tartu), Valga maakond (Valga), Viljandi maakond (Viljandi), Voru maakond (Voru)
*note:* county centers are in parentheses
**Independence:** 6 September 1991 (from Soviet Union)
**National holiday:** Independence Day, 24 February (1918)
**Constitution:** adopted 28 June 1992
**Legal system:** based on civil law system; no judicial review of legislative acts
**Suffrage:** 18 years of age; universal
**Executive branch:**
*chief of state:* President Lennart MERI (since 21 October 1992); election last held 20 September 1992; (next to be held NA 1997); results—no candidate received majority; newly elected Parliament elected Lennart MERI (21 October 1992)
*head of government:* Prime Minister Mart

---

43

LAAR (since 21 October 1992)
*cabinet:* Council of Ministers; appointed by the prime minister, authorized by the legislature
**Legislative branch:** unicameral
*Parliament (Riigikogu):* elections last held 20 September 1992; (next to be held NA); results—Fatherland 21%, Safe Haven 14%, Popular Front 13%, M 10%, ENIP 8%, ERP 7%, ERL 7%, EP 2%, other 18%; seats—(101 total) Fatherland 29, Safe Haven 18, Popular Front 15, M 12, ENIP 10, ERP 8, ERL 8, EP 1
**Judicial branch:** Supreme Court
**Political parties and leaders:** National Coalition Party 'Pro Patria' (Isamaa of Fatherland), Mart LAAR, president, made up of 4 parties: Christian Democratic Party (KDE), Aivar KALA, chairman; Christian Democratic Union (KDL), Illar HALLASTE, chairman; Conservative People's Party (KR), Enn TARTO, chairman; Republican Coalition Party (VK), Leo STARKOV, chairman; Moderates (M), made up of two parties: Estonian Social Democratic Party (ESDB), Marju LAURISTIN, chairman; Estonian Rural Center Pary (EMK), Ivar RAIG, chairman; Estonian National Independence Party (ENIP), Tunne KELAM, chairman; Liberal Democratic Party (LDP), Paul-Eerik RUMMO, chairman; Safe Haven, made up of three parties: Estonian Coalition Party (EK), Tiit VAHI, chairman; Estonian Rural Union (EM), Arvo SIRENDI, chairman; Estonian Democratic Justice Union/ Estonian Pensioners' League (EDO/EPU), Harri KARTNER, chairman; Estonian Centrist Party (EK), Edgar SAVISAAR, chairman; Estonian Democratic Labor Party (EDT), Vaino VALJAS, chairman; Estonian Green Party (ERL), Tonu OJA; Estonian Royalist Party (ERP), Kalle KULBOK, chairman; Entrepreneurs' Party (EP), Tiit MADE; Estonian Citizen (EKL), Juri TOOMEPUU, chairman
**Member of:** BIS, CBSS, CCC, CE, CSCE, EBRD, ECE, FAO, IAEA, IBRD, ICAO, ICFTU, IFC, ILO, IMF, IMO, INTERPOL, IOC, ISO (correspondent), ITU, NACC, UN, UNCTAD, UNESCO, UPU, WHO, WMO
**Diplomatic representation in US:**
*chief of mission:* Ambassador Toomas

Hendrik ILVES
*chancery:* 1030 15th Street NW, Washington, DC 20005, Suite 1000
*telephone:* (202) 789-0320
*FAX:* (202) 789-0471
*consulate(s) general:* New York
**US diplomatic representation:**
*chief of mission:* Ambassador Robert C. FRASURE
*embassy:* Kentmanni 20, Tallin EE 0001
*mailing address:* use embassy street address
*telephone:* 011-[372] (6) 312-021 through 024
*FAX:* [372] (6) 312-025
**Flag:** pre-1940 flag restored by Supreme Soviet in May 1990—three equal horizontal bands of blue (top), black, and white

**U.S. Government Contacts:**

**U.S. Trade Desk:** (202) 482-4915

# FINLAND

300 km

Gulf of Bothnia

Ivalo
Rovaniemi
Oulu
Vaasa  Kuopio
Joensuu
Tampere
Aland
Islands  Turku  Kotka
HELSINKI

## Economy

**Overview:** Finland has a highly industrialized, largely free market economy, with per capita output two-thirds of the US figure. Its key economic sector is manufacturing—principally the wood, metals, and engineering industries. Trade is important, with the export of goods representing about 30% of GDP. Except for timber and several minerals, Finland depends on imports of raw materials, energy, and some components for manufactured goods. Because of the climate, agricultural development is limited to maintaining self-sufficiency in basic products. The economy, which experienced an average of 4.9% annual growth between 1987 and 1989, sank into deep recession in 1991 as growth contracted by 6.5%. The recession—which continued in 1992 with growth contracting by 4.1%—has been caused by economic overheating, depressed foreign markets, and the dismantling of the barter system between Finland and the former Soviet Union under which Soviet oil and gas had been exchanged for Finnish manufactured goods. The Finnish Government has proposed efforts to increase industrial competitiveness and efficiency by an increase in exports to Western markets, cuts in public expenditures, partial privatization of state enterprises, and changes in monetary policy. In June 1991 Helsinki had tied the markka to the European Union's (EU) European Currency Unit (ECU) to promote stability. Ongoing speculation resulting from a lack of confidence in the government's policies forced Helsinki to devalue the markka by about 12% in November 1991 and to indefinitely break the link in September 1992. The devaluations have boosted the competitiveness of Finnish exports to the extent the recession bottomed out in 1993 with renewed economic growth expected in 1994. Unemployment probably will remain a serious problem during the next few years, with the majority of Finnish firms facing a weak domestic market and the troubled German and Swedish export markets. Declining revenues, increased transfer payments, and extensive funding to bail out the banking system pushed the central government's budget deficit to nearly 13% in 1993. Helsinki continues to harmonize its economic policies with those of the EU during Finland's current EU membership bid. In early 1995, Finland is expected to join the European Union (formerly the European Community), thus broadening European economic unity.

**National product:** GDP—purchasing power equivalent—$81.1 billion (1993)

**National product real growth rate:** -2.6% (1993)

**National product per capita:** $16,100 (1993)

**Inflation rate (consumer prices):** 2.1% (1992)

**Unemployment rate:** 22% (1993)

**Budget:**
*revenues:* $26.8 billion
*expenditures:* $40.6 billion, including capital expenditures of $NA (1992)

**Exports:** $23.4 billion (f.o.b., 1993)
*commodities:* timber, paper and pulp, ships, machinery, clothing and footwear

*partners:* EC 53.2% (Germany 15.6%, UK 10.7%), EFTA 19.5% (Sweden 12.8%), US 5.9%, Japan 1.3%, Russia 2.8% (1992)
**Imports:** $18 billion (c.i.f., 1993 est.)
*commodities:* foodstuffs, petroleum and petroleum products, chemicals, transport equipment, iron and steel, machinery, textile yarn and fabrics, fodder grains
*partners:* EC 47.2% (Germany 16.9%, UK 8.7%), EFTA 19.0% (Sweden 11.7%), US 6.1%, Japan 5.5%, Russia 7.1% (1992)
**External debt:** $30 billion (December 1993)
**Industrial production:** growth rate 7.6% (1992 est.)
**Electricity:**
*capacity:* 13,500,000 kW
*production:* 55.3 billion kWh
*consumption per capita:* 11,050 kWh (1992)
**Industries:** metal products, shipbuilding, forestry and wood processing (pulp, paper), copper refining, foodstuffs, chemicals, textiles, clothing
**Agriculture:** accounts for 5% of GDP (including forestry); livestock production, especially dairy cattle, predominates; forestry is an important export earner and a secondary occupation for the rural population;
main crops—cereals, sugar beets, potatoes; 85% self-sufficient, but short of foodgrains and fodder grains; annual fish catch about 160,000 metric tons
**Economic aid:**
*donor:* ODA and OOF commitments (1970-89), $2.7 billion
**Currency:** 1 markka (FMk) or Finmark = 100 pennia
**Exchange rates:** markkaa (FMk) per US$1—5.6920 (January 1994), 5.7123 (1993), 4.4794 (1992), 4.0440 (1991), 3.8235 (1990), 4.2912 (1989)
**Fiscal year:** calendar year

---

**Communications**

**Railroads:** 5,924 km total; Finnish State Railways (VR) operate a total of 5,863 km 1,524-mm gauge, of which 480 km are multiple track and 1,710 km are electrified

**Highways:**
*total:* 76,631 km (1991)
*paved:* bituminous concrete, bituminous treated soil 46,745 km
*unpaved:* gravel 29,886 km
**Inland waterways:** 6,675 km total (including Saimaa Canal); 3,700 km suitable for steamers
**Pipelines:** natural gas 580 km
**Ports:** Helsinki, Oulu, Pori, Rauma, Turku
**Merchant marine:** 93 ships (1,000 GRT or over) totaling 1,040,905 GRT/1,143,276 DWT, passenger 3, short-sea passenger 9, cargo 20, refrigerated cargo 1, roll-on/roll-off cargo 30, oil tanker 15, chemical tanker 5, liquefied gas 3, bulk 7
**Airports:**
*total:* 160
*usable:* 157
*with permanent-surface runways:* 66
*with runways over 3,659 m:* 0
*with runways 2,440-3,659 m:* 26
*with runways 1,220-2,439 m:* 20
**Telecommunications:** good service from cable and microwave radio relay network; 3,140,000 telephones; broadcast stations—6 AM, 105 FM, 235 TV; 1 submarine cable; INTELSAT satellite transmission service via Swedish earth station and a receive-only INTELSAT earth station near Helsinki

---

**Defense Forces**

**Branches:** Army, Navy, Air Force, Frontier Guard (including Coast Guard)
**Manpower availability:** males age 15-49 1,323,322; fit for military service 1,089,300; reach military age (17) annually 33,594 (1994 est.)
**Defense expenditures:** exchange rate conversion—$1.93 billion, about 2% of GDP (1992)

---

**Geography**

**Location:** Nordic State, Northern Europe, bordering the Baltic Sea between Sweden and Russia
**Map references:** Arctic Region, Europe,

Standard Time Zones of the World
**Area:**
*total area:* 337,030 sq km
*land area:* 305,470 sq km
*comparative area:* slightly smaller than Montana
**Land boundaries:** total 2,628 km, Norway 729 km, Sweden 586 km, Russia 1,313 km
**Coastline:** 1,126 km (excludes islands and coastal indentations)
**Maritime claims:**
*contiguous zone:* 6 nm
*continental shelf:* 200-m depth or to depth of exploitation
*exclusive fishing zone:* 12 nm
*territorial sea:* 4 nm
**International disputes:** none
**Climate:** cold temperate; potentially subarctic, but comparatively mild because of moderating influence of the North Atlantic Current, Baltic Sea, and more than 60,000 lakes
**Terrain:** mostly low, flat to rolling plains interspersed with lakes and low hills
**Natural resources:** timber, copper, zinc, iron ore, silver
**Land use:**
*arable land:* 8%
*permanent crops:* 0%
*meadows and pastures:* 0%
*forest and woodland:* 76%
*other:* 16%
**Irrigated land:** 620 sq km (1989 est.)
**Environment:**
*current issues:* air pollution from manufacturing and power plants contributing to acid rain; water pollution from industrial wastes, agricultural chemicals; habitat loss threatens wildlife populations
*natural hazards:* NA
*international agreements:* party to—Air Pollution, Air Pollution-Nitrogen Oxides, Air Pollution-Sulphur, Air Pollution-Volatile Organic Compounds, Antarctic Treaty, Endangered Species, Environmental Modification, Hazardous Wastes, Marine Dumping, Marine Life Conservation, Nuclear Test Ban, Ozone Layer Protection, Ship Pollution, Tropical Timber, Wetlands, Whaling; signed, but not ratified—Antarctic-Environmental Protocol, Biodiversity, Climate Change, Law of the Sea
**Note:** long boundary with Russia; Helsinki is northernmost national capital on European continent; population concentrated on small southwestern coastal plain

---

## People

**Population:** 5,068,931 (July 1994 est.)
**Population growth rate:** 0.34% (1994 est.)
**Birth rate:** 12.41 births/1,000 population (1994 est.)
**Death rate:** 9.84 deaths/1,000 population (1994 est.)
**Net migration rate:** 0.81 migrant(s)/1,000 population (1994 est.)
**Infant mortality rate:** 5.3 deaths/1,000 live births (1994 est.)
**Life expectancy at birth:**
*total population:* 75.93 years
*male:* 72.18 years
*female:* 79.86 years (1994 est.)
**Total fertility rate:** 1.79 children born/woman (1994 est.)
**Nationality:**
*noun:* Finn(s)
*adjective:* Finnish
**Ethnic divisions:** Finn, Swede, Lapp, Gypsy, Tatar
**Religions:** Evangelical Lutheran 89%, Greek Orthodox 1%, none 9%, other 1%
**Languages:** Finnish 93.5% (official), Swedish 6.3% (official), small Lapp- and Russian-speaking minorities
**Literacy:** age 15 and over can read and write (1980 est.)
*total population:* 100%
*male:* NA%
*female:* NA%
**Labor force:** 2.533 million
*by occupation:* public services 30.4%, industry 20.9%, commerce 15.0%, finance, insurance, and business services 10.2%, agriculture and forestry 8.6%, transport and communications 7.7%, construction 7.2%

## Government

**Names:**
*conventional long form:* Republic of Finland
*conventional short form:* Finland
*local long form:* Suomen Tasavalta
*local short form:* Suomi
**Digraph:** FI
**Type:** republic
**Capital:** Helsinki
**Administrative divisions:** 12 provinces (laanit, singular—laani); Ahvenanmaa, Hame, Keski-Suomi, Kuopio, Kymi, Lappi, Mikkeli, Oulu, Pohjois-Karjala, Turku ja Pori, Uusimaa, Vaasa
**Independence:** 6 December 1917 (from Soviet Union)
**National holiday:** Independence Day, 6 December (1917)
**Constitution:** 17 July 1919
**Legal system:** civil law system based on Swedish law; Supreme Court may request legislation interpreting or modifying laws; accepts compulsory ICJ jurisdiction, with reservations
**Suffrage:** 18 years of age; universal
**Executive branch:**
*chief of state:* President Martti AHTISAARI (since 1 March 1994); election last held 31 January—6 February 1994 (next to be held January 2000); results—Martti AHTISAARI 54%, Elisabeth REHN 46%
*head of government:* Prime Minister Esko AHO (since 26 April 1991); Deputy Prime Minister Pertti SALOLAINEN (since at least January 1992)
*cabinet:* Council of State (Valtioneuvosto); appointed by the president, responsible to Parliament
**Legislative branch:** unicameral
*Parliament (Eduskunta):* elections last held 17 March 1991 (next to be held March 1995); results—Center Party 24.8%, Social Democratic Party 22.1%, National Coalition (Conservative) Party 19.3%, Leftist Alliance (Communist) 10.1%, Green League 6.8%, Swedish People's Party 5.5%, Rural 4.8%, Finnish Christian League 3.1%, Liberal People's Party 0.8%; seats—(200 total) Center Party 55, Social Democratic Party 48, National

Coalition (Conservative) Party 40, Leftist Alliance (Communist) 19, Swedish People's Party 12, Green League 10, Finnish Christian League 8, Rural 7, Liberal People's Party 1
**Judicial branch:** Supreme Court (Korkein Oikeus)
**Political parties and leaders:**
*government coalition:* Center Party, Esko AHO; National Coalition (conservative) Party, Perti SALOLAINEN; Swedish People's Party, (Johan) Ole NORRBACK; Finnish Christian League, Toimi KANKAANNIEMI
*other parties:* Social Democratic Party, Paavo LIPPONEN, acting chairman; Leftist Alliance (Communist) People's Democratic League and Democratic Alternative, Claes ANDERSON; Green League, Pekka SAURI; Rural Party, Tina MAKELA; Liberal People's Party, Kalle MAATTA
**Other political or pressure groups:** Finnish Communist Party-Unity, Yrjo HAKANEN; Constitutional Rightist Party; Finnish Pensioners Party; Communist Workers Party, Timo LAHDENMAKI
**Member of:** AfDB, AG (observer), AsDB, Australia Group, BIS, CBSS, CCC, CE, CERN, COCOM (cooperating), CSCE, EBRD, ECE, EFTA, ESA (associate), FAO, G-9, GATT, IADB, IAEA, IBRD, ICAO, ICC, ICFTU, IDA, IEA, IFAD, IFC, ILO, IMF, IMO, INMARSAT, INTELSAT, INTERPOL, IOC, IOM, ISO, ITU, LORCS, MTCR, NAM (guest), NC, NEA, NIB, NSG, OAS (observer), OECD, PCA, UN, UNCTAD, UNDOF, UNESCO, UNFICYP, UNHCR, UNIDO, UNIFIL, UNIKOM, UNMOGIP, UNPROFOR, UNTSO, UPU, WFTU, WHO, WIPO, WMO, WTO, ZC
**Diplomatic representation in US:**
*chief of mission:* Ambassador Jukka VALTASAARI
*chancery:* 3216 New Mexico Avenue NW, Washington, DC 20016
*telephone:* (202) 363-2430
*FAX:* (202) 363-8233
*consulate(s) general:* Los Angeles and New York
**US diplomatic representation:**
*chief of mission:* Ambassador John H. KELLY
*embassy:* Itainen Puistotie 14A, SF-00140, Helsinki

*mailing address:* APO AE 09723
*telephone:* [358] (0) 171931
*FAX:* [358] (0) 174681
**Flag:** white with a blue cross that extends to the edges of the flag; the vertical part of the cross is shifted to the hoist side in the style of the DANNEBROG (Danish flag)

## U.S. Government Contacts:

**U.S. Trade Desk**: (202) 482-3254

**American Embassy Commercial Section**
Itained Puistotie 14A
SF-00140 Helsinki, Finland
APO AE 09723
Tel: 358-0-171-821
Fax: 358-0-635-332

## Finland Government Contacts:

**Invest in Finland Bureau**
P.O. Box 908
00101 Helsinki, Finland
Tel: 358-0-695-9285
Fax: 358-0-694-7934

## Travel:

**International Hotels in Country:**
Helsinki:
Inter-Continental, Tel: 3580/90/40551, Fax: 3580/90/405-5255
Ramada Presidentti, Tel: 3580/90/6911, Fax: 3580/90/694-7886
Strand Inter-Continental, Tel: 3580/90/39351, Fax: 3580/90/761362.

# FRANCE

## Economy

**Overview:** One of the world's most developed economies, France has substantial agricultural resources and a highly diversified modern industrial sector. Large tracts of fertile land, the application of modern technology, and subsidies have combined to make it the leading agricultural producer in Western Europe. Largely self-sufficient in agricultural products, France is a major exporter of wheat and dairy products. The industrial sector generates about one-quarter of GDP, and the growing services sector has become crucial to the economy. Although French GDP contracted by 0.7% in 1993, the economy showed signs of life by yearend. GDP growth, however, will remain sluggish in 1994—perhaps reaching only 1.0%. Rapidly increasing unemployment will still pose a major problem for the government. Paris remains committed to maintaining the franc-deutsche mark parity, which has kept French interest rates high despite France's low inflation. Although the pace of economic integration within the European Community has slowed down, integration presumably will remain a major force shaping the fortunes of the various economic sectors.

**National product:** GDP—purchasing power equivalent—$1.05 trillion (1993)

**National product real growth rate:** -0.7% (1993)

**National product per capita:** $18,200 (1993)

**Inflation rate (consumer prices):** 2.1% (1993)

**Unemployment rate:** 12.2% (May 1994)

**Budget:**
*revenues:* $220.5 billion
*expenditures:* $249.1 billion, including capital expenditures of $47 billion (1993 budget)

**Exports:** $270.5 billion (f.o.b., 1993)
*commodities:* machinery and transportation equipment, chemicals, foodstuffs, agricultural products, iron and steel products, textiles and clothing
*partners:* Germany 18.6%, Italy 11.0%, Spain 11.0%, Belgium-Luxembourg 9.1%, UK 8.8%, Netherlands 7.9%, US 6.4%, Japan 2.0%, former USSR 0.7% (1991 est.)

**Imports:** $250.2 billion (c.i.f., 1993)
*commodities:* crude oil, machinery and equipment, agricultural products, chemicals, iron and steel products
*partners:* Germany 17.8%, Italy 10.9%, US 9.5%, Netherlands 8.9%, Spain 8.8%, Belgium-Luxembourg 8.5%, UK 7.5%, Japan 4.1%, former USSR 1.3% (1991 est.)

**External debt:** $300 billion (1993 est.)

**Industrial production:** growth rate -4.3% (1993)

**Electricity:**
*capacity:* 110 million kW
*production:* 426 billion kWh
*consumption per capita:* 7,430 kWh (1992)

**Industries:** steel, machinery, chemicals, automobiles, metallurgy, aircraft, electronics, mining, textiles, food processing, tourism

**Agriculture:** accounts for 4% of GDP (including fishing and forestry); one of the world's top five wheat producers; other principal products—beef, dairy products, cereals, sugar beets, potatoes, wine grapes; self-sufficient for most temperate-zone foods; shortages include fats and oils and tropical produce, but overall net exporter of farm products; fish catch of 850,000 metric tons ranks among world's top 20 countries and is all used domestically

**Economic aid:**
*donor:* ODA and OOF commitments (1970-89), $75.1 billion

**Currency:** 1 French franc (F) = 100 centimes

**Exchange rates:** French francs (F) per US$1—5.9205 (January 1994), 5.6632 (1993), 5.2938 (1992), 5.6421 (1991), 5.4453 (1990), 6.3801 (1989)

**Fiscal year:** calendar year

## Communications

**Railroads:** French National Railways (SNCF) operates 34,322 km 1,435-mm standard gauge; 12,434 km electrified, 15,132 km double or multiple track; 99 km of various gauges (1,000-mm), privately owned and operated

**Highways:**
*total:* 1,510,750 km
*paved:* 747,750 km (including 7,450 km of controlled access divided highway)
*unpaved:* 763,000 km

**Inland waterways:** 14,932 km; 6,969 km heavily traveled

**Pipelines:** crude oil 3,059 km; petroleum products 4,487 km; natural gas 24,746 km

**Ports:** coastal—Bordeaux, Boulogne, Brest, Cherbourg, Dunkerque, Fos-Sur-Mer, Le Havre, Marseille, Nantes, Sete, Toulon; inland—Rouen

**Merchant marine:** 124 ships (1,000 GRT or over) totaling 3,226,175 GRT/5,109,375 DWT, short-sea passenger 7, cargo 10, container 21, multifunction large-load carrier 1, roll-on/roll-off cargo 21, oil tanker 37, chemical tanker 8, liquefied gas 6, specialized tanker 3, passenger 1, bulk 9
*note:* France also maintains a captive register for French-owned ships in the Kerguelen Islands (French Southern and Antarctic Lands) and French Polynesia

**Airports:**
*total:* 472
*usable:* 461
*with permanent-surface runways:* 258
*with runways over 3,659 m:* 3
*with runways 2,440-3,659 m:* 37
*with runways 1,220-2,439 m:* 136

**Telecommunications:** highly developed; extensive cable and microwave radio relay networks; large-scale introduction of optical-fiber systems; satellite systems for domestic traffic; 39,200,000 telephones; broadcast stations—41 AM, 800 (mostly repeaters) FM, 846 (mostly repeaters) TV; 24 submarine coaxial cables; 2 INTELSAT earth stations (with total of 5 antennas—2 for the Indian Ocean INTELSAT and 3 for the Atlantic Ocean INTELSAT); HF radio communications with more than 20 countries; INMARSAT service; EUTELSAT TV service

## Defense Forces

**Branches:** Army, Navy (including Naval Air), Air Force, National Gendarmerie

**Manpower availability:** males age 15-49 14,717,461; fit for military service 12,265,874; reach military age (18) annually 376,485 (1994 est.)

**Defense expenditures:** exchange rate conversion—$36.6 billion, 3.1% of GDP (1993 est.)

## Geography

**Location:** Western Europe, bordering the North Atlantic Ocean between Spain and Germany

**Map references:** Europe, Standard Time Zones of the World

**Area:**
*total area:* 547,030 sq km
*land area:* 545,630 sq km
*comparative area:* slightly more than twice the size of Colorado
*note:* includes Corsica and the rest of metropolitan France, but excludes the overseas administrative divisions

**Land boundaries:** total 2,892.4 km, Andorra

60 km, Belgium 620 km, Germany 451 km, Italy 488 km, Luxembourg 73 km, Monaco 4.4 km, Spain 623 km, Switzerland 573 km
**Coastline:** 3,427 km (mainland 2,783 km, Corsica 644 km)
**Maritime claims:**
*contiguous zone:* 12-24 nm
*exclusive economic zone:* 200 nm
*territorial sea:* 12 nm
**International disputes:** Madagascar claims Bassas da India, Europa Island, Glorioso Islands, Juan de Nova Island, and Tromelin Island; Comoros claims Mayotte; Mauritius claims Tromelin Island; Seychelles claims Tromelin Island; Suriname claims part of French Guiana; Mexico claims Clipperton Island; territorial claim in Antarctica (Adelie Land); Saint Pierre and Miquelon is focus of maritime boundary dispute between Canada and France
**Climate:** generally cool winters and mild summers, but mild winters and hot summers along the Mediterranean
**Terrain:** mostly flat plains or gently rolling hills in north and west; remainder is mountainous, especially Pyrenees in south, Alps in east
**Natural resources:** coal, iron ore, bauxite, fish, timber, zinc, potash
**Land use:**
*arable land:* 32%
*permanent crops:* 2%
*meadows and pastures:* 23%
*forest and woodland:* 27%
*other:* 16%
**Irrigated land:** 11,600 sq km (1989 est.)
**Environment:**
*current issues:* some forest damage from acid rain; air pollution from industrial and vehicle emissions; water pollution from urban wastes, agricultural runoff
*natural hazards:* NA
*international agreements:* party to—Air Pollution, Air Pollution-Nitrogen Oxides, Air Pollution-Sulphur, Antarctic-Environmental Protocol, Antarctic Treaty, Climate Change, Endangered Species, Hazardous Wastes, Marine Dumping, Marine Life Conservation, Ozone Layer Protection, Ship Pollution, Tropical Timber, Wetlands, Whaling; signed, but not ratified—Air Pollution-Volatile Organic Compounds, Biodiversity, Law of the Sea
**Note:** largest West European nation; occasional warm tropical wind known as mistral

---

## People

**Population:** 57,840,445 (July 1994 est.)
**Population growth rate:** 0.47% (1994 est.)
**Birth rate:** 13.13 births/1,000 population (1994 est.)
**Death rate:** 9.3 deaths/1,000 population (1994 est.)
**Net migration rate:** 0.86 migrant(s)/1,000 population (1994 est.)
**Infant mortality rate:** 6.6 deaths/1,000 live births (1994 est.)
**Life expectancy at birth:**
*total population:* 78.19 years
*male:* 74.27 years
*female:* 82.3 years (1994 est.)
**Total fertility rate:** 1.8 children born/woman (1994 est.)
**Nationality:**
*noun:* Frenchman(men), Frenchwoman(women)
*adjective:* French
**Ethnic divisions:** Celtic and Latin with Teutonic, Slavic, North African, Indochinese, Basque minorities
**Religions:** Roman Catholic 90%, Protestant 2%, Jewish 1%, Muslim (North African workers) 1%, unaffiliated 6%
**Languages:** French 100%, rapidly declining regional dialects and languages (Provencal, Breton, Alsatian, Corsican, Catalan, Basque, Flemish)
**Literacy:** age 15 and over can read and write (1980 est.)
*total population:* 99%
*male:* NA%
*female:* NA%
**Labor force:** 24.17 million
*by occupation:* services 61.5%, industry 31.3%, agriculture 7.2% (1987)

## Government

**Names:**
*conventional long form:* French Republic
*conventional short form:* France
*local long form:* Republique Francaise
*local short form:* France
**Digraph:** FR
**Type:** republic
**Capital:** Paris
**Administrative divisions:** 22 regions
(regions, singular—region); Alsace, Aquitaine,
Auvergne, Basse-Normandie, Bourgogne,
Bretagne, Centre, Champagne-Ardenne,
Corse, Franche-Comte, Haute-Normandie, Ile-
de-France, Languedoc-Roussillon, Limousin,
Lorraine, Midi-Pyrenees, Nord-Pas-de-Calais,
Pays de la Loire, Picardie, Poitou-Charentes,
Provence-Alpes-Cote d'Azur, Rhone-Alpes
*note:* the 22 regions are subdivided into 96
departments; see separate entries for the
overseas departments (French Guiana,
Guadeloupe, Martinique, Reunion) and the
territorial collectivities (Mayotte, Saint Pierre
and Miquelon)
**Dependent areas:** Bassas da India,
Clipperton Island, Europa Island, French
Polynesia, French Southern and Antarctic
Lands, Glorioso Islands, Juan de Nova Island,
New Caledonia, Tromelin Island, Wallis and
Futuna
*note:* the US does not recognize claims to
Antarctica
**Independence:** 486 (unified by Clovis)
**National holiday:** National Day, Taking of
the Bastille, 14 July (1789)
**Constitution:** 28 September 1958, amended
concerning election of president in 1962,
amended to comply with provisions of EC
Maastricht Treaty in 1992; amended to tighten
immigration laws 1993
**Legal system:** civil law system with
indigenous concepts; review of administrative
but not legislative acts
**Suffrage:** 18 years of age; universal
**Executive branch:**
*chief of state:* President Francois
MITTERRAND (since 21 May 1981); election
last held 8 May 1988 (next to be held by May
1995); results—Second Ballot Francois

MITTERRAND 54%, Jacques CHIRAC 46%
*head of government:* Prime Minister Edouard
BALLADUR (since 29 March 1993)
*cabinet:* Council of Ministers; appointed by
the president on the suggestion of the prime
minister
**Legislative branch:** bicameral Parliament
(Parlement)
*Senate (Senat):* elections last held 27
September 1992 (next to be held September
1995—nine-year term, elected by thirds every
three years); results—percent of vote by party
NA; seats—(321 total; 296 metropolitan
France, 13 for overseas departments and
territories, and 12 for French nationals abroad)
RPR 91, UDF 142 (UREI 51, UC 68, RDE 23),
PS 66, PCF 16, independents 2, other 4
*National Assembly (Assemblee Nationale):*
elections last held 21 and 28 March 1993 (next
to be held NA 1998); results - percent of vote
by party NA; seats—(577 total) RPR 247, UDF
213, PS 67, PCF 24, independents 26
**Judicial branch:** Constitutional Court (Cour
Constitutionnelle)
**Political parties and leaders:** Rally for the
Republic (RPR), Jacques CHIRAC; Union for
French Democracy (UDF, federation of UREI,
UC, RDE), Valery Giscard d'ESTAING;
Republican Party (PR), Gerard LONGUET;
Center for Social Democrats (CDS), Pierre
MEHAIGNERIE; Radical (RAD), Yves
GALLAND; Socialist Party (PS), Michel
ROCARD; Left Radical Movement (MRG),
Jean-Francois HORY; Communist Party
(PCF), Robert HUE; National Front (FN),
Jean-Marie LE PEN; Union of Republican and
Independents (UREI); Centrist Union (UC);
Democratic Assembly (RDE); The Greens,
Antoine WAECHTER, Jean-Louis VIDAL,
Guy CAMBOT; Generation Ecology (GE),
Brice LALONDE
**Other political or pressure groups:**
Communist-controlled labor union
(Confederation Generale du Travail—CGT)
nearly 2.4 million members (claimed);
Socialist-leaning labor union (Confederation
Francaise Democratique du Travail or CFDT)
about 800,000 members (est.); independent
labor union (Force Ouvriere) 1 million
members (est.); independent white-collar

union (Confederation Generale des Cadres) 340,000 members (claimed); National Council of French Employers (Conseil National du Patronat Francais—CNPF or Patronat)
**Member of:** ACCT, AfDB, AG (observer), AsDB, Australia Group, BDEAC, BIS, CCC, CDB (non-regional), CE, CERN, COCOM, CSCE, EBRD, EC, ECA (associate), ECE, ECLAC, EIB, ESA, ESCAP, FAO, FZ, GATT, G-5, G-7, G-10, IADB, IAEA, IBRD, ICAO, ICC, ICFTU, IDA, IEA, IFAD, IFC, ILO, IMF, IMO, INMARSAT, INTELSAT, INTERPOL, IOC, IOM, ISO, ITU, LORCS, MINURSO, MTCR, NACC, NATO, NEA, NSG, OAS (observer), OECD, ONUSAL, PCA, SPC, UN, UNCTAD, UNESCO, UNHCR, UNIDO, UNIFIL, UNIKOM, UNOSOM, UNPROFOR, UNRWA, UN Security Council, UNTAC, UN Trusteeship Council, UNTSO, UPU, WCL, WEU, WFTU, WHO, WIPO, WMO, WTO, ZC
**Diplomatic representation in US:**
*chief of mission:* Ambassador Jacques ANDREANI
*chancery:* 4101 Reservoir Road NW, Washington, DC 20007
*telephone:* (202) 944-6000
*consulate(s) general:* Atlanta, Boston, Chicago, Honolulu, Houston, Los Angeles, Miami, New Orleans, New York, San Francisco, and San Juan (Puerto Rico)
**US diplomatic representation:**
*chief of mission:* Ambassador Pamela C. HARRIMAN
*embassy:* 2 Avenue Gabriel, 75382 Paris Cedex 08
*mailing address:* Unit 21551, Paris; APO AE 09777
*telephone:* [33] (1) 4296-12-02 or 42-61-80-75
*FAX:* [33] (1) 4266-9783
*consulate(s) general:* Bordeaux, Marseille, Strasbourg
**Flag:** three equal vertical bands of blue (hoist side), white, and red; known as the French Tricouleur (Tricolor); the design and colors are similar to a number of other flags, including those of Belgium, Chad, Ireland, Cote d'Ivoire, and Luxembourg; the official flag for all French dependent areas

## U.S. Government Contacts:

**U.S. Trade Desk:** (202) 482-6008

**American Embassy Commercial Section**
2 Avenue Gabriel
75382 Paris Cedex 08
Paris, France
APO AE 09777
Tel: 33-1-42-96-1202
Fax: 33-1-4266-4827

**American Consulate General - Marseille Commercial Section**
No. 9 Rue Armeny 13006
13006 Marseilles, France
Tel: 33-91-54-92-00

**American Consulate General - Strasbourg Commercial Section**
15 Avenue D'Alsace
67082 Strasbourg Cedex
Strasbourg, France
APO New York 09777
Tel: 33-88-35-31-04

## France Government Contacts:

**Embassy of France Commercial Section**
4101 Reservoir Road, N.W.
Washington, DC 20007
Tel: (202) 944-6000

## Chambers of Commerce & Organizations:

**American Chamber of Commerce in France**
21 AVenue George V
F-75008 Paris, France
Tel: 33-1-47237028
Fax: 33-1-47201862

## Legal Services:

**Jobard-Chemla & Associes**
Association d'Avocats
50 Boulevard de Courcelles
75017 Paris, France
Tel: 331-42-67-11-70
Fax: 331-42-67-11-83

General Practice in French and International
Law. Foreign Investments, Mergers and
Acquisitions, Corporate, Banking Law, Tax
Law, Agency Franchise, Liscensing, Unfair
Competition, Antitrust.

**Vogel & Vogel**
15, Rue Greuze
75116 Paris, France
Tel: 331-45-53-50-28
Fax: 331-47-55-85-33
*Antitrust Law, European Community Law,
International Business Law, Mergers and
Acquisitions, Product Distribution Law,
Products Liability Law, Unfair Competition
Law.*

**Law Offices of Sylvie J. Volnay**
44 Rue des Belles Feuilles
Paris 75016, France
Tel: 331-45-53-19-19
Fax: 331-47-55-17-85
*Trademark and Intellectual Property Law,
Franchising, European Community Law,
Antitrust Distribution, Unfair Competition,
Economic Regulations, Environment, General
Commercial and Trade Law.*

**Travel:**

**International Airlines to Country:**
American, Continental, Northwest, TWA,
United, USAir

**International Hotels in Country:**
Paris:
L'Hotel, Left bank, Tel: 331-43-25-27-22, Fax:
331-43-25-64-81
Le Bristol, West Paris, Tel: 331-42-66-91-45,
Fax: 331-42-66-68-68
Crillon, West Paris, Tel: 331-44-71-15-00, Fax:
331-44-71-15-02
Grand Hotel Inter-Continental, Central Paris,
Tel: 331-40-07-32-32, Fax: 331-42-66-12-51
Ritz, Central Paris, Tel: 331-42-60-38-30, Fax:
331-42-86-00-91.

# FORMER YUGOSLAVA REP. OF MACEDONIA

Macedonia has proclaimed independent statehood but has not been formally recognized as a state by the United States.

## Economy

**Overview:** The Former Yugoslav Republic of Macedonia, although the poorest republic in the former Yugoslav federation, can meet basic food and energy needs through its own agricultural and coal resources. Its economic decline will continue unless ties are reforged or enlarged with its neighbors Serbia and Montenegro, Albania, Greece, and Bulgaria. The economy depends on outside sources for all of its oil and gas and its modern machinery and parts. Continued political turmoil, both internally and in the region as a whole, prevents any swift readjustments of trade patterns and economic programs. The country's industrial output and GDP are expected to decline further in 1994. The Former Yugoslav Republic of Macedonia's geographical isolation, technological backwardness, and potential political instability place it far down the list of countries of interest to Western investors. Resolution of the dispute with Greece and an internal commitment to economic reform would help to encourage foreign investment over the long run. In the immediate future, the worst scenario for the economy would be the spread of fighting across its borders.

**National product:** GDP—purchasing power equivalent—$2.2 billion (1993 est.)

**National product real growth rate:** -14.7% (1992 est.)

**National product per capita:** $1,000 (1993 est.)

**Inflation rate (consumer prices):** 13% monthly average (1993 est.)

**Unemployment rate:** 27% (1993 est.)

**Budget:**

*revenues:* $NA

*expenditures:* $NA, including capital expenditures of $NA

**Exports:** $889 million (1993)

*commodities:* manufactured goods 40%, machinery and transport equipment 14%, miscellaneous manufactured articles 23%, raw materials 7.6%, food (rice) and live animals 5.7%, beverages and tobacco 4.5%, chemicals 4.7% (1990)

*partners:* principally Serbia and Montenegro and the other former Yugoslav republics, Germany, Greece, Albania

**Imports:** $963 million (1993)

*commodities:* fuels and lubricants 19%, manufactured goods 18%, machinery and transport equipment 15%, food and live animals 14%, chemicals 11.4%, raw materials 10%, miscellaneous manufactured articles 8.0%, beverages and tobacco 3.5% (1990)

*partners:* other former Yugoslav republics, Greece, Albania, Germany, Bulgaria

**External debt:** $840 million (1992)

**Industrial production:** growth rate -14% (1993 est.)

**Electricity:**

*capacity:* 1,600,000 kW

*production:* 6.3 billion kWh

*consumption per capita:* 2,900 kWh (1992)

**Industries:** low levels of technology predominate, such as, oil refining by distillation only; produces basic liquid fuels, coal, metallic chromium, lead, zinc, and ferronickel; light industry produces basic textiles, wood products, and tobacco

**Agriculture:** provides 12% of GDP and meets the basic needs for food; principal crops are rice, tobacco, wheat, corn, and millet; also grown are cotton, sesame, mulberry leaves, citrus fruit, and vegetables; The Former Yugoslav Republic of Macedonia is one of the seven legal cultivators of the opium poppy for the world pharmaceutical industry, including some exports to the US; agricultural production is highly labor intensive

**Illicit drugs:** limited illicit opium cultivation; transshipment point for Asian heroin

**Economic aid:**

*recipient:* US $10 million (for humanitarian and technical assistance)

EC promised a 100 ECU million economic aid package (1993)

**Currency:** the denar, which was adopted by the Macedonian legislature 26 April 1992, was initially issued in the form of a coupon pegged to the German mark; subsequently repegged to a basket of seven currencies

**Exchange rates:** denar per US$1—865 (October 1992)

**Fiscal year:** calendar year

## Communications

**Railroads:** NA

**Highways:**

*total:* 10,591 km

*paved:* 5,091 km

*unpaved:* gravel 1,404 km; earth 4,096 km (1991)

**Inland waterways:** NA km

**Pipelines:** none

**Ports:** none; landlocked

**Airports:**

*total:* 16

*usable:* 16

*with permanent-surface runways:* 10

*with runways over 3,659 m:* 0

*with runways 2,440-3,659 m:* 2

*with runways 1,220-2,439 m:* 2

**Telecommunications:** 125,000 telephones; broadcast stations—6 AM, 2 FM, 5 (2 relays) TV; 370,000 radios, 325,000 TV; satellite communications ground stations—none

## Defense Forces

**Branches:** Army, Navy, Air and Air Defense Force, Police Force

**Manpower availability:** males age 15-49 604,257; fit for military service 489,746; reach military age (19) annually 19,539 (1994 est.)

**Defense expenditures:** 7 billion denars, NA% of GNP (1993 est.); note—conversion of the military budget into US dollars using the prevailing exchange rate could produce misleading results

## Geography

**Location:** Balkan State, Southeastern Europe, between Serbia and Montenegro and Greece

**Map references:** Ethnic Groups in Eastern Europe, Europe, Standard Time Zones of the World

**Area:**

*total area:* 25,333 sq km

*land area:* 24,856 sq km

*comparative area:* slightly larger than Vermont

**Land boundaries:** total 748 km, Albania 151 km, Bulgaria 148 km, Greece 228 km, Serbia and Montenegro 221 km (all with Serbia)

**Coastline:** 0 km (landlocked)

**Maritime claims:** none; landlocked

**International disputes:** Greece claims republic's name implies territorial claims against Aegean Macedonia

**Climate:** hot, dry summers and autumns and relatively cold winters with heavy snowfall

**Terrain:** mountainous territory covered with deep basins and valleys; there are three large lakes, each divided by a frontier line

**Natural resources:** chromium, lead, zinc, manganese, tungsten, nickel, low-grade iron ore, asbestos, sulphur, timber

**Land use:**

*arable land:* 5%

*permanent crops:* 5%

*meadows and pastures:* 20%

*forest and woodland:* 30%

*other:* 40%

**Irrigated land:** NA sq km

**Environment:**

*current issues:* air pollution from metallurgical

plants
*natural hazards:* high seismic risks
*international agreements:* party to—Ozone Layer Protection
**Note:** landlocked; major transportation corridor from Western and Central Europe to Aegean Sea and Southern Europe to Western Europe

## People

**Population:** 2,213,785 (July 1994 est.)
**Population growth rate:** 0.89% (1994 est.)
**Birth rate:** 15.59 births/1,000 population (1994 est.)
**Death rate:** 6.72 deaths/1,000 population (1994 est.)
**Net migration rate:** 0 migrant(s)/1,000 population (1994 est.)
**Infant mortality rate:** 27.8 deaths/1,000 live births (1994 est.)
**Life expectancy at birth:**
*total population:* 73.59 years
*male:* 71.51 years
*female:* 75.85 years (1994 est.)
**Total fertility rate:** 1.98 children born/woman (1994 est.)
**Nationality:**
*noun:* Macedonian(s)
*adjective:* Macedonian
**Ethnic divisions:** Macedonian 65%, Albanian 22%, Turkish 4%, Serb 2%, Gypsies 3%, other 4%
**Religions:** Eastern Orthodox 67%, Muslim 30%, other 3%
**Languages:** Macedonian 70%, Albanian 21%, Turkish 3%, Serbo-Croatian 3%, other 3%
**Literacy:**
*total population:* NA%
*male:* NA%
*female:* NA%
**Labor force:** 507,324
*by occupation:* agriculture 8%, manufacturing and mining 40% (1990)

## Government

**Names:**
*conventional long form:* The Former Yugoslav

Republic of Macedonia
*conventional short form:* none
*local long form:* Republika Makedonija
*local short form:* Makedonija
**Abbreviation:** F.Y.R.O.M.
**Digraph:** MK
**Type:** emerging democracy
**Capital:** Skopje
**Administrative divisions:** 34 counties (opstinas, singular—opstina) Berovo, Bitola, Brod, Debar, Delcevo, Gevgelija, Gostivar, Kavadarci, Kicevo, Kocani, Kratovo, Kriva Palanka, Krusevo, Kumanovo, Murgasevo, Negotino, Ohrid, Prilep, Probistip, Radovis, Resen, Skopje-Centar, Skopje-Cair, Skopje-Karpos, Skopje-Kisela Voda, Skopje-Gazi Baba, Stip, Struga, Strumica, Sveti Nikole, Tetovo, Titov Veles, Valandovo, Vinica
**Independence:** 17 September 1991 (from Yugoslavia)
**National holiday:** NA
**Constitution:** adopted 17 November 1991, effective 20 November 1991
**Legal system:** based on civil law system; judicial review of legislative acts
**Suffrage:** 18 years of age; universal
**Executive branch:**
*chief of state:* President Kiro GLIGOROV (since 27 January 1991); election last held 27 January 1991 (next to be held NA); results—Kiro GLIGOROV was elected by the Assembly
*head of government:* Prime Minister Branko CRVENKOVSKI (since 4 September 1992), Deputy Prime Ministers Jovan ANDONOV (since NA March 1991), Risto IVANOV (since NA), and Becir ZUTA (since NA March 1991)
*cabinet:* Council of Ministers; elected by the majority vote of all the deputies in the Sobranje
**Legislative branch:** unicameral
*Assembly (Sobranje):* elections last held 11 and 25 November and 9 December 1990 (next to be held November 1994); results—percent of vote by party NA; seats—(120 total) VMRO-DPMNE 32, SDSM 29, PDPM 23, SRSM 19, SPM 4, DP 4, SJM 2, others 7
**Judicial branch:** Constitutional Court, Judicial Court of the Republic
**Political parties and leaders:** Social-Democratic Alliance of Macedonia (SDSM;

former Communist Party), Branko
CRVENKOVSKI, president; Party for
Democratic Prosperity (PDPM); National
Democratic Party (PDP), Ilijas HALINI,
president; Alliance of Reform Forces of
Macedonia—Liberal Party (SRSM-LP), Stojan
ANDOV, president; Socialist Party of
Macedonia (SPM), Kiro POPOVSKI,
president; Internal Macedonian Revolutionary
Organization—Democratic Party for
Macedonian National Unity (VMRO-
DPMNE), Ljupco GEORGIEVSKI, president;
Party of Yugoslavs in Macedonia (SJM), Milan
DURCINOV, president; Democratic Party
(DP), Petal GOSEV, president

**Other political or pressure groups:**
Movement for All Macedonian Action
(MAAK); Democratic Party of Serbs;
Democratic Party of Turks; Party for
Democratic Action (Slavic Muslim)

**Member of:** CE (guest), CSCE (observer),
EBRD, ECE, ICAO, ILO, IMF, INTELSAT
(nonsignatory user), ITU, UN, UNCTAD,
UNESCO, UNIDO, UPU, WHO, WIPO,
WMO

**Diplomatic representation in US:** the US
recognized The Former Yugoslav Republic of
Macedonia on 9 February 1994

**US diplomatic representation:** the US
recognized The Former Yugoslav Republic of
Macedonia on 9 February 1994

**Flag:** 16-point gold sun (Vergina, Sun)
centered on a red field

# GERMANY

## Economy

**Overview:** With the collapse of communism in Eastern Europe in 1989, prospects seemed bright for a fairly rapid incorporation of East Germany into the highly successful West German economy. The Federal Republic, however, continues to experience difficulties in integrating and modernizing eastern Germany, and the tremendous costs of unification pushed western Germany into its deepest recession since World War II. The western German economy shrank by 1.9% in 1993 as the Bundesbank maintained high interest rates to offset the inflationary effects of large government deficits and high wage settlements. Eastern Germany grew by 7.1% in 1993 but this was from a shrunken base. Despite government transfers to the east amounting to nearly $110 billion annually, a self-sustaining economy in the region is still some years away. The bright spots are eastern Germany's construction, transportation, telecommunications, and service sectors, which have experienced strong growth. Western Germany has an advanced market economy and is a world leader in exports. It has a highly urbanized and skilled population that enjoys excellent living standards, abundant leisure time, and comprehensive social welfare benefits. Western Germany is relatively poor in natural resources, coal being the most important mineral. Western Germany's world-class companies manufacture technologically advanced goods. The region's economy is mature: services and manufacturing account for the dominant share of economic activity, and raw materials and semimanufactured goods constitute a large portion of imports. In recent years, manufacturing has accounted for about 31% of GDP, with other sectors contributing lesser amounts. Gross fixed investment in 1993 accounted for about 20.5% of GDP. GDP in the western region is now $19,400 per capita, or 78% of US per capita GDP. Eastern Germany's economy appears to be changing from one anchored on manufacturing into a more service-oriented economy. The German government, however, is intent on maintaining a manufacturing base in the east and is considering a policy for subsidizing industrial cores in the region. Eastern Germany's share of all-German GDP is only 8% and eastern productivity is just 30% that of the west even though eastern wages are at roughly 70% of western levels. The privatization agency for eastern Germany, Treuhand, has privatized more than 90% of the 13,000 firms under its control and will likely wind down operations in 1994. Private investment in the region continues to be lackluster, resulting primarily from the deepening recession in western Germany and excessively high eastern wages. Eastern Germany has one of the world's largest reserves of low-grade lignite coal but little else in the way of mineral resources. The quality of statistics from eastern Germany is improving, yet many gaps remain; the federal government began producing all-German data for select economic statistics at the start of 1992. The most challenging economic problem is promoting eastern Germany's economic reconstruction—specifically, finding the right mix of fiscal, monetary, regulatory, and tax policies that will spur investment in eastern Germany—without destabilizing western Germany's economy or damaging relations with West European partners. The government hopes a "solidarity pact" among labor unions, business, state governments, and the SPD opposition will provide the right mix of wage restraints, investment incentives, and spending cuts to stimulate eastern recovery. Finally, the homogeneity of the German economic culture has been changed by the admission of large numbers of immigrants.

**National product:**
*Germany:* GDP—purchasing power equivalent—$1.331 trillion (1993)
*western:* GDP—purchasing power equivalent—$1.218 trillion (1993)
*eastern:* GDP—purchasing power equivalent—$112.7 billion (1993)

**National product real growth rate:**
*Germany:* -1.2% (1993)
*western:* -1.9% (1993)
*eastern:* 7.1% (1993)

**National product per capita:**
*Germany:* $16,500 (1993)
*western:* $19,400 (1993)
*eastern:* $6,300 (1993)

**Inflation rate (consumer prices):**
*western:* 4.2% (1993)
*eastern:* 8.9% (1993 est.)

**Unemployment rate:**
*western:* 8.1% (December 1993)
*eastern:* 15.4% (December 1993)

**Budget:**
*revenues:* $918 billion
*expenditures:* $972 billion, including capital expenditures of $NA (1992)

**Exports:** $392 billion (f.o.b., 1993)
*commodities:* manufactures 89.0% (including machines and machine tools, chemicals, motor vehicles, iron and steel products), agricultural products 5.4%, raw materials 2.2%, fuels 1.3% (1922)
*partners:* EC 51.3% (France 11.1%, Netherlands 8.3%, Italy 8.2%, UK 7.9%, Belgium-Luxembourg 7.5%), EFTA 13.3%, US 6.8%, Eastern Europe 5.0%, OPEC 3.3% (1993)

**Imports:** $374.6 billion (f.o.b., 1993)
*commodities:* manufactures 74.9%, agricultural products 10.3%, fuels 7.4%, raw materials 5.5% (1992)
*partners:* EC 49.7 (France 11.0%, Netherlands 9.2%, Italy 8.8%, UK 6.6%, Belgium-Luxembourg 6.7%), EFTA 12.7%, US 5.9%, Japan 5.2%, Eastern Europe 4.8%, OPEC 2.6% (1993)

**External debt:** $NA

**Industrial production:**
*western:* growth rates -7% (1993)
*eastern:* $NA

**Electricity:**
*capacity:* 134,000,000 kW
*production:* 580 billion kWh
*consumption per capita:* 7,160 kWh (1992)

**Industries:**
*western:* among world's largest producers of iron, steel, coal, cement, chemicals, machinery, vehicles, machine tools, electronics; food and beverages
*eastern:* metal fabrication, chemicals, brown coal, shipbuilding, machine building, food and beverages, textiles, petroleum refining

**Agriculture:**
*western:* accounts for about 2% of GDP (including fishing and forestry); diversified crop and livestock farming; principal crops and livestock include potatoes, wheat, barley, sugar beets, fruit, cabbage, cattle, pigs, poultry; net importer of food
*eastern:* accounts for about 10% of GDP (including fishing and forestry); principal crops—wheat, rye, barley, potatoes, sugar beets, fruit; livestock products include pork, beef, chicken, milk, hides and skins; net importer of food

**Illicit drugs:** source of precursor chemicals for South American cocaine processors; transshipment point for Southwest Asian heroin and Latin American cocaine for West European markets

**Economic aid:**
*western-donor:* ODA and OOF commitments (1970-89), $75.5 billion
*eastern-donor:* bilateral to non-Communist less developed countries (1956-89) $4 billion

**Currency:** 1 deutsche mark (DM) = 100 pfennige

**Exchange rates:** deutsche marks (DM) per US$1—1.7431 (January 1994), 1.6533 (1993), 1.5617 (1992), 1.6595 (1991), 1.6157 (1990), 1.8800 (1989)
**Fiscal year:** calendar year

## Communications

**Railroads:**
*western:* 31,443 km total; 27,421 km government owned, 1.435-meter standard gauge (12,491 km double track, 11,501 km electrified); 4,022 km nongovernment owned, including 3,598 km 1.435-meter standard gauge (214 km electrified) and 424 km 1.000-meter gauge (186 km electrified)
*eastern:* 14,025 km total; 13,750 km 1.435-meter standard gauge, 275 km 1.000-meter or other narrow gauge; 3,830 (est.) km 1.435-meter standard gauge double-track; 3,475 km overhead electrified (1988)
**Highways:**
*total:* 625,600 km (1991 est.); western—501,000 km (1990 est.); eastern—124,600 km (1988 est.)
*paved:* 543,200 km, including 10,814 km of expressways; western—495,900 km, including 8,959 km of expressways; eastern—47,300 km, including 1,855 km of expressways
*unpaved:* 82,400 km; western—5,000 km earth; eastern—77,400 km gravel and earth
**Inland waterways:**
*western:* 5,222 km, of which almost 70% are usable by craft of 1,000-metric-ton capacity or larger; major rivers include the Rhine and Elbe; Kiel Canal is an important connection between the Baltic Sea and North Sea
*eastern:* 2,319 km (1988)
**Pipelines:** crude oil 3,644 km; petroleum products 3,946 km; natural gas 97,564 km (1988)
**Ports:** coastal—Bremerhaven, Brunsbuttel, Cuxhaven, Emden, Bremen, Hamburg, Kiel, Lubeck, Wilhelmshaven, Rostock, Wismar, Stralsund, Sassnitz; inland—31 major on Rhine and Elbe rivers
**Merchant marine:** 485 ships (1,000 GRT or over) totaling 4,541,441 GRT/5,835,511 DWT, short-sea passenger 5, passenger 3, cargo 241, refrigerated cargo 7, container 132, roll-on/roll-off cargo 20, railcar carrier 5, barge carrier 7, oil tanker 7, chemical tanker 20, liquefied gas tanker 16, combination bulk 6, bulk 11, combination ore/oil 5
*note:* the German register includes ships of the former East and West Germany
**Airports:**
*total:* 590
*usable:* 583
*with permanent-surface runways:* 308
*with runways over 3,659 m:* 5
*with runways 2,440-3,659 m:* 85
*with runways 1,220-2,439 m:* 97
**Telecommunications:**
*western:* highly developed, modern telecommunication service to all parts of the country; fully adequate in all respects; 40,300,000 telephones; intensively developed, highly redundant cable and microwave radio relay networks, all completely automatic; broadcast stations—80 AM, 470 FM, 225 (6,000 repeaters) TV; 6 submarine coaxial cables; satellite earth stations—12 Atlantic Ocean INTELSAT antennas, 2 Indian Ocean INTELSAT antennas, EUTELSAT, and domestic systems; 2 HF radiocommunication centers; tropospheric links
*eastern:* badly needs modernization; 3,970,000 telephones; broadcast stations—23 AM, 17 FM, 21 TV (15 Soviet TV repeaters); 6,181,860 TVs; 6,700,000 radios; 1 satellite earth station operating in INTELSAT and Intersputnik systems

## Defense Forces

**Branches:** Army, Navy, Air Force
**Manpower availability:** males age 15-49 20,253,482; fit for military service 17,506,468; reach military age (18) annually 418,124 (1994 est.)
**Defense expenditures:** exchange rate conversion—$42.4 billion, 2.2% of GDP (1992)

## Geography

**Location:** Central Europe, bordering the North Sea between France and Poland
**Map references:** Arctic Region, Europe,

Standard Time Zones of the World
**Area:**
*total area:* 356,910 sq km
*land area:* 349,520 sq km
*comparative area:* slightly smaller than Montana
*note:* includes the formerly separate Federal Republic of Germany, the German Democratic Republic, and Berlin following formal unification on 3 October 1990
**Land boundaries:** total 3,621 km, Austria 784 km, Belgium 167 km, Czech Republic 646 km, Denmark 68 km, France 451 km, Luxembourg 138 km, Netherlands 577 km, Poland 456 km, Switzerland 334 km
**Coastline:** 2,389 km
**Maritime claims:**
*continental shelf:* 200-m depth or to depth of exploitation
*exclusive fishing zone:* 200 nm
*territorial sea:* 3 nm in North Sea and Schleswig-Holstein coast of Baltic Sea (extends, at one point, to 16 nm in the Helgolander Bucht); 12 nm in remainder of Baltic Sea
**International disputes:** none
**Climate:** temperate and marine; cool, cloudy, wet winters and summers; occasional warm, tropical foehn wind; high relative humidity
**Terrain:** lowlands in north, uplands in center, Bavarian Alps in south
**Natural resources:** iron ore, coal, potash, timber, lignite, uranium, copper, natural gas, salt, nickel
**Land use:**
*arable land:* 34%
*permanent crops:* 1%
*meadows and pastures:* 16%
*forest and woodland:* 30%
*other:* 19%
**Irrigated land:** 4,800 sq km (1989 est.)

**Environment:**
*current issues:* emissions from coal-burning utilities and industries in the southeast and lead emissions from vehicle exhausts (the result of continued use of leaded fuels) contribute to air pollution; acid rain, resulting from sulfur dioxide emissions, is damaging forests; heavy pollution in the Baltic Sea from raw sewage and industrial effluents from rivers in eastern Germany
*natural hazards:* NA
*international agreements:* party to—Air Pollution, Air Pollution-Nitrogen Oxides, Air Pollution-Sulphur, Antarctic Treaty, Biodiversity, Climate Change, Endangered Species, Environmental Modification, Marine Dumping, Nuclear Test Ban, Ozone Layer Protection, Ship Pollution, Tropical Timber, Wetlands, Whaling; signed, but not ratified—Air Pollution-Volatile Organic Compounds, Antarctic-Environmental Protocol, Hazardous Wastes
**Note:** strategic location on North European Plain and along the entrance to the Baltic Sea

---

**People**

**Population:** 81,087,506 (July 1994 est.)
**Population growth rate:** 0.36% (1994 est.)
**Birth rate:** 11.04 births/1,000 population (1994 est.)
**Death rate:** 10.89 deaths/1,000 population (1994 est.)
**Net migration rate:** 3.39 migrant(s)/1,000 population (1994 est.)
**Infant mortality rate:** 6.5 deaths/1,000 live births (1994 est.)
**Life expectancy at birth:**
*total population:* 76.34 years
*male:* 73.22 years
*female:* 79.64 years (1994 est.)
**Total fertility rate:** 1.47 children born/ woman (1994 est.)
**Nationality:**
*noun:* German(s)
*adjective:* German
**Ethnic divisions:** German 95.1%, Turkish 2.3%, Italians 0.7%, Greeks 0.4%, Poles 0.4%, other 1.1% (made up largely of people fleeing the war in the former Yugoslavia)
**Religions:** Protestant 45%, Roman Catholic 37%, unaffiliated or other 18%
**Languages:** German
**Literacy:** age 15 and over can read and write (1977 est.)
*total population:* 99%
*male:* NA%
*female:* NA%

**Labor force:** 36.75 million
*by occupation:* industry 41%, agriculture 6%, other 53% (1987)

---

# Government

**Names:**
*conventional long form:* Federal Republic of Germany
*conventional short form:* Germany
*local long form:* Bundesrepublik Deutschland
*local short form:* Deutschland
**Digraph:** GM
**Type:** federal republic
**Capital:** Berlin
*note:* the shift from Bonn to Berlin will take place over a period of years with Bonn retaining many administrative functions and several ministries
**Administrative divisions:** 16 states (laender, singular—land); Baden-Wurttemberg, Bayern, Berlin, Brandenburg, Bremen, Hamburg, Hessen, Mecklenburg-Vorpommern, Niedersachsen, Nordrhein-Westfalen, Rheinland-Pfalz, Saarland, Sachsen, Sachsen-Anhalt, Schleswig-Holstein, Thuringen
**Independence:** 18 January 1871 (German Empire unification); divided into four zones of occupation (UK, US, USSR, and later, France) in 1945 following World War II; Federal Republic of Germany (FRG or West Germany) proclaimed 23 May 1949 and included the former UK, US, and French zones; German Democratic Republic (GDR or East Germany) proclaimed 7 October 1949 and included the former USSR zone; unification of West Germany and East Germany took place 3 October 1990; all four power rights formally relinquished 15 March 1991
**National holiday:** German Unity Day (Day of Unity), 3 October (1990)
**Constitution:** 23 May 1949, known as Basic Law; became constitution of the united German people 3 October 1990
**Legal system:** civil law system with indigenous concepts; judicial review of legislative acts in the Federal Constitutional Court; has not accepted compulsory ICJ jurisdiction

**Suffrage:** 18 years of age; universal
**Executive branch:**
*chief of state:* President Dr. Richard von WEIZSACKER (since 1 July 1984); note— presidential elections were held on 23 May 1994; Roman HERZOG was the winner and will be inaugurated 1 July 1994
*head of government:* Chancellor Dr. Helmut KOHL (since 4 October 1982)
*cabinet:* Cabinet; appointed by the president upon the proposal of the chancellor
**Legislative branch:** bicameral chamber (no official name for the two chambers as a whole)
*Federal Assembly (Bundestag):* last held 2 December 1990 (next to be held by 16 October 1994); results—CDU 36.7%, SPD 33.5%, FDP 11.0%, CSU 7.1%, Green Party (West Germany) 3.9%, PDS 2.4%, Republikaner 2.1%, Alliance 90/Green Party (East Germany) 1.2%, other 2.1%; seats—(662 total) CDU 268, CSU 51, SPD 239, FDP 79, PDS 17, Greens/Alliance '90 8; elected by direct popular vote under a system combining direct and proportional representation; a party must win 5% of the national vote or 3 direct mandates to gain representation
*Federal Council (Bundesrat):* State governments are directly represented by votes; each has 3 to 6 votes depending on size and are required to vote as a block; current composition: votes—(68 total) SPD-led states 37, CDU-led states 31
**Judicial branch:** Federal Constitutional Court (Bundesverfassungsgericht)
**Political parties and leaders:** Christian Democratic Union (CDU), Helmut KOHL, chairman; Christian Social Union (CSU), Theo WAIGEL, chairman; Free Democratic Party (FDP), Klaus KINKEL, chairman; Social Democratic Party (SPD), Rudolf SCHARPING, chairman; Alliance '90/Greens, Ludger VOLMER, Marianne BIRTHLER, co-chairmen; Party of Democratic Socialism (PDS), Lothar BISKY, chairman; Republikaner, Franz SCHOENHUBER; National Democratic Party (NPD), Guenter DECKERT; Communist Party (DKP), Rolf PRIEMER
**Other political or pressure groups:** expellee, refugee, and veterans groups

**Member of:** AfDB, AG (observer), AsDB, Australian Group, BDEAC, BIS, CBSS, CCC, CDB (non-regional), CE, CERN, COCOM, CSCE, EBRD, EC, ECE, EIB, ESA, FAO, G-5, G-7, G-10, GATT, IADB, IAEA, IBRD, ICAO, ICC, ICFTU, IDA, IEA, IFAD, IFC, ILO, IMF, IMO, INMARSAT, INTELSAT, INTERPOL, IOC, IOM, ISO, ITU, LORCS, MTCR, NACC, NAM (guest), NATO, NEA, NSG, OAS (observer), OECD, PCA, UN, UNCTAD, UNESCO, UNIDO, UNHCR, UNOMIG, UNOSOM, UNTAC, UPU, WEU, WHO, WIPO, WMO, WTO, ZC

**Diplomatic representation in US:**
*chief of mission:* Ambassador Immo STABREIT
*chancery:* 4645 Reservoir Road NW, Washington, DC 20007
*telephone:* (202) 298-4000
*FAX:* (202) 298-4249
*consulate(s) general:* Atlanta, Boston, Chicago, Detroit, Houston, Los Angeles, Miami, New York, San Francisco, Seattle
*consulate(s):* Manila (Trust Territories of the Pacific Islands) and Wellington (America Samoa)

**US diplomatic representation:**
*chief of mission:* Ambassador Richard C. HOLBROOKE
*embassy:* Deichmanns Avenue 29, 53170 Bonn
*mailing address:* Unit 21701, Bonn; APO AE 09080
*telephone:* [49] (228) 3391
*FAX:* [49] (228) 339-2663
*branch office:* Berlin
*consulate(s) general:* Frankfurt, Hamburg, Leipzig, Munich, and Stuttgart
**Flag:** three equal horizontal bands of black (top), red, and yellow

---

**U.S. Government Contacts:**

**U.S. Trade Desk**: (202) 482-2435

**American Embassy Commercial Section**
Delchmannasaue
5300 Bonn 2, Germany
APO AE 09080
Tel: 49-228-339-2895
Fax: 49-228-334-649

**American Embassy Office - Berlin**
**Commercial Section**
Neustaedtische Kirchstrasse 4-5
D-1080 Berlin, Germany
APO AE 09235
Tel: 49-30-819-7888
Fax: 37-2-229-2167

**U.S. Commercial Office - Dusseldorf**
Emmanuel-Leutze-Strasse 1B
4000 Dusseldorf 11, Germany
Tel: 49-211-596-798
Fax: 49-211-594-897

**American Consulate General - Frankfurt am Main Commercial Section**
Siesmayerstrasse 21
6000 Frankfurt, Germany
APO AE 09213
Tel: 49-69-7535-2453
Fax: 49-69-748204

**American Consulate General - Hamburg Commercial Section**
Alsterufer 27/28
2000 Hamburg 36, Germany
APO AE 09215
Tel: 49-40-4117-304
Fax: 49-40-410-6958

**American Consulate General - Munich Commercial Section**
Koeniginstrasse 5
8000 Muenchen 22, Germany
APO AE 09108
Tel: 49-89-2888-748
Fax: 49-89-285-261

**American Consulate General - Stuttgart Commercial Section**
Urbanstrasse 7
7000 Stuttgart, Germany
APO AE 09154
Tel: 49-711-246-513
Fax: 49-711-234-350

---

**Germany Government Contacts:**

**Embassy of the Federal Republic of Germany**
4645 Reservoir Road, N.W.
Washington, DC 20007
Tel: 202-298-4000

**Chambers of Commerce & Organizations:**

**American Chamber of Commerce in Germany**
Rossmarkt 12, Postfach 21 23
D-6000 Frankfurt 1, Germany
Tel: 49-69-283-401
Fax: 49-69-285-632

**Legal Services:**
**Carlos Claussen & Partner**
Josef-Orlopp-Strasse 89-91
10365 Berlin, Germany
Tel: 00-49-30-558-83-98
Fax: 00-49-30-558-81-16
*Commercial, Corporation, Common Market, Unfair Competition, Insurance, Trademark, Copyright, International Private Law, Litigation and Arbitration.*

**Meilicke & Partner**
Poppelsdorfer Allee 106
53115 Bonn, Germany
Tel: 49 0228-631635
Fax: 49 0228-659306
*Taxaxtion, Corporation, Reorganization, Mergers and Acquisitions, International Business Law, Anti-Trust, EEC Law, Competition, Civil Litigation, Labor Law, Environmental and Banking, Media Law.*

**Redeker Schon Dahs & Sellner**
Oxfordstrasse 24
53111 Bonn, Germany
Tel: 49 0228 7-26—25-0
Fax: 49 0228-65-04-79
*Administrative, Anit-Trust, Corporate and Commercial, Construction, Media and Copyright, Domestic and International Tax, Trade, Litigation and Appeals.*

**Travel:**

**International Airlines to Country:**
American, Continental, Northwest, TWA, United, USAir

**International Hotels in Country**
Munich:
Bayerischer Hof, Tel: 49089/21200, Fax: 49089/212-0906
Rafael, Tel: 49089/290980, Fax: 49089/222539
Vier Jahreszeiten, Tel: 49089/2303-9693.

# GREECE

## Economy

**Overview:** Greece has a mixed capitalist economy with the basic entrepreneurial system overlaid in 1981-89 by a socialist system that enlarged the public sector from 55% of GDP in 1981 to about 70% in 1989. Since then, the public sector has been reduced to about 60% of GDP. Tourism continues as a major source of foreign exchange, and agriculture is self-sufficient except for meat, dairy products, and animal feedstuffs. Over the last decade, real GDP growth has averaged 1.6% a year, compared with the European Union average of 2.2%. Inflation is four times the EU average, and the national debt has reached 140% of GDP, the highest in the EU. Prime Minister PAPANDREOU will probably only make limited progress correcting the economy's problems of high inflation, large budget deficit, and decaying infrastructure. His economic program suggests that although he will shun his expansionary policies of the 1980s, he will avoid tough measures needed to slow inflation or reduce the state's role in the economy. He has limited the previous government's privatization plans, for example, and has called for generous welfare spending and real wage increases. In 1994, the GDP growth rate is likely to remain low, and inflation probably will accelerate, remaining the highest in the EU. PAPANDREOU'S failure to improve the country's economic performance will further strain relations with the EU. Since Greece's accession to the then EC in 1981, Athens' heavy reliance on EU aid—amounting to about 6% of Greek GDP annually—and its poor use of Union funds have riled Brussels. Its ailing economy will continue to be a drag on European economic and monetary union.

**National product:** GDP—purchasing power equivalent—$93.2 billion (1993)

**National product real growth rate:** 1% (1993)

**National product per capita:** $8,900 (1993)

**Inflation rate (consumer prices):** 14.4% (1993)

**Unemployment rate:** 9.5% (1993)

**Budget:**

*revenues:* $28.3 billion

*expenditures:* $37.6 billion, including capital expenditures of $5.2 billion (1994)

**Exports:** $6 billion (f.o.b., 1992)

*commodities:* manufactured goods 53%, foodstuffs 34%, fuels 5%

*partners:* Germany 23%, Italy 18%, France 7%, UK 7%, US 4% (1992)

**Imports:** $23.3 billion (c.i.f., 1992)

*commodities:* manufactured goods 72%, foodstuffs 15%, fuels 10%

*partners:* Germany 20%, Italy 14%, France 8%, Netherlands 7%, Japan 6% (1992)

**External debt:** $23.1 billion (1992)

**Industrial production:** growth rate -1.3% (1992); accounts for 20% of GDP

**Electricity:**

*capacity:* 10,500,000 kW

*production:* 36.4 billion kWh

*consumption per capita:* 3,610 kWh (1992)

**Industries:** food and tobacco processing, textiles, chemicals, metal products, tourism, mining, petroleum

**Agriculture:** including fishing and forestry, accounts for 15% of GDP and 24% of the labor force; principal products—wheat, corn, barley, sugar beets, olives, tomatoes, wine, tobacco, potatoes; self-sufficient in food except meat, dairy products, and animal feedstuffs

**Illicit drugs:** illicit producer of cannabis and limited opium; mostly for domestic production; serves as a gateway to Europe for traffickers smuggling cannabis and heroin from the Middle East and Southwest Asia to the West and precursor chemicals to the East; transshipment point for Southwest Asian heroin transiting the Balkan route

**Economic aid:**
*recipient:* US commitments, including Ex-Im (FY70-81), $525 million; Western (non-US) countries, ODA and OOF bilateral commitments (1970-89), $1.39 billion

**Currency:** 1 drachma (Dr) = 100 lepta

**Exchange rates:** drachmae (Dr) per US$1—250.28 (January 1994), 229.26 (1993), 190.62 (1992), 182.27 (1991), 158.51 (1990), 162.42 (1989)

**Fiscal year:** calendar year

## Communications

**Railroads:** 2,479 km total; 1,565 km 1,435-mm standard gauge, of which 36 km electrified and 100 km double track; 892 km 1,000-mm gauge; 22 km 750-mm narrow gauge; all government owned

**Highways:**
*total:* 38,938 km
*paved:* 16,090 km
*unpaved:* crushed stone, gravel 13,676 km; improved earth 5,632 km; unimproved earth 3,540 km

**Inland waterways:** 80 km; system consists of three coastal canals; including the Corinth Canal (6 km) which crosses the Isthmus of Corinth connecting the Gulf of Corinth with the Saronic Gulf and shortens the sea voyage from the Adriatic to Piraievs (Piraeus) by 325 km; and three unconnected rivers

**Pipelines:** crude oil 26 km; petroleum products 547 km

**Ports:** Piraievs (Piraeus), Thessaloniki

**Merchant marine:** 1,059 ships (1,000 GRT or over) totaling 29,343,367 GRT/54,249,294 DWT, passenger 15, short-sea passenger 65, passenger-cargo 2, cargo 117, container 36, roll-on/roll-off cargo 17, refrigerated cargo 11, vehicle carrier 1, oil tanker 251, chemical tanker 20, liquefied gas 6, combination ore/oil 38, specialized tanker 3, bulk 453, combination bulk 23, livestock carrier 1
*note:* ethnic Greeks also own large numbers of ships under the registry of Liberia, Panama, Cyprus, Malta, and The Bahamas

**Airports:**
*total:* 78
*usable:* 77
*with permanent-surface runways:* 63
*with runways over 3,659 m:* 0
*with runways 2,440-3,659 m:* 20
*with runways 1,220-2,439 m:* 24

**Telecommunications:** adequate, modern networks reach all areas; 4,080,000 telephones; microwave radio relay carries most traffic; extensive open-wire network; submarine cables to off-shore islands; broadcast stations—29 AM, 17 (20 repeaters) FM, 361 TV; tropospheric links, 8 submarine cables; 1 satellite earth station operating in INTELSAT (1 Atlantic Ocean and 1 Indian Ocean antenna), and EUTELSAT systems

## Defense Forces

**Branches:** Hellenic Army, Hellenic Navy, Hellenic Air Force, National Guard, Police

**Manpower availability:** males age 15-49 2,645,859; fit for military service 2,025,212; reach military age (21) annually 74,484 (1994 est.)

**Defense expenditures:** exchange rate conversion—$4.2 billion, 5.1% of GDP (1992)

## Geography

**Location:** Balkan State, Southern Europe, bordering the Mediterranean Sea between Turkey and Bulgaria

**Map references:** Africa, Europe, Standard Time Zones of the World

**Area:**

*total area:* 131,940 sq km
*land area:* 130,800 sq km
*comparative area:* slightly smaller than Alabama
**Land boundaries:** total 1,210 km, Albania 282 km, Bulgaria 494 km, Turkey 206 km, The Former Yugoslav Republic of Macedonia 228 km
**Coastline:** 13,676 km
**Maritime claims:**
*continental shelf:* 200-m depth or to depth of exploitation
*territorial sea:* 6 nm, but Greece has threatened to claim 12 nm
**International disputes:** air, continental shelf, and territorial water disputes with Turkey in Aegean Sea; Cyprus question; dispute with The Former Yugoslav Republic of Macedonia over name and symbol implying territorial claim
**Climate:** temperate; mild, wet winters; hot, dry summers
**Terrain:** mostly mountains with ranges extending into sea as peninsulas or chains of islands
**Natural resources:** bauxite, lignite, magnesite, petroleum, marble
**Land use:**
*arable land:* 23%
*permanent crops:* 8%
*meadows and pastures:* 40%
*forest and woodland:* 20%
*other:* 9%
**Irrigated land:** 11,900 sq km (1989 est.)
**Environment:**
*current issues:* air pollution; water pollution
*natural hazards:* subject to severe earthquakes
*international agreements:* party to—Air Pollution, Antarctic Treaty, Environmental Modification, Marine Dumping, Nuclear Test Ban, Ozone Layer Protection, Ship Pollution, Tropical Timber, Wetlands; signed, but not ratified—Air Pollution-Nitrogen Oxides, Air Pollution-Volatile Organic Compounds, Antarctic-Environmental Protocol, Biodiversity, Climate Change, Hazardous Wastes, Law of the Sea
**Note:** strategic location dominating the Aegean Sea and southern approach to Turkish Straits; a peninsular country, possessing an archipelago of about 2,000 islands

## People

**Population:** 10,564,630 (July 1994 est.)
**Population growth rate:** 0.84% (1994 est.)
**Birth rate:** 10.5 births/1,000 population (1994 est.)
**Death rate:** 9.32 deaths/1,000 population (1994 est.)
**Net migration rate:** 7.21 migrant(s)/1,000 population (1994 est.)
**Infant mortality rate:** 8.6 deaths/1,000 live births (1994 est.)
**Life expectancy at birth:**
*total population:* 77.71 years
*male:* 75.2 years
*female:* 80.35 years (1994 est.)
**Total fertility rate:** 1.45 children born/ woman (1994 est.)
**Nationality:**
*noun:* Greek(s)
*adjective:* Greek
**Ethnic divisions:** Greek 98%, other 2%
*note:* the Greek Government states there are no ethnic divisions in Greece
**Religions:** Greek Orthodox 98%, Muslim 1.3%, other 0.7%
**Languages:** Greek (official), English, French
**Literacy:** age 15 and over can read and write (1990 est.)
*total population:* 93%
*male:* 98%
*female:* 89%
**Labor force:** 4.083 million
*by occupation:* services 48%, agriculture 24%, industry 28% (1993)

## Government

**Names:**
*conventional long form:* Hellenic Republic
*conventional short form:* Greece
*local long form:* Elliniki Dhimokratia
*local short form:* Ellas
*former:* Kingdom of Greece
**Digraph:** GR
**Type:** presidential parliamentary government; monarchy rejected by referendum 8 December 1974
**Capital:** Athens
**Administrative divisions:** 52 prefectures

(nomoi, singular—nomos); Aitolia kai Akarnania, Akhaia, Argolis, Arkadhia, Arta, Attiki, Dhodhekanisos, Dhrama, Evritania, Evros, Evvoia, Florina, Fokis, Fthiotis, Grevena, Ilia, Imathia, Ioannina, Iraklion, Kardhitsa, Kastoria, Kavala, Kefallinia, Kerkira, Khalkidhiki, Khania, Khios, Kikladhes, Kilkis, Korinthia, Kozani, Lakonia, Larisa, Lasithi, Lesvos, Levkas, Magnisia, Messinia, Pella, Pieria, Piraievs, Preveza, Rethimni, Rodhopi, Samos, Serrai, Thesprotia, Thessaloniki, Trikala, Voiotia, Xanthi, Zakinthos, autonomous region: Agion Oros (Mt. Athos)

**Independence:** 1829 (from the Ottoman Empire)

**National holiday:** Independence Day, 25 March (1821) (proclamation of the war of independence)

**Constitution:** 11 June 1975

**Legal system:** based on codified Roman law; judiciary divided into civil, criminal, and administrative courts

**Suffrage:** 18 years of age; universal and compulsory

**Executive branch:**

*chief of state:* President Konstantinos KARAMANLIS (since 5 May 1990); election last held 4 May 1990 (next to be held May 1995); results—Konstantinos KARAMANLIS was elected by Parliament

*head of government:* Prime Minister Andreas PAPANDREOU (since 10 October 1993)

*cabinet:* Cabinet; appointed by the president on recommendation of the prime minister

**Legislative branch:** unicameral

*Chamber of Deputies (Vouli ton Ellinon):* elections last held 10 October 1993 (next to be held by NA October 1997); results—PASOK 46.88%, ND 39.30%, Political Spring 4.87%, KKE 4.54%, and Progressive Left Coalition 2.94%; seats—(300 total) PASOK 170, ND 111, Political Spring 10, KKE 9

**Judicial branch:** Supreme Judicial Court, Special Supreme Tribunal

**Political parties and leaders:** New Democracy (ND; conservative), Miltiades EVERT; Panhellenic Socialist Movement (PASOK), Andreas PAPANDREOU; Progressive Left Coalition, Maria DAMANAKI; Democratic Renewal

(DIANA), Konstantinos STEFANOPOULOS; Communist Party (KKE), Aleka PAPARIGA; Ecologist-Alternative List, leader rotates; Political Spring, Antonis SAMARAS

**Member of:** Australian Group, BIS, BSEC, CCC, CE, CERN, COCOM, CSCE, EBRD, EC, ECE, EIB, FAO, G-6, GATT, IAEA, IBRD, ICAO, ICC, ICFTU, IDA, IEA, IFAD, IFC, ILO, IMF, IMO, INMARSAT, INTELSAT, INTERPOL, IOC, IOM, ISO, ITU, LORCS, MINURSO, MTCR, NACC, NAM (guest), NATO, NEA, NSG, OAS (observer), OECD, PCA, UN, UNCTAD, UNESCO, UNHCR, UNIDO, UNIKOM, UNOMIG, UNOSOM, UPU, WEU (associate), WFTU, WHO, WIPO, WMO, WTO, ZC

**Diplomatic representation in US:**

*chief of mission:* Ambassador Loucas TSILAS

*chancery:* 2221 Massachusetts Avenue NW, Washington, DC 20008

*telephone:* (202) 939-5800

*FAX:* (202) 939-5824

*consulate(s) general:* Atlanta, Boston, Chicago, Houston, Los Angeles, New York, and San Francisco

*consulate(s):* New Orleans

**US diplomatic representation:**

*chief of mission:* Ambassador Thomas M.T. NILES

*embassy:* 91 Vasilissis Sophias Boulevard, 10160 Athens

*mailing address:* PSC 108, Athens; APO AE 09842

*telephone:* [30] (1) 721-2951 or 721-8401

*FAX:* [30] (1) 645-6282

*consulate(s) general:* Thessaloniki

**Flag:** nine equal horizontal stripes of blue alternating with white; there is a blue square in the upper hoist-side corner bearing a white cross; the cross symbolizes Greek Orthodoxy, the established religion of the country

---

**U.S. Government Contacts:**

**U.S. Trade Desk:** (202) 482-3945

**American Embassy Commercial Section**
91 Vasillis Sophias Boulevard
10160 Athens, Greece
APO AE 09842

Tel: 30-1-723-9705
Fax: 30-1-723-9705

## Greece Government Contacts:

### General Iretorate for Private Investments
Syntagma Sq. 101 80 Athens
Tel: 30-1-216326
Fax: 30-1-3230801

## Chambers of Commerce & Organizations:

### American-Hellenic Chamber of Commerce
16 Kanari Street, 3rd Floor
Athens 106 74, Greece
Tel: 30-1-36-18-385
     30-1-36-36-407
Fax: 30-1-36-10-170

## Legal Services:

### Theodore G. Mitrakos
109 Alkiviadou Street
Piraeus 185 32, Greece
Tel: 30-411-22-42
Fax: 30-411-22-43
*General Civil Law Practice (Torts, Reality, Probate and Estates); Commercial and Corporate Law; Admiralty and Maritime matters.*

### G. and A. Dimopoulos and Associates
3 Korai Street
Athens, 105 64, Greece
Tel: (301) 3225985
    (301) 3222692
Fax: (301) 3228564
*General Legal Practice. Civil and Commercial Law including Patent, Trademark, Unfair Competition Law.*

## Travel:

### International Hotels in Country:
Athens:
Astir Palace, Tel: 3001/896-0211, Fax: 3001/896-2582
Athenaeum Inter-Continental, Tel: 3001/902-3666, Fax: 3001/924-3011
Athens Hilton, Tel: 3001/725-0201, Fax: 3001/725-3110.

# HUNGARY

125 km

## Economy

**Overview:** Hungary is still in the midst of a difficult transition from a command to a market economy. Its economic reforms during the Communist era gave it a head start on this process, particularly in terms of attracting foreign investors—Hungary has accounted for about half of all foreign direct investment in Eastern Europe since 1989. Nonetheless, the economy continued to contract in 1993, with real GDP falling perhaps 1%. Although the privatization process has lagged, in December 1993 Hungary carried out the largest privatization yet in Eastern Europe, selling a controlling interest in the Matav telecommunications firm to private investors—including a 30% share to a US-German consortium for $875 million. Overall, about half of GDP now originates in the private sector. Unemployment rose to about 13% in 1993 while inflation remained above 20%, and falling exports pushed the trade deficit to about $3 billion. The government hopes that economic recovery in Western Europe in 1994 will boost exports, lower the trade deficit, and help jump-start the economy. The budget, however, is likely to remain a serious concern;

depressed tax revenue pushed up the budget deficit in 1993.
**National product:** GDP—purchasing power equivalent—$57 billion (1993 est.)
**National product real growth rate:** -1% (1993 est.)
**National product per capita:** $5,500 (1993 est.)
**Inflation rate (consumer prices):** 23% (1993 est.)
**Unemployment rate:** 13% (1993)
**Budget:**
*revenues:* $10.2 billion
*expenditures:* $12.5 billion, including capital expenditures of $NA (1993 est.)
**Exports:** $8.9 billion (f.o.b., 1993 est.)
*commodities:* raw materials, semi-finished goods, chemicals 39.6%, machinery 14.5%, consumer goods 22.3%, food and agriculture 20.0%, fuels and energy 3.6% (January-June 1993)
*partners:* EC 49.8% (Germany 27.8%, Italy 9.5%), Austria 10.7%, the FSU 13.1%, Eastern Europe 9.8% (1992)
**Imports:** $12.5 billion (f.o.b., 1993 est.)
*commodities:* fuels and energy 13.9%, raw materials, semi-finished goods, chemicals 35.9%, machinery 22.4%, consumer goods 21.8%, food and agriculture 6.0% (January-June 1993)
*partners:* EC 42.8% (Germany 23.6%, Italy 6.3%), Austria 14.4%, the FSU 16.8%, Eastern Europe 9.2%
**External debt:** $24.7 billion (November 1993)
**Industrial production:** growth rate 4% (1993 est.)
**Electricity:**
*capacity:* 7,200,000 kW
*production:* 30 billion kWh
*consumption per capita:* 3,000 kWh (1992)
**Industries:** mining, metallurgy, construction materials, processed foods, textiles, chemicals (especially pharmaceuticals), buses, automobiles

**Agriculture:** including forestry, accounts for 15% of GDP and 16% of employment; highly diversified crop and livestock farming; principal crops—wheat, corn, sunflowers, potatoes, sugar beets; livestock—hogs, cattle, poultry, dairy products; self-sufficient in food output

**Illicit drugs:** transshipment point for Southeast Asia heroin transiting the Balkan route

**Economic aid:**

*recipient:* assistance pledged by OECD countries since 1989 about $9 billion

**Currency:** 1 forint (Ft) = 100 filler

**Exchange rates:** forints per US$1—93.46 (September 1993), 92.5 (1993), 78.99 (1992), 74.74 (1991), 63.21 (1990), 59.07 (1989)

**Fiscal year:** calendar year

## Communications

**Railroads:** 7,765 km total; 7,508 km 1.435-meter standard gauge, 222 km narrow gauge (mostly 0.760-meter), 35 km 1.520-meter broad gauge; 1,236 km double track, 2,249 km electrified; all government owned (1990)

**Highways:**

*total:* 130,224 km

*paved:* 61,948 km

*unpaved:* 68,276 km (1988)

**Inland waterways:** 1,622 km (1988)

**Pipelines:** crude oil 1,204 km; natural gas 4,387 km (1991)

**Ports:** Budapest and Dunaujvaros are river ports on the Danube; coastal outlets are Rostock (Germany), Gdansk (Poland), Gdynia (Poland), Szczecin (Poland), Galati (Romania), and Braila (Romania)

**Merchant marine:** 10 cargo ships (1,000 GRT or over) and 1 bulk totaling 46,121 GRT/ 61,613 DWT

**Airports:**

*total:* 126

*usable:* 65

*with permanent-surface runways:* 12

*with runways over 3,659 m:* 1

*with runways 2,440-3,659 m:* 18

*with runways 1,060-2,439 m:* 31

*note:* a C-130 can land on a 1,060-m airstrip

**Telecommunications:** automatic telephone network based on microwave radio relay system; 1,128,800 phones (1991); telephone density is at 19.4 per 100 inhabitants; 49% of all phones are in Budapest; 608,000 telephones on order (1991); 12-15 year wait for a phone; 14,213 telex lines (1991); broadcast stations— 32 AM, 15 FM, 41 TV (8 Soviet TV repeaters); 4.2 million TVs (1990); 1 satellite ground station using INTELSAT and Intersputnik

## Defense Forces

**Branches:** Ground Forces, Air and Air Defense Forces, Border Guard, Territorial Defense

**Manpower availability:** males age 15-49 2,636,888; fit for military service 2,105,628; reach military age (18) annually 90,134 (1994 est.)

**Defense expenditures:** 66.5 billion forints, NA% of GNP (1993 est.); note—conversion of defense expenditures into US dollars using the current exchange rate could produce misleading results

## Geography

**Location:** Central Europe, between Slovakia and Romania

**Map references:** Ethnic Groups in Eastern Europe, Europe

**Area:**

*total area:* 93,030 sq km

*land area:* 92,340 sq km

*comparative area:* slightly smaller than Indiana

**Land boundaries:** total 1,989 km, Austria 366 km, Croatia 329 km, Romania 443 km, Serbia and Montenegro 151 km (all with Serbia), Slovakia 515 km, Slovenia 82 km, Ukraine 103 km

**Coastline:** 0 km (landlocked)

**Maritime claims:** none; landlocked

**International disputes:** Gabcikovo Dam dispute with Slovakia

**Climate:** temperate; cold, cloudy, humid winters; warm summers

**Terrain:** mostly flat to rolling plains

**Natural resources:** bauxite, coal, natural gas, fertile soils
**Land use:**
*arable land:* 50.7%
*permanent crops:* 6.1%
*meadows and pastures:* 12.6%
*forest and woodland:* 18.3%
*other:* 12.3%
**Irrigated land:** 1,750 sq km (1989)
**Environment:**
*current issues:* air pollution; industrial and municipal pollution of Lake Balaton
*natural hazards:* levees are common along many streams, but flooding occurs almost every year
*international agreements:* party to—Air Pollution, Air Pollution-Nitrogen Oxides, Air Pollution-Sulphur, Antarctic Treaty, Biodiversity, Climate Change, Endangered Species, Environmental Modification, Hazardous Wastes, Marine Dumping, Nuclear Test Ban, Ozone Layer Protection, Ship Pollution, Wetlands; signed, but not ratified— Air Pollution-Volatile Organic Compounds, Antarctic-Environmental Protocol, Law of the Sea
**Note:** landlocked; strategic location astride main land routes between Western Europe and Balkan Peninsula as well as between Ukraine and Mediterranean basin

---

## People

**Population:** 10,319,113 (July 1994 est.)
**Population growth rate:** -0.03% (1994 est.)
**Birth rate:** 12.46 births/1,000 population (1994 est.)
**Death rate:** 12.72 deaths/1,000 population (1994 est.)
**Net migration rate:** 0 migrant(s)/1,000 population (1994 est.)
**Infant mortality rate:** 12.5 deaths/1,000 live births (1994 est.)
**Life expectancy at birth:**
*total population:* 71.37 years
*male:* 67.37 years
*female:* 75.58 years (1994 est.)
**Total fertility rate:** 1.83 children born/ woman (1994 est.)

**Nationality:**
*noun:* Hungarian(s)
*adjective:* Hungarian
**Ethnic divisions:** Hungarian 89.9%, Gypsy 4%, German 2.6%, Serb 2%, Slovak 0.8%, Romanian 0.7%
**Religions:** Roman Catholic 67.5%, Calvinist 20%, Lutheran 5%, atheist and other 7.5%
**Languages:** Hungarian 98.2%, other 1.8%
**Literacy:** age 15 and over can read and write (1980)
*total population:* 99%
*male:* 99%
*female:* 98%
**Labor force:** 5.4 million
*by occupation:* services, trade, government, and other 44.8%, industry 29.7%, agriculture 16.1%, construction 7.0% (1991)

---

## Government

**Names:**
*conventional long form:* Republic of Hungary
*conventional short form:* Hungary
*local long form:* Magyar Koztarsasag
*local short form:* Magyarorszag
**Digraph:** HU
**Type:** republic
**Capital:** Budapest
**Administrative divisions:** 38 counties (megyek, singular—megye) and 1 capital city* (fovaros); Bacs-Kiskun, Baranya, Bekes, Bekescsaba, Borsod-Abauj-Zemplen, Budapest*, Csongrad, Debrecen, Dunaujvaros, Eger, Fejer, Gyor, Gyor-Moson-Sopron, Hajdu-Bihar, Heves, Hodmezovasarhely, Jasz-Nagykun-Szolnok, Kaposvar, Kecskemet, Komarom-Esztergom, Miskolc, Nagykanizsa, Nograd, Nyiregyhaza, Pecs, Pest, Somogy, Sopron, Szabolcs-Szatmar-Bereg, Szeged, Szekesfehervar, Szolnok, Szombathely, Tatabanya, Tolna, Vas, Veszprem, Zala, Zalaegerszeg
**Independence:** 1001 (unification by King Stephen I)
**National holiday:** St. Stephen's Day (National Day), 20 August (commemorates the founding of Hungarian state circa 1000 A.D.)
**Constitution:** 18 August 1949, effective 20

August 1949, revised 19 April 1972; 18 October 1989 revision ensured legal rights for individuals and constitutional checks on the authority of the prime minister and also established the principle of parliamentary oversight

**Legal system:** in process of revision, moving toward rule of law based on Western model

**Suffrage:** 18 years of age; universal

**Executive branch:**

*chief of state:* President Arpad GONCZ (since 3 August 1990; previously interim president from 2 May 1990); election last held 3 August 1990 (next to be held NA 1995); results— President GONCZ elected by parliamentary vote; note—President GONCZ was elected by the National Assembly with a total of 295 votes out of 304 as interim President from 2 May 1990 until elected President

*head of government:* Prime Minister Peter BOROSS (since 12 December 1993 on the death of Jozsef ANTALL); new prime minister will probably be Gyula HORN

*cabinet:* Council of Ministers; elected by the National Assembly on recommendation of the president

**Legislative branch:** unicameral

*National Assembly (Orszaggyules):* elections last held on 8 and 29 May 1994 (next to be held spring 1998); results—percent of vote by party NA; seats—(386 total) Hungarian Socialist Party 209, Alliance of Free Democrats 70, Hungarian Democratic Forum 37, Independent Smallholders 26, Christian Democratic People's Party 22, Federation of Young Democrats 20, other 2

**Judicial branch:** Constitutional Court

**Political parties and leaders:** Democratic Forum, Sandor LESZAK, chairman; Independent Smallholders (FKGP), Jozsef TORGYAN, president; Hungarian Socialist Party (MSZP), Gyula HORN, president; Christian Democratic People's Party (KDNP), Dr. Lazlo SURJAN, president; Federation of Young Democrats (FIDESZ), Viktor ORBAN, chairman; Alliance of Free Democrats (SZDSZ), Ivan PETO, chairman

*note:* the Hungarian Socialist (Communist) Workers' Party (MSZMP) renounced Communism and became the Hungarian

Socialist Party (MSZP) in October 1989; there is still a small MSZMP

**Member of:** Australian Group, BIS, CCC, CE, CEI, CERN, COCOM (cooperating), CSCE, EBRD, ECE, FAO, G-9, GATT, IAEA, IBRD, ICAO, IDA, IFC, ILO, IMF, IMO, INTELSAT, INTERPOL, IOC, IOM, ISO, ITU, LORCS, MTCR, NACC, NAM (guest), NSG, OAS (observer), PCA, UN, UNAVEM II, UNCTAD, UNESCO, UNHCR, UNIDO, UNIKOM, UNOMOZ, UNOMUR, UNOSOM, UNTAC, UPU, WFTU, WHO, WIPO, WMO, WTO, ZC

**Diplomatic representation in US:**

*chief of mission:* Ambassador Pal TAR

*chancery:* 3910 Shoemaker Street NW, Washington, DC 20008

*telephone:* (202) 362-6730

*FAX:* (202) 966-8135

*consulate(s) general:* Los Angeles and New York

**US diplomatic representation:**

*chief of mission:* Ambassador Donald BLINKEN

*embassy:* V. Szabadsag Ter 12, Budapest

*mailing address:* Am Embassy, Unit 1320, Budapest; APO AE 09213

*telephone:* [36] (1) 112-6450

*FAX:* [36] (1) 132-8934

**Flag:** three equal horizontal bands of red (top), white, and green

---

**U.S. Government Contacts:**

**U.S. Trade Desk:** (202) 482-4915

**American Embassy Commercial Section**
Baiza Utca 31
H-1062 Budapest, Hungary
APO AE 09213 (BUD)
Tel: 36-1-122-8600
Fax: 36-1-142-2529

---

**Chambers of Commerce**

**American Chamber of Commerce in Hungary**
Dozsa Gyorgy ut. 84/A, Room 222
1068 Budapest, Hungary
Tel: (36 1) 142-7518
Fax: (36 1) 269-6016

# ICELAND

125 km

*Greenland Sea*

*North Atlantic Ocean*

## Economy

**Overview:** Iceland's Scandinavian-type economy is basically capitalistic, but with an extensive welfare system, relatively low unemployment, and comparatively even distribution of income. The economy is heavily dependent on the fishing industry, which provides nearly 75% of export earnings and employs 12% of the workforce. In the absence of other natural resources—except energy—Iceland's economy is vulnerable to changing world fish prices. Iceland's economy has been in recession since 1988. The recession continued in 1993 due to a third year of cutbacks in fishing quotas as well as falling world prices for the country's main exports: fish and fish products, aluminum, and ferrosilicon. Real GDP declined 3.3% in 1992 and rose slightly, by 0.4%, in 1993. The center-right government's economic goals include reducing the budget and current account deficits, limiting foreign borrowing, containing inflation, revising agricultural and fishing policies, diversifying the economy, and privatizing state-owned industries. The recession has led to a wave of bankruptcies and mergers throughout the economy, as well as the highest unemployment of the post-World War II period. Inflation, previously a serious problem, declined from double digit rates in the 1980s to only 3.7% in 1992-93.

**National product:** GDP—purchasing power equivalent—$4.2 billion (1993)

**National product real growth rate:** 0.4% (1993 est.)

**National product per capita:** $16,000 (1993)

**Inflation rate (consumer prices):** 4% (1993)

**Unemployment rate:** 4.5% (1993 est.)

**Budget:**

*revenues:* $1.8 billion

*expenditures:* $1.9 billion, including capital expenditures of $191 million (1992)

**Exports:** $1.5 billion (f.o.b., 1992)

*commodities:* fish and fish products, animal products, aluminum, ferrosilicon, diatomite

*partners:* EC 68% (UK 25%, FRG 12%), US 11%, Japan 8% (1992)

**Imports:** $1.5 billion (c.i.f., 1992)

*commodities:* machinery and transportation equipment, petroleum products, foodstuffs, textiles

*partners:* EC 53% (Germany 14%, Denmark 10%, UK 9%), Norway 14%, US 9% (1992)

**External debt:** $3.9 billion (1992 est.)

**Industrial production:** growth rate 1.75% (1991 est.)

**Electricity:**

*capacity:* 1,063,000 kW

*production:* 5.165 billion kWh

*consumption per capita:* 19,940 kWh (1992)

**Industries:** fish processing, aluminum smelting, ferro-silicon production, geothermal power

**Agriculture:** accounts for about 15% of GDP; fishing is most important economic activity, contributing nearly 75% to export earnings; principal crops—potatoes, turnips; livestock—cattle, sheep; self-sufficient in crops; fish catch of about 1.1 million metric tons in 1992

**Economic aid:**
*recipient:* US commitments, including Ex-Im
(FY70-81), $19.1 million
**Currency:** 1 Icelandic krona (IKr) = 100
aurar
**Exchange rates:** Icelandic kronur (IKr) per
US$1—72.971 (January 1994), 67.603 (1993),
57.546 (1992), 58.996 (1991), 58.284 (1990),
57.042 (1989)
**Fiscal year:** calendar year

---

## Communications

**Highways:**
*total:* 12,537 km
*paved:* 2,690 km
*unpaved:* gravel, earth 9,847 km
**Ports:** Reykjavik, Akureyri, Hafnarfjordhur,
Keflavik, Seydhisfjordhur, Siglufjordhur,
Vestmannaeyjar
**Merchant marine:** 8 ships (1,000 GRT or
over) totaling 33,212 GRT/47,359 DWT, cargo
2, refrigerated cargo 2, roll-on/roll-off cargo 2,
oil tanker 1, chemical tanker 1
**Airports:**
*total:* 90
*usable:* 84
*with permanent-surface runways:* 9
*with runways over 3,659 m:* 0
*with runways 2,440-3,659 m:* 1
*with runways 1,220-2,439 m:* 12
**Telecommunications:** adequate domestic
service; coaxial and fiber-optical cables and
microwave radio relay for trunk network;
140,000 telephones; broadcast stations—5
AM, 147 (transmitters and repeaters) FM, 202
(transmitters and repeaters) TV; 2 submarine
cables; 1 Atlantic Ocean INTELSAT earth
station carries all international traffic; a second
INTELSAT earth station is scheduled to be
operational in 1993

---

## Defense Forces

**Branches:** Police, Coast Guard
*note:* no armed forces, Iceland's defense is
provided by the US-manned Icelandic Defense
Force (IDF) headquartered at Keflavik
**Manpower availability:** males age 15-49
70,074; fit for military service 62,197
**Defense expenditures:** none

---

## Geography

**Location:** Nordic State, Northern Europe, in
the North Atlantic Ocean, between Greenland
and Norway
**Map references:** Arctic Region, Europe,
North America, Standard Time Zones of the
World
**Area:**
*total area:* 103,000 sq km
*land area:* 100,250 sq km
*comparative area:* slightly smaller than
Kentucky
**Land boundaries:** 0 km
**Coastline:** 4,988 km
**Maritime claims:**
*continental shelf:* 200 nm or the edge of
continental margin
*exclusive economic zone:* 200 nm
*territorial sea:* 12 nm
**International disputes:** Rockall continental
shelf dispute involving Denmark, Ireland, and
the UK (Ireland and the UK have signed a
boundary agreement in the Rockall area)
**Climate:** temperate; moderated by North
Atlantic Current; mild, windy winters; damp,
cool summers
**Terrain:** mostly plateau interspersed with
mountain peaks, icefields; coast deeply
indented by bays and fiords
**Natural resources:** fish, hydropower,
geothermal power, diatomite
**Land use:**
*arable land:* 1%
*permanent crops:* 0%
*meadows and pastures:* 20%
*forest and woodland:* 1%
*other:* 78%
**Irrigated land:** NA sq km
**Environment:**
*current issues:* water pollution from fertilizer
runoff; inadequate wastewater treatment
*natural hazards:* subject to earthquakes and
volcanic activity
*international agreements:* party to—Air
Pollution, Climate Change, Law of the Sea,
Marine Dumping, Nuclear Test Ban, Ozone
Layer Protection, Ship Pollution, Wetlands;
signed, but not ratified—Biodiversity,
Environmental Modification, Marine Life
Conservation

**Note:** strategic location between Greenland and Europe; westernmost European country; more land covered by glaciers than in all of continental Europe

## People

**Population:** 263,599 (July 1994 est.)
*note:* population data estimates based on average growth rate may differ slightly from official population data because of volatile migration rates
**Population growth rate:** 0.9% (1994 est.)
**Birth rate:** 16.41 births/1,000 population (1994 est.)
**Death rate:** 6.72 deaths/1,000 population (1994 est.)
**Net migration rate:** -0.73 migrant(s)/1,000 population (1994 est.)
**Infant mortality rate:** 4 deaths/1,000 live births (1994 est.)
**Life expectancy at birth:**
*total population:* 78.83 years
*male:* 76.57 years
*female:* 81.21 years (1994 est.)
**Total fertility rate:** 2.11 children born/woman (1994 est.)
**Nationality:**
*noun:* Icelander(s)
*adjective:* Icelandic
**Ethnic divisions:** homogeneous mixture of descendants of Norwegians and Celts
**Religions:** Evangelical Lutheran 96%, other Protestant and Roman Catholic 3%, none 1% (1988)
**Languages:** Icelandic
**Literacy:** age 15 and over can read and write (1976 est.)
*total population:* 100%
*male:* NA%
*female:* NA%
**Labor force:** 127,900
*by occupation:* commerce, transportation, and services 60.0%, manufacturing 12.5%, fishing and fish processing 11.8%, construction 10.8%, agriculture 4.0% (1990)

## Government

**Names:**
*conventional long form:* Republic of Iceland
*conventional short form:* Iceland
*local long form:* Lyoveldio Island
*local short form:* Island
**Digraph:** IC
**Type:** republic
**Capital:** Reykjavik
**Administrative divisions:** 23 counties (syslar, singular—sysla) and 14 independent towns* (kaupstadhir, singular—kaupstadhur); Akranes*, Akureyri*, Arnessysla, Austur-Bardhastrandarsysla, Austur-Hunavatnssysla, Austur-Skaftafellssysla, Borgarfjardharsysla, Dalasysla, Eyjafjardharsysla, Gullbringusysla, Hafnarfjordhur*, Husavik*, Isafjordhur*, Keflavik*, Kjosarsysla, Kopavogur*, Myrasysla, Neskaupstadhur*, Nordhur-Isafjardharsysla, Nordhur-Mulasys-la, Nordhur-Thingeyjarsysla, Olafsfjordhur*, Rangarvallasysla, Reykjavik*, Saudharkrokur*, Seydhisfjordhur*, Siglufjordhur*, Skagafjardharsysla, Snaefellsnes-og Hnappadalssysla, Strandasysla, Sudhur-Mulasysla, Sudhur-Thingeyjarsysla, Vesttmannaeyjar*, Vestur-Bardhastrandarsysla, Vestur-Hunavatnssysla, Vestur-Isafjardharsysla, Vestur-Skaftafellssysla
**Independence:** 17 June 1944 (from Denmark)
**National holiday:** Anniversary of the Establishment of the Republic, 17 June (1944)
**Constitution:** 16 June 1944, effective 17 June 1944
**Legal system:** civil law system based on Danish law; does not accept compulsory ICJ jurisdiction
**Suffrage:** 18 years of age; universal
**Executive branch:**
*chief of state:* President Vigdis FINNBOGADOTTIR (since 1 August 1980); election last held on 29 June 1988 (next scheduled for June 1996); results—there was no election in 1992 as President Vigdis FINNBOGADOTTIR was unopposed
*head of government:* Prime Minister David ODDSSON (since 30 April 1991)
*cabinet:* Cabinet; appointed by the president

**Legislative branch:** unicameral
*Parliament (Althing):* elections last held on 20
April 1991 (next to be held by April 1995);
results—Independence Party 38.6%,
Progressive Party 18.9%, Social Democratic
Party 15.5%, People's Alliance 14.4%,
Womens List 8.3%, Liberals 1.2%, other 3.1%;
seats—(63 total) Independence 26, Progressive
13, Social Democratic 10, People's Alliance 9,
Womens List 5
**Judicial branch:** Supreme Court
(Haestirettur)
**Political parties and leaders:** Independence
Party (conservative), David ODDSSON;
Progressive Party, Steingrimur
HERMANNSSON; Social Democratic Party,
Jon Baldvin HANNIBALSSON; People's
Alliance (left socialist), Olafur Ragnar
GRIMSSON; Women's List
**Member of:** Australian Group, BIS, CCC,
CE, CSCE, EBRD, ECE, EFTA, FAO, GATT,
IAEA, IBRD, ICAO, ICC, ICFTU, IDA, IFC,
ILO, IMF, IMO, INMARSAT, INTELSAT,
INTERPOL, IOC, ISO, ITU, LORCS, MTCR,
NACC, NATO, NC, NEA, NIB, OECD, PCA,
UN, UNCTAD, UNESCO, UPU, WEU
(associate), WHO, WIPO, WMO
**Diplomatic representation in US:**
*chief of mission:* Ambassador Einar
BENEDIKTSSON
*chancery:* 2022 Connecticut Avenue NW,
Washington, DC 20008
*telephone:* (202) 265-6653 through 6655
*FAX:* (202) 265-6656
*consulate(s) general:* New York
**US diplomatic representation:**
*chief of mission:* Ambassador Parker W.
BORG
*embassy:* Laufasvegur 21, Box 40, Reykjavik
*mailing address:* US Embassy, PSC 1003, Box
40, Reykjavik; FPO AE 09728-0340
*telephone:* [354] (1) 629100
*FAX:* [354] (1) 629139
**Flag:** blue with a red cross outlined in white
that extends to the edges of the flag; the vertical
part of the cross is shifted to the hoist side in
the style of the Dannebrog (Danish flag)

**U.S. Government Contacts:**

**U.S. Trade Desk**: (202) 482-3254

**Travel:**

**International Hotels in Country:**
Reykjavik:
Holt, Tel: 3541/552-5700, Fax: 3541/562-
3025
Saga, Tel: 3541/552-9900, Fax: 3541/562-
3928.

# IRELAND

## Economy

**Overview:** The economy is small and trade dependent. Agriculture, once the most important sector, is now dwarfed by industry, which accounts for 37% of GDP, about 80% of exports, and employs 28% of the labor force. Since 1987, real GDP growth, led by exports, has averaged 4% annually. Over the same period, inflation has fallen sharply and chronic trade deficits have been transformed into annual surpluses. Unemployment remains a serious problem, however, and job creation is the main focus of government policy. To ease unemployment, Dublin aggressively courts foreign investors and recently created a new industrial development agency to aid small indigenous firms. Government assistance is constrained by Dublin's continuing deficit reduction measures.

**National product:** GDP—purchasing power equivalent—$46.3 billion (1993)

**National product real growth rate:** 2.7% (1993)

**National product per capita:** $13,100 (1993)

**Inflation rate (consumer prices):** 2.7% (1994 est.)

**Unemployment rate:** 16% (1994 est.)

**Budget:**
*revenues:* $16 billion
*expenditures:* $16.6 billion, including capital expenditures of $1.6 billion (1992 est.)

**Exports:** $28.3 billion (f.o.b., 1992)
*commodities:* chemicals, data processing equipment, industrial machinery, live animals, animal products
*partners:* EC 75% (UK 32%, Germany 13%, France 10%), US 9%

**Imports:** $23.3 billion (c.i.f., 1992)
*commodities:* food, animal feed, data processing equipment, petroleum and petroleum products, machinery, textiles, clothing
*partners:* EC 66% (UK 41%, Germany 8%, Netherlands 4%), US 15%

**External debt:** $17.6 billion (1992)

**Industrial production:** growth rate 11.5% (1992); accounts for 37% of GDP

**Electricity:**
*capacity:* 5,000,000 kW
*production:* 14.5 billion kWh
*consumption per capita:* 4,120 kWh (1992)

**Industries:** food products, brewing, textiles, clothing, chemicals, pharmaceuticals, machinery, transportation equipment, glass and crystal

**Agriculture:** accounts for 8% of GDP and 13% of the labor force; principal crops—turnips, barley, potatoes, sugar beets, wheat; livestock—meat and dairy products; 85% self-sufficient in food; food shortages include bread grain, fruits, vegetables

**Illicit drugs:** transshipment point for hashish from North Africa to the UK and Netherlands

**Economic aid:**
*donor:* ODA commitments (1980-89), $90 million

**Currency:** 1 Irish pound (£Ir) = 100 pence

**Exchange rates:** Irish pounds (£Ir) per US$1—0.6978 (January 1994), 0.6816 (1993), 0.5864 (1992), 0.6190 (1991), 0.6030 (1990), 0.7472 (1989)

**Fiscal year:** calendar year

## Communications

**Railroads:** Irish National Railways (CIE) operates 1,947 km 1.602-meter gauge, government owned; 485 km double track; 37 km electrified

**Highways:**

*total:* 92,294 km

*paved:* 87,422 km

*unpaved:* gravel, crushed stone 4,872 km

**Inland waterways:** limited for commercial traffic

**Pipelines:** natural gas 225 km

**Ports:** Cork, Dublin, Waterford

**Merchant marine:** 53 ships (1,000 GRT or over) totaling 139,278 GRT/173,325 DWT, short-sea passenger 3, cargo 32, refrigerated cargo 2, container 4, oil tanker 3, specialized tanker 3, chemical tanker 2, bulk 4

**Airports:**

*total:* 44

*usable:* 42

*with permanent-surface runways:* 14

*with runways over 3,659 m:* 0

*with runways 2,440-3,659 m:* 2

*with runways 1,220-2,439 m:* 7

**Telecommunications:** modern system using cable and digital microwave circuits; 900,000 telephones; broadcast stations—9 AM, 45 FM, 86 TV; 2 coaxial submarine cables; 1 Atlantic Ocean INTELSAT earth station

## Defense Forces

**Branches:** Army (including Naval Service and Air Corps), National Police (Garda Siochana)

**Manpower availability:** males age 15-49 914,052; fit for military service 739,288; reach military age (17) annually 33,809 (1994 est.)

**Defense expenditures:** exchange rate conversion—$569 million, 1%-2% of GDP (1993 est.)

## Geography

**Location:** Western Europe, in the North Atlantic Ocean, across the Irish Sea from Great Britain

**Map references:** Europe, Standard Time Zones of the World

**Area:**

*total area:* 70,280 sq km

*land area:* 68,890 sq km

*comparative area:* slightly larger than West Virginia

**Land boundaries:** total 360 km, UK 360 km

**Coastline:** 1,448 km

**Maritime claims:**

*continental shelf:* not specified

*exclusive fishing zone:* 200 nm

*territorial sea:* 12 nm

**International disputes:** Northern Ireland question with the UK; Rockall continental shelf dispute involving Denmark, Iceland, and the UK (Ireland and the UK have signed a boundary agreement in the Rockall area)

**Climate:** temperate maritime; modified by North Atlantic Current; mild winters, cool summers; consistently humid; overcast about half the time

**Terrain:** mostly level to rolling interior plain surrounded by rugged hills and low mountains; sea cliffs on west coast

**Natural resources:** zinc, lead, natural gas, petroleum, barite, copper, gypsum, limestone, dolomite, peat, silver

**Land use:**

*arable land:* 14%

*permanent crops:* 0%

*meadows and pastures:* 71%

*forest and woodland:* 5%

*other:* 10%

**Irrigated land:** NA sq km

**Environment:**

*current issues:* water pollution, especially of lakes, from agricultural runoff

*natural hazards:* NA

*international agreements:* party to—Air Pollution, Environmental Modification, Hazardous Wastes, Marine Dumping, Nuclear Test Ban, Ozone Layer Protection, Tropical Timber, Wetlands, Whaling; signed, but not ratified—Air Pollution-Nitrogen Oxides, Biodiversity, Climate Change, Endangered Species, Law of the Sea, Marine Life Conservation

**Note:** strategic location on major air and sea routes between North American and northern

Europe; over 40% of the population resides
within 60 miles of Dublin

## People

**Population:** 3,539,296 (July 1994 est.)
**Population growth rate:** 0.3% (1994 est.)
**Birth rate:** 14.21 births/1,000 population
(1994 est.)
**Death rate:** 8.59 deaths/1,000 population
(1994 est.)
**Net migration rate:** -2.67 migrant(s)/1,000
population (1994 est.)
**Infant mortality rate:** 7.4 deaths/1,000 live
births (1994 est.)
**Life expectancy at birth:**
*total population:* 75.68 years
*male:* 72.85 years
*female:* 78.68 years (1994 est.)
**Total fertility rate:** 1.99 children born/
woman (1994 est.)
**Nationality:**
*noun:* Irishman(men), Irishwoman(men), Irish
(collective plural)
*adjective:* Irish
**Ethnic divisions:** Celtic, English
**Religions:** Roman Catholic 93%, Anglican
3%, none 1%, unknown 2%, other 1% (1981)
**Languages:** Irish (Gaelic), spoken mainly in
areas located along the western seaboard,
English is the language generally used
**Literacy:** age 15 and over can read and write
(1981 est.)
*total population:* 98%
*male:* NA%
*female:* NA%
**Labor force:** 1.37 million
*by occupation:* services 57.0%, manufacturing
and construction 28%, agriculture, forestry,
and fishing 13.5%, energy and mining 1.5%
(1992)

## Government

**Names:**
*conventional long form:* none
*conventional short form:* Ireland
**Digraph:** EI
**Type:** republic

**Capital:** Dublin
**Administrative divisions:** 26 counties;
Carlow, Cavan, Clare, Cork, Donegal, Dublin,
Galway, Kerry, Kildare, Kilkenny, Laois,
Leitrim, Limerick, Longford, Louth, Mayo,
Meath, Monaghan, Offaly, Roscommon, Sligo,
Tipperary, Waterford, Westmeath, Wexford,
Wicklow
**Independence:** 6 December 1921 (from UK)
**National holiday:** Saint Patrick's Day, 17
March
**Constitution:** 29 December 1937; adopted 1
July 1937 by plebecite
**Legal system:** based on English common law,
substantially modified by indigenous concepts;
judicial review of legislative acts in Supreme
Court; has not accepted compulsory ICJ
jurisdiction
**Suffrage:** 18 years of age; universal
**Executive branch:**
*chief of state:* President Mary Bourke
ROBINSON (since 9 November 1990);
election last held 9 November 1990 (next to be
held November 1997); results—Mary Bourke
ROBINSON 52.8%, Brian LENIHAN 47.2%
*head of government:* Prime Minister Albert
REYNOLDS (since 11 February 1992)
*cabinet:* Cabinet; appointed by president with
previous nomination of the prime minister and
approval of the House of Representatives
**Legislative branch:** bicameral Parliament
(Oireachtas)
*Senate (Seanad Eireann):* elections last held
on NA February 1992 (next to be held February
1997); results—percent of vote by party NA;
seats—(60 total, 49 elected) Fianna Fail 26,
Fine Gael 16, Labor 9, Progressive Democrats
2, Democratic Left 1, independents 6
*House of Representatives (Dail Eireann):*
elections last held on 25 November 1992 (next
to be held by June 1995); results—Fianna Fail
39.1%, Fine Gael 24.5%, Labor Party 19.3%,
Progressive Democrats 4.7%, Democratic Left
2.8%, Sinn Fein 1.6%, Workers' Party 0.7%,
independents 5.9%; seats—(166 total) Fianna
Fail 68, Fine Gael 45, Labor Party 33,
Progressive Democrats 10, Democratic Left 4,
Greens 1, independents 5
**Judicial branch:** Supreme Court

**Political parties and leaders:** Democratic Left, Proinsias DE ROSSA; Fianna Fail, Albert REYNOLDS; Labor Party, Richard SPRING; Fine Gael, John BRUTON; Communist Party of Ireland, Michael O'RIORDAN; Sinn Fein, Gerry ADAMS; Progressive Democrats, Desmond O'MALLEY
*note:* Prime Minister REYNOLDS heads a coalition consisting of the Fianna Fail and the Labor Party
**Member of:** Australian Group, BIS, CCC, CE, COCOM (cooperating), CSCE, EBRD, EC, ECE, EIB, ESA, FAO, GATT, IAEA, IBRD, ICAO, ICC, IDA, IEA, IFAD, IFC, ILO, IMF, IMO, INTELSAT, INTERPOL, IOC, ISO, ITU, LORCS, MINURSO, MTCR, NEA, NSG, OECD, ONUSAL, UN, UNAVEM II, UNCTAD, UNESCO, UNFICYP, UNIDO, UNIFIL, UNIKOM, UNOSOM, UNPROFRO, UNTAC, UNTSO, UPU, WEU (observer), WHO, WIPO, WMO, ZC
**Diplomatic representation in US:**
*chief of mission:* Ambassador Dermot A. GALLAGHER
*chancery:* 2234 Massachusetts Avenue NW, Washington, DC 20008
*telephone:* (202) 462-3939
*consulate(s) general:* Boston, Chicago, New York, and San Francisco
**US diplomatic representation:**
*chief of mission:* Ambassador Jean Kennedy SMITH
*embassy:* 42 Elgin Road, Ballsbridge, Dublin
*mailing address:* use embassy street address
*telephone:* [353] (1) 6687122
*FAX:* [353] (1) 6689946
**Flag:** three equal vertical bands of green (hoist side), white, and orange; similar to the flag of the Cote d'Ivoire, which is shorter and has the colors reversed—orange (hoist side), white, and green; also similar to the flag of Italy, which is shorter and has colors of green (hoist side), white, and red

---

**U.S. Government Contacts:**

**U.S. Trade Desk:** (202) 482-2177

**American Embassy Commercial Section**
42 Elgin Road
Ballsbridge
Dublin, Ireland
c/o U.S. Department of State (Dublin)
Washington, DC 20521-5290
Tel: 353-1-687-122
Fax: 353-1-608-469

---

**Ireland Government Contacts:**

**Embassy of Ireland Commercial Section**
2234 Massachusetts Avenue, N.W.
Washington, DC 20008
Tel: (202) 462-3939

---

**Chambers of Commerce & Organizations:**

**American Chamber of Commerce in Ireland**
20 College Green
Dublin 2, Ireland
Tel: 353-1-79-37-33

---

**Travel:**

**International Hotels in Country:**
Dublin:
Conrad, Tel: 3531/676-5555, Fax: 3531/676-5076
Shelbourne, Tel: 3531/676-6471, Fax: 3531/661-6006.

# ITALY

## Economy

**Overview:** Since World War II the Italian economy has changed from one based on agriculture into a ranking industrial economy, with approximately the same total and per capita output as France and the UK. The country is still divided into a developed industrial north, dominated by private companies, and an undeveloped agricultural south, dominated by large public enterprises. Services account for 48% of GDP, industry 35%, agriculture 4%, and public administration 13%. Most raw materials needed by industry and over 75% of energy requirements must be imported. After growing at an annual average rate of 3% in 1983-90, growth slowed to about 1% in 1991 and 1992 and fell by 0.7% in 1993. In the second half of 1992, Rome became unsettled by the prospect of not qualifying to participate in EC plans for economic and monetary union later in the decade; thus it finally began to address its huge fiscal imbalances. Thanks to the determination of Prime Ministers AMATO and CIAMPI, the government adopted a fairly stringent budget for 1993 and 1994, abandoned its highly inflationary wage indexation system, and started to scale back its extremely generous social welfare programs, including pension and health care benefits. Monetary officials were forced to withdraw the lira from the European monetary system in September 1992 when it came under extreme pressure in currency markets. For the 1990s, Italy faces the problems of refurbishing a tottering communications system, curbing pollution in major industrial centers, and adjusting to the new competitive forces accompanying the ongoing economic integration of the European Union.

**National product:** GDP—purchasing power equivalent—$967.6 billion (1993)

**National product real growth rate:** -0.7% (1993)

**National product per capita:** $16,700 (1993)

**Inflation rate (consumer prices):** 4.2% (1993)

**Unemployment rate:** 11.3% (January 1994)

**Budget:**
*revenues:* $302 billion
*expenditures:* $391 billion, including capital expenditures of $48 billion (1993 est.)

**Exports:** $178.2 billion (f.o.b., 1992)
*commodities:* metals, textiles and clothing, production machinery, motor vehicles, transportation equipment, chemicals, other
*partners:* EC 58.3%, US 6.8%, OPEC 5.1% (1992)

**Imports:** $188.5 billion (f.o.b., 1992)
*commodities:* industrial machinery, chemicals, transport equipment, petroleum, metals, food, agricultural products
*partners:* EC 58.8%, OPEC 6.1%, US 5.5% (1992)

**External debt:** $67 billion (1993 est.)

**Industrial production:** growth rate -2.8% (1993 est.); accounts for almost 35% of GDP

**Electricity:**
*capacity:* 58,000,000 kW
*production:* 235 billion kWh
*consumption per capita:* 4,060 kWh (1992)

**Industries:** machinery, iron and steel, chemicals, food processing, textiles, motor vehicles, clothing, footwear, ceramics
**Agriculture:** accounts for about 4% of GDP and about 9.8% of the work force; self-sufficient in foods other than meat, dairy products, and cereals; principal crops—fruits, vegetables, grapes, potatoes, sugar beets, soybeans, grain, olives; fish catch of 525,000 metric tons in 1990
**Illicit drugs:** important gateway country for Latin American cocaine and Southwest Asian heroin entering the European market
**Economic aid:**
*donor:* ODA and OOF commitments (1970-89), $25.9 billion
**Currency:** 1 Italian lira (Lit) = 100 centesimi
**Exchange rates:** Italian lire (Lit) per US$1— 1,700.2 (January 1994), 1,573.7 (1993), 1,232.4 (1992), 1,240.6 (1991), 1,198.1 (1990), 1,372.1 (1989)
**Fiscal year:** calendar year

## Communications

**Railroads:** 20,011 km total; 16,066 km 1.435-meter government-owned standard gauge (8,999 km electrified); 3,945 km privately owned—2,100 km 1.435-meter standard gauge (1,155 km electrified) and 1,845 km 0.950-meter narrow gauge (380 km electrified)
**Highways:**
*total:* 298,000 km
*paved:* 270,000 km (including nearly 7,000 km of expressways)
*unpaved:* gravel, crushed stone 23,000 km; earth 5,000 km
**Inland waterways:** 2,400 km for various types of commercial traffic, although of limited overall value
**Pipelines:** crude oil 1,703 km; petroleum products 2,148 km; natural gas 19,400 km
**Ports:** Cagliari (Sardinia), Genoa, La Spezia, Livorno, Naples, Palermo (Sicily), Taranto, Trieste, Venice
**Merchant marine:** 474 ships (1,000 GRT or over) totaling 6,055,779 GRT/8,924,779 DWT, passenger 8, short-sea passenger 34, cargo 72, refrigerated cargo 2, container 20,

roll-on/roll-off cargo 62, vehicle carrier 7, multifunction large-load carrier 1, oil tanker 129, chemical tanker 34, liquefied gas 39, specialized tanker 10, combination ore/oil 5, bulk 50, combination bulk 1
**Airports:**
*total:* 137
*usable:* 132
*with permanent-surface runways:* 92
*with runways over 3,659 m:* 2
*with runways 2,440-3,659 m:* 36
*with runways 1,220-2,439 m:* 39
**Telecommunications:** modern, well-developed, fast; 25,600,000 telephones; fully automated telephone, telex, and data services; high-capacity cable and microwave radio relay trunks; broadcast stations—135 AM, 28 (1,840 repeaters) FM, 83 (1,000 repeaters) TV; international service by 21 submarine cables, 3 satellite earth stations operating in INTELSAT with 3 Atlantic Ocean antennas and 2 Indian Ocean antennas; also participates in INMARSAT and EUTELSAT systems

## Defense Forces

**Branches:** Army, Navy, Air Force, Carabinieri
**Manpower availability:** males age 15-49 14,921,411; fit for military service 12,982,445; reach military age (18) annually 403,017 (1994 est.)
**Defense expenditures:** exchange rate conversion—$24.5 billion, 2% of GDP (1992)

## Geography

**Location:** Southern Europe, a peninsula extending into the central Mediterranean Sea
**Map references:** Africa, Europe, Standard Time Zones of the World
**Area:**
*total area:* 301,230 sq km
*land area:* 294,020 sq km
*comparative area:* slightly larger than Arizona
*note:* includes Sardinia and Sicily
**Land boundaries:** total 1,899.2 km, Austria 430 km, France 488 km, Holy See (Vatican City) 3.2 km, San Marino 39 km, Slovenia 199

km, Switzerland 740 km
**Coastline:** 4,996 km
**Maritime claims:**
*continental shelf:* 200-m depth or to depth of exploitation
*territorial sea:* 12 nm
**International disputes:** none
**Climate:** predominantly Mediterranean; Alpine in far north; hot, dry in south
**Terrain:** mostly rugged and mountainous; some plains, coastal lowlands
**Natural resources:** mercury, potash, marble, sulfur, dwindling natural gas and crude oil reserves, fish, coal
**Land use:**
*arable land:* 32%
*permanent crops:* 10%
*meadows and pastures:* 17%
*forest and woodland:* 22%
*other:* 19%
**Irrigated land:** 31,000 sq km (1989 est.)
**Environment:**
*current issues:* air pollution from industrial emissions such as sulfur dioxide; coastal and inland rivers polluted from industrial and agricultural effluents; acid rain damaging lakes
*natural hazards:* regional risks include landslides, mudflows, avalanches, earthquakes, volcanic eruptions, flooding; land subsidence in Venice
*international agreements:* party to—Air Pollution, Air Pollution-Nitrogen Oxides, Air Pollution-Sulphur, Antarctic Treaty, Endangered Species, Environmental Modification, Hazardous Wastes, Marine Dumping, Nuclear Test Ban, Ozone Layer Protection, Ship Pollution, Tropical Timber, Wetlands; signed, but not ratified—Air Pollution-Volatile Organic Compounds, Antarctic-Environmental Protocol, Biodiversity, Climate Change, Law of the Sea
**Note:** strategic location dominating central Mediterranean as well as southern sea and air approaches to Western Europe

---

## People

**Population:** 58,138,394 (July 1994 est.)
**Population growth rate:** 0.21% (1994 est.)

**Birth rate:** 10.79 births/1,000 population (1994 est.)
**Death rate:** 9.71 deaths/1,000 population (1994 est.)
**Net migration rate:** 1.03 migrant(s)/1,000 population (1994 est.)
**Infant mortality rate:** 7.6 deaths/1,000 live births (1994 est.)
**Life expectancy at birth:**
*total population:* 77.64 years
*male:* 74.44 years
*female:* 81.04 years (1994 est.)
**Total fertility rate:** 1.39 children born/woman (1994 est.)
**Nationality:**
*noun:* Italian(s)
*adjective:* Italian
**Ethnic divisions:** Italian (includes small clusters of German-, French-, and Slovene-Italians in the north and Albanian-Italians and Greek-Italians in the south), Sicilians, Sardinians
**Religions:** Roman Catholic 98%, other 2%
**Languages:** Italian, German (parts of Trentino-Alto Adige region are predominantly German speaking), French (small French-speaking minority in Valle d'Aosta region), Slovene (Slovene-speaking minority in the Trieste-Gorizia area)
**Literacy:** age 15 and over can read and write (1990 est.)
*total population:* 97%
*male:* 98%
*female:* 96%
**Labor force:** 23.988 million
*by occupation:* services 58%, industry 32.2%, agriculture 9.8% (1988)

---

## Government

**Names:**
*conventional long form:* Italian Republic
*conventional short form:* Italy
*local long form:* Repubblica Italiana
*local short form:* Italia
*former:* Kingdom of Italy
**Digraph:** IT
**Type:** republic
**Capital:** Rome

**Administrative divisions:** 20 regions (regioni, singular—regione); Abruzzi, Basilicata, Calabria, Campania, Emilia-Romagna, Friuli-Venezia Giulia, Lazio, Liguria, Lombardia, Marche, Molise, Piemonte, Puglia, Sardegna, Sicilia, Toscana, Trentino-Alto Adige, Umbria, Valle d'Aosta, Veneto

**Independence:** 17 March 1861 (Kingdom of Italy proclaimed)

**National holiday:** Anniversary of the Republic, 2 June (1946)

**Constitution:** 1 January 1948

**Legal system:** based on civil law system, with ecclesiastical law influence; appeals treated as trials de novo; judicial review under certain conditions in Constitutional Court; has not accepted compulsory ICJ jurisdiction

**Suffrage:** 18 years of age, universal (except in senatorial elections, where minimum age is 25)

**Executive branch:**

*chief of state:* President Oscar Luigi SCALFARO (since 28 May 1992)

*head of government:* Prime Minister Silvio BERLUSCONI (since 11 May 1994)

*cabinet:* Council of Ministers; appointed by the president

**Legislative branch:** bicameral Parliament (Parlamento)

*Senate (Senato della Repubblica):* elections last held 27-28 March 1994 (next expected to be held by spring 2001); results—percent of vote by party NA; seats—(326 total; 315 elected, 11 appointed senators-for-life) PDS 61, Northern League 60, National Alliance 48, Forza Italia 36, Popular Party 31, Communist Refounding 18, Greens and The Network 13, Socialist Party 13, Christian Democratic Center 12, Democratic Alliance 8, Christian Socialists 5, Pact for Italy 4, Radical Party 1, others 5

*Chamber of Deputies (Camera dei Deputati):* elections last held 27-28 March 1994 (next expected to be held by spring 2001); results—percent of vote by party NA; seats—(630 total) Northern League 117, PDS 114, Forza Italia 113, National Alliance 109, Communist Refounding 39, Christian Democratic Center 33, Popular Party 33, Greens and The Network 20, Democratic Alliance 18, Socialist Party 16, Pact for Italy 13, Christian Socialists 5

**Judicial branch:** Constitutional Court (Corte Costituzionale)

**Political parties and leaders:**

*Rightists:* Forza Italia, Silvio BERLUSCONI; National Alliance (was Italian Social Movement—MSI—until January 1994), Gianfranco FINI, party secretary; Lega Nord (Northern League), Umberto BOSSI, president

*Leftists:* Democratic Party of the Left (PDS—was Communist Party, or PCI, until January 1991), Achille OCCHETTO, secretary; Communist Refounding, Fausto BERTINOTTI; Greens, Carlo RIPA di MEARA; Radical Party, Marco PANNELLA; Italian Socialist Party, Ottaviano DELTURCO; The Network, Leoluca ORLANDO; Christian Socialists, Ermanno GORRIERI

*Centrists:* Pact for Italy, Mario SEGNI; Popular Party, Rosa JERVOLINO; Christian Democratic Center, Pier Ferdinando CASINI

**Other political or pressure groups:** the Roman Catholic Church; three major trade union confederations (CGIL—formerly Communist dominated, CISL—Christian Democratic, and UIL—Social Democratic, Socialist, and Republican); Italian manufacturers and merchants associations (Confindustria, Confcommercio); organized farm groups (Confcoltivatori, Confagricoltura)

**Member of:** AfDB, AG (observer), Australia Group, AsDB, BIS, CCC, CDB (non-regional), CE, CEI, CERN, COCOM, CSCE, EBRD, EC, ECE, ECLAC, EIB, ESA, FAO, G-7, G-10, GATT, IADB, IAEA, IBRD, ICAO, ICC, ICFTU, IDA, IFAD, IEA, IFC, ILO, IMF, IMO, INMARSAT, INTELSAT, INTERPOL, IOC, IOM, ISO, ITU, LAIA (observer), LORCS, MINURSO, MTCR, NACC, NATO, NEA, NSG, OAS (observer), OECD, ONUSAL, PCA, UN, UNCTAD, UNESCO, UNHCR, UNIDO, UNIFIL, UNIKOM, UNMOGIP, UNOSOM, UNTAC, UNTSO, UPU, WCL, WEU, WHO, WIPO, WMO, WTO, ZC

**Diplomatic representation in US:**

*chief of mission:* Ambassador Boris BIANCHERI-CHIAPPORI

*chancery:* 1601 Fuller Street NW,

Washington, DC 20009
*telephone:* (202) 328-5500
*consulate(s) general:* Boston, Chicago,
Houston, Miami, New York, Los Angeles,
Philadelphia, San Francisco
*consulate(s):* Detroit, New Orleans, and
Newark (New Jersey)
**US diplomatic representation:**
*chief of mission:* Ambassador Reginald
BARTHOLOMEW
*embassy:* Via Veneto 119/A, 00187-Rome
*mailing address:* PSC 59, Box 100, Rome;
APO AE 09624
*telephone:* [39] (6) 46741
*FAX:* [39] (6) 488-2672
*consulate(s) general:* Florence, Milan, Naples
**Flag:** three equal vertical bands of green
(hoist side), white, and red; similar to the flag
of Ireland, which is longer and is green (hoist
side), white, and orange; also similar to the flag
of the Cote d'Ivoire, which has the colors
reversed—orange (hoist side), white, and green

---

**U.S. Government Contacts:**

**U.S. Trade Desk**: (202) 482-2177

**American Embassy Commercial Section**
Via Veneto 119/A
00187 Rome, Italy
APO AE 09624
Tel: 39-6-4674-2202
Fax: 39-6-4674-2113

**American Consulate General - Milan
Commercial Section**
Via Principe Amedeo, 2/10
20121 Milan, Italy
Box M, APO AE 09624
Tel: 39-2-498-2241
Fax: 39-2-481-4161

---

**Italy Government Contacts:**

**Embassy of Italy Commercial Section**
1601 Fuller Street, N.W.
Washington, DC 20009
Tel: (202) 328-5500

**Ministero delle Finanze**

Viale Boston, Roma
Tel: 39-06-59971

**Ministero dell'Industria,
del Commercio e dell'Artigianato
Via Molise 2, Roma**
Tel: 39-06-47051
Fax: 39-06-4744048

**Istituto Nazionale**
per il Commercio Estero (I.C.E.)
Head office Roma
Via LIszt, 21 - 00144 Roma
Tel: 39-06-59929591
Fax: 39-06-596474438 - 59926900
Director of Cooperation Section:
Cesare Fritelli

**Instituto Assistenza Sviluppo Meridione -
IASM**
Viale Pilsudski, 124
00197 ROMA
Tel: 011-39-6/84721
Fax: 011-39-6/872898
Chairman:
Gasparino Caviglioli

---

**Chambers of Commerce &
Organizations:**

**American Chamber of Commerce in Italy**
Via Cantu 1
20123 Milan, Italy
Tel: 39-2-869-0661
Fax: 39-2-805-7737

---

**Legal Services:**

**Calabi & Frigessi di Rattalma**
Via Montenapoleone 20
20121 Milan, Italy
Tel: 39-2-76022178
Fax: 39-2-782743
*General Civil and Corporate Practice,
Securities, Insurance and Banking Law,
International and EEC Law, Intellectual
Property Law.*

**Cappello & Associati**
47, Piazza Barberini
00187 Rome, Italy

Tel: 39-6-4824781
       39-6-4820650
Fax: 39-6-4881327
*Copyright Law, Franchise, EEC Law, General
Commercial and Company Law, International
Taxation, Joint Ventures. General Legal
Practice.*

## Travel:

**International Airlines to Country:**
American, Continental, TWA, United

**International Hotels in Country:**
Rome:
Cavalieri Hilton, Tel: 3906/35091, Fax:
3906/315-12241
Hassler-Villa Medici, Tel: 3906/678-2651, Fax:
3906/678-9991
Majestic, Tel: 3906/48641, Fax: 3906/488-
0984.

# LATVIA

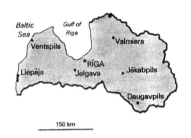

Baltic Sea, Gulf of Riga, Ventspils, Valmiera, *RĪGA, Jelgava, Liepāja, Jēkabpils, Daugavpils

150 km

## Economy

**Overview:** Latvia is rapidly becoming a dynamic market economy, rivaled only by Estonia among the former Soviet states in the speed of its transformation. The transition has been painful with GDP falling over 45% in 1992-93, according to official statistics, and industrial production experiencing even steeper declines. Nevertheless, the government's tough monetary policies and reform program, which foster the development of the private sector and market mechanisms, have kept inflation low, created a dynamic private sector—much of which is not captured in official statistics—and expanded trade ties with the West. Much of agriculture is already privatized and the government plans to step up the pace of privatization of state enterprises. The economy is now poised for recovery and will benefit from the country's strategic location on the Baltic Sea, its well-educated population, and its diverse—albeit largely obsolete—industrial structure.

**National product:** GDP—purchasing power equivalent—$13.2 billion (1993 estimate from the UN International Comparison Program, as extended to 1991 and published in the World Bank's World Development Report 1993; and as extrapolated to 1993 using official Latvian statistics, which are very uncertain because of major economic changes since 1990)

**National product real growth rate:** -5% (1993 est.)

**National product per capita:** $4,810 (1993 est.)

**Inflation rate (consumer prices):** 2% per month (1993 average)

**Unemployment rate:** 5.6% (December 1993)

**Budget:**
*revenues:* $NA
*expenditures:* $NA, including capital expenditures of $NA

**Exports:** $429 million from non-FSU countries (f.o.b., 1992)
*commodities:* oil products, timber, ferrous metals, dairy products, furniture, textiles
*partners:* Russia, other CIS countries, Western Europe

**Imports:** $NA
*commodities:* fuels, cars, ferrous metals, chemicals
*partners:* Russia, other CIS countries, Western Europe

**External debt:** $NA

**Industrial production:** growth rate -38% (1992 est.)

**Electricity:**
*capacity:* 2,140,000 kW
*production:* 5.8 billion kWh
*consumption per capita:* 2,125 kWh (1992)

**Industries:** employs 41% of labor force; highly diversified; dependent on imports for energy, raw materials, and intermediate products; produces buses, vans, street and railroad cars, synthetic fibers, agricultural machinery, fertilizers, washing machines, radios, electronics, pharmaceuticals, processed foods, textiles

**Agriculture:** employs 16% of labor force; principally dairy farming and livestock feeding; products—meat, milk, eggs, grain,

90

sugar beets, potatoes, vegetables; fishing and fish packing

**Illicit drugs:** transshipment point for illicit drugs from Central and Southwest Asia and Latin America to Western Europe; limited producer of illicit opium; mostly for domestic consumption; also produces illicit amphetamines for export

**Economic aid:** $NA

**Currency:** 1 lat = 100 cents; introduced NA March 1993

**Exchange rates:** lats per US$1—0.5917 (January 1994), 1.32 (March 1993)

**Fiscal year:** calendar year

## Communications

**Railroads:** 2,400 km (1,524-mm gauge); 270 km electrified

**Highways:**

*total:* 59,500 km

*paved and graveled:* 33,000 km

*unpaved:* earth 26,500 km (1990)

**Inland waterways:** 300 km perennially navigable

**Pipelines:** crude oil 750 km, refined products 780 km, natural gas 560 km (1992)

**Ports:** coastal—Riga, Ventspils, Liepaja; inland—Daugavpils

**Merchant marine:** 93 ships (1,000 GRT or over) totaling 850,840 GRT/1,107,403 DWT, cargo 15, refrigerated cargo 27, container 2, roll-on/roll-off cargo 8, oil tanker 41

**Airports:**

*total:* 50

*usable:* 15

*with permanent-surface runways:* 11

*with runways over 3,659 m:* 0

*with runways 2,440-3,659 m:* 7

*with runways 1,060-2,439 m:* 7

*note:* a C-130 can land on a 1,060-m airstrip

**Telecommunications:** Latvia is better provided with telephone service than most of the other former Soviet republics; subscriber circuits 660,000; subscriber density 240 per 1,000 persons (1993); an NMT-450 analog cellular telephone network covers 75% of Latvia's population; international traffic carried by leased connection to the Moscow international gateway switch and through the new Ericsson AXE local/transit digital telephone exchange in Riga and through the Finnish cellular net; electronic mail capability by Sprint data network; broadcasting services NA

## Defense Forces

**Branches:** Ground Forces, Navy, Air Force, Security Forces (internal and border troops), Border Guard, Home Guard (Zemessardze)

**Manpower availability:** males age 15-49 652,444; fit for military service 514,055; reach military age (18) annually 18,803 (1994 est.)

**Defense expenditures:** 176 million rubles, 3%-5% of GDP; note—conversion of the military budget into US dollars using the prevailing exchange rate could produce misleading results

## Geography

**Location:** Eastern Europe, bordering on the Baltic Sea, between Sweden and Russia

**Map references:** Arctic Region, Asia, Europe, Standard Time Zones of the World

**Area:**

*total area:* 64,100 sq km

*land area:* 64,100 sq km

*comparative area:* slightly larger than West Virginia

**Land boundaries:** total 1,078 km, Belarus 141 km, Estonia 267 km, Lithuania 453 km, Russia 217 km

**Coastline:** 531 km

**Maritime claims:**

*exclusive economic zone:* 200 nm

*territorial sea:* 12 nm

**International disputes:** the Abrene section of border ceded by the Latvian Soviet Socialist Republic to Russia in 1944

**Climate:** maritime; wet, moderate winters

**Terrain:** low plain

**Natural resources:** minimal; amber, peat, limestone, dolomite

**Land use:**

*arable land:* 27%

*permanent crops:* 0%

*meadows and pastures:* 13%
*forest and woodland:* 39%
*other:* 21%
**Irrigated land:** 160 sq km (1990)
**Environment:**
*current issues:* air and water pollution because of a lack of waste conversion equipment; Gulf of Riga and Daugava River heavily polluted; contamination of soil and groundwater with chemicals and petroleum products at military bases
*natural hazards:* NA
*international agreements:* party to—Hazardous Wastes, Ship Pollution; signed, but not ratified—Biodiversity, Climate Change

## People

**Population:** 2,749,211 (July 1994 est.)
**Population growth rate:** 0.5% (1994 est.)
**Birth rate:** 13.84 births/1,000 population (1994 est.)
**Death rate:** 12.61 deaths/1,000 population (1994 est.)
**Net migration rate:** 3.74 migrant(s)/1,000 population (1994 est.)
**Infant mortality rate:** 21.5 deaths/1,000 live births (1994 est.)
**Life expectancy at birth:**
*total population:* 69.44 years
*male:* 64.37 years
*female:* 74.75 years (1994 est.)
**Total fertility rate:** 1.98 children born/woman (1994 est.)
**Nationality:**
*noun:* Latvian(s)
*adjective:* Latvian
**Ethnic divisions:** Latvian 51.8%, Russian 33.8%, Byelorussian 4.5%, Ukrainian 3.4%, Polish 2.3%, other 4.2%
**Religions:** Lutheran, Roman Catholic, Russian Orthodox
**Languages:** Lettish (official), Lithuanian, Russian, other
**Literacy:** age 9-49 can read and write (1970)
*total population:* 100%
*male:* 100%
*female:* 100%
**Labor force:** 1.407 million

*by occupation:* industry and construction 41%, agriculture and forestry 16%, other 43% (1990)

## Government

**Names:**
*conventional long form:* Republic of Latvia
*conventional short form:* Latvia
*local long form:* Latvijas Republika
*local short form:* Latvija
*former:* Latvian Soviet Socialist Republic
**Digraph:** LG
**Type:** republic
**Capital:** Riga
**Administrative divisions:** 26 counties (singular—rajons) and 7 municipalities*: Aizkraukles Rajons, Aluksnes Rajons, Balvu Rajons, Bauskas Rajons, Cesu Rajons, Daugavpils*, Daugavpils Rajons, Dobeles Rajons, Gulbenes Rajons, Jekabpils Rajons, Jelgava*, Jelgavas Rajons, Jurmala*, Kraslavas Rajons, Kuldigas Rajons, Leipaja*, Liepajas Rajons, Limbazu Rajons, Ludzas Rajons, Madonas Rajons, Ogres Rajons, Preiju Rajons, Rezekne*, Rezeknes Rajons, Riga*, Rigas Rajons, Saldus Rajons, Talsu Rajons, Tukuma Rajons, Valkas Rajons, Valmieras Rajons, Ventspils*, Ventspils Rajons
**Independence:** 6 September 1991 (from Soviet Union)
**National holiday:** Independence Day, 18 November (1918)
**Constitution:** newly elected Parliament in 1993 restored the 1933 constitution
**Legal system:** based on civil law system
**Suffrage:** 18 years of age; universal
**Executive branch:**
*chief of state:* President Guntis ULMANIS (since 7 July 1993); Saeima elected President ULMANIS in the third round of balloting on 7 July 1993
*head of government:* Prime Minister Valdis BIRKAVS (since 20 July 1993)
*cabinet:* Council of Ministers; appointed by the Supreme Council
**Legislative branch:** unicameral
*Parliament (Saeima):* elections last held 5-6 June 1993 (next to be held NA June 1996); results—percent of vote by party NA; seats—

(100 total) LC 36, LNNK 15, Concord for
Latvia 13, LZS 12, Equal Rights 7, LKDS 6,
TUB 6, DCP 5
**Judicial branch:** Supreme Court
**Political parties and leaders:** Latvian Way
Union (LC), Valdis BIRKAVS; Latvian
Farmers Union (LZS), Alvars BERKIS;
Latvian National Independence Movement
(LNNK), Andrejs KRASTINS, Aristids
LAMBERGS, cochairmen; Concord for
Latvia, Janis JURKANS; Equal Rights, Sergejs
DIMANIS; Christian Democrat Union
(LKDS), Peteris CIMDINS, Andris
SAULITIS, Janis RUSKO; Fatherland and
Freedom (TUB), Maris GRINBLATS, Roberts
MILBERGS, Oigerts DZENTIS; Democratic
Center (DCP), Ints CALITIS; Popular Front of
Latvia (LTF), Uldis AUGSTKALNS
**Member of:** BIS, CBSS, CCC, CE (guest),
CSCE, EBRD, ECE, FAO, IBRD, ICAO, IDA,
IFC, ILO, IMF, IMO, INTELSAT
(nonsignatory user), INTERPOL, IOC, IOM
(observer), ITU, LORCS, NACC, UN,
UNCTAD, UNESCO, UNIDO, UPU, WHO,
WIPO, WMO
**Diplomatic representation in US:**
*chief of mission:* Ambassador Ojars Eriks
KALNINS
*chancery:* 4325 17th Street NW, Washington,
DC 20011
*telephone:* (202) 726-8213 and 8214
**US diplomatic representation:**
*chief of mission:* Ambassador Ints M. SILINS
*embassy:* Raina Boulevard 7, Riga 226050
*mailing address:* use embassy street address
*telephone:* 46-9-882-0046
*FAX:* 46-9-882-0047
**Flag:** two horizontal bands of maroon (top
and bottom), white (middle, narrower than
other two bands)

**Chambers of Commerce &
Organizations:**

**American Chamber of Commerce in Latvia**
Jauniela 24, Room 205
Riga, Republic of Latvia
Tel: 371-2-215-205
Fax: 371-882-0090

# LIECHTENSTEIN

5 km

Ruggell

Nendeln

Schaan

VADUZ

Malbun

Balzers

## Economy

**Overview:** The prosperous economy is based primarily on small-scale light industry and tourism. Industry accounts for 53% of total employment, the service sector 45% (mostly based on tourism), and agriculture and forestry 2%. The sale of postage stamps to collectors is estimated at $10 million annually. Low business taxes (the maximum tax rate is 20%) and easy incorporation rules have induced about 25,000 holding or so-called letter box companies to establish nominal offices in Liechtenstein. Such companies, incorporated solely for tax purposes, provide 30% of state revenues. The economy is tied closely to Switzerland's economy in a customs union, and incomes and living standards parallel those of the more prosperous Swiss groups.

**National product:** GDP—purchasing power equivalent—$630 million (1990 est.)

**National product real growth rate:** NA%

**National product per capita:** $22,300 (1990 est.)

**Inflation rate (consumer prices):** 5.4% (1990)

**Unemployment rate:** 1.5% (1990)

**Budget:**

*revenues:* $259 million

*expenditures:* $292 million, including capital expenditures of $NA (1990 est.)

**Exports:** $NA

*commodities:* small specialty machinery, dental products, stamps, hardware, pottery

*partners:* EFTA countries 20.9% (Switzerland 15.4%), EC countries 42.7%, other 36.4% (1990)

**Imports:** $NA

*commodities:* machinery, metal goods, textiles, foodstuffs, motor vehicles

*partners:* NA

**External debt:** $NA

**Industrial production:** growth rate NA%

**Electricity:**

*capacity:* 23,000 kW

*production:* 150 million kWh

*consumption per capita:* 5,230 kWh (1992)

**Industries:** electronics, metal manufacturing, textiles, ceramics, pharmaceuticals, food products, precision instruments, tourism

**Agriculture:** livestock, vegetables, corn, wheat, potatoes, grapes

**Economic aid:** none

**Currency:** 1 Swiss franc, franken, or franco (SwF) = 100 centimes, rappen, or centesimi

**Exchange rates:** Swiss francs, franken, or franchi (SwF) per US$1—1.4715 (January 1994), 1.4776 (1993), 1.4062 (1992), 1.4340 (1991), 1.3892 (1990), 1.6359 (1989)

**Fiscal year:** calendar year

## Communications

**Railroads:** 18.5 km 1.435-meter standard gauge, electrified; owned, operated, and included in statistics of Austrian Federal Railways

**Highways:**

*total:* 322.93 km

*paved:* 322.93 km

**Airports:** none

**Telecommunications:** limited, but sufficient automatic telephone system; 25,400 telephones; linked to Swiss networks by cable and radio relay for international telephone, radio, and TV services

## Defense Forces

**Note:** defense is responsibility of Switzerland

## Geography

**Location:** Central Europe, between Austria and Switzerland
**Map references:** Europe, Standard Time Zones of the World
**Area:**
*total area:* 160 sq km
*land area:* 160 sq km
*comparative area:* about 0.9 times the size of Washington, DC
**Land boundaries:** total 78 km, Austria 37 km, Switzerland 41 km
**Coastline:** 0 km (landlocked)
**Maritime claims:** none; landlocked
**International disputes:** claims 620 square miles of Czech territory confiscated from its royal family in 1918; the Czech Republic insists that restitution does not go back before February 1948, when the Communists seized power
**Climate:** continental; cold, cloudy winters with frequent snow or rain; cool to moderately warm, cloudy, humid summers
**Terrain:** mostly mountainous (Alps) with Rhine Valley in western third
**Natural resources:** hydroelectric potential
**Land use:**
*arable land:* 25%
*permanent crops:* 0%
*meadows and pastures:* 38%
*forest and woodland:* 19%
*other:* 18%
**Irrigated land:** NA sq km
**Environment:**
*current issues:* NA
*natural hazards:* NA
*international agreements:* party to—Air Pollution, Air Pollution-Nitrogen Oxides, Air Pollution-Sulphur, Air Pollution-Volatile Organic Compounds, Hazardous Wastes, Ozone Layer Protection, Wetlands; signed, but not ratified—Biodiversity, Climate Change, Law of the Sea
**Note:** landlocked; variety of microclimatic variations based on elevation

## People

**Population:** 30,281 (July 1994 est.)
**Population growth rate:** 1.26% (1994 est.)
**Birth rate:** 13.08 births/1,000 population (1994 est.)
**Death rate:** 6.6 deaths/1,000 population (1994 est.)
**Net migration rate:** 6.11 migrant(s)/1,000 population (1994 est.)
**Infant mortality rate:** 5.3 deaths/1,000 live births (1994 est.)
**Life expectancy at birth:**
*total population:* 77.46 years
*male:* 73.76 years
*female:* 81.03 years (1994 est.)
**Total fertility rate:** 1.46 children born/woman (1994 est.)
**Nationality:**
*noun:* Liechtensteiner(s)
*adjective:* Liechtenstein
**Ethnic divisions:** Alemannic 95%, Italian and other 5%
**Religions:** Roman Catholic 87.3%, Protestant 8.3%, unknown 1.6%, other 2.8% (1988)
**Languages:** German (official), Alemannic dialect
**Literacy:** age 10 and over can read and write (1981)
*total population:* 100%
*male:* 100%
*female:* 100%
**Labor force:** 19,905 of which 11,933 are foreigners; 6,885 commute from Austria and Switzerland to work each day
*by occupation:* industry, trade, and building 53.2%, services 45%, agriculture, fishing, forestry, and horticulture 1.8% (1990)

## Government

**Names:**
*conventional long form:* Principality of Liechtenstein

*conventional short form:* Liechtenstein
*local long form:* Furstentum Liechtenstein
*local short form:* Liechtenstein
**Digraph:** LS
**Type:** hereditary constitutional monarchy
**Capital:** Vaduz
**Administrative divisions:** 11 communes
(gemeinden, singular—gemeinde); Balzers,
Eschen, Gamprin, Mauren, Planken, Ruggell,
Schaan, Schellenberg, Triesen, Triesenberg,
Vaduz
**Independence:** 23 January 1719 (Imperial
Principality of Liechtenstein established)
**National holiday:** Assumption Day, 15
August
**Constitution:** 5 October 1921
**Legal system:** local civil and penal codes;
accepts compulsory ICJ jurisdiction, with
reservations
**Suffrage:** 18 years of age; universal
**Executive branch:**
*chief of state:* Prince Hans ADAM II (since 13
November 1989; assumed executive powers 26
August 1984); Heir Apparent Prince ALOIS
von und zu Liechtenstein (born 11 June 1968)
*head of government:* Mario FRICK (since 15
December 1993); Deputy Head of Government
Dr. Thomas BUECHEL (since 15 December
1993)
*cabinet:* Cabinet; elected by the Diet,
confirmed by the sovereign
**Legislative branch:** unicameral
*Diet (Landtag):* elections last held on 24
October 1993 (next to be held by March 1997);
results—VU 50.1%, FBP 41.3%, FL 8.5%;
seats—(25 total) VU 13, FBP 11, FL 1
**Judicial branch:** Supreme Court (Oberster
Gerichtshof) for criminal cases, Superior Court
(Obergericht) for civil cases
**Political parties and leaders:** Fatherland
Union (VU), Dr. Otto HASLER; Progressive
Citizens' Party (FBP), Emanuel VOGT; Free
Electoral List (FL)
**Member of:** CE, CSCE, EBRD, ECE, EFTA,
IAEA, INTELSAT, INTERPOL, IOC, ITU,
LORCS, UN, UNCTAD, UPU, WCL, WIPO
**Diplomatic representation in US:** in routine
diplomatic matters, Liechtenstein is
represented in the US by the Swiss Embassy

**US diplomatic representation:** the US has
no diplomatic or consular mission in
Liechtenstein, but the US Consul General at
Zurich (Switzerland) has consular
accreditation at Vaduz
**Flag:** two equal horizontal bands of blue (top)
and red with a gold crown on the hoist side of
the blue band

---

**Travel:**

**International Hotels in Country:**
Gorifon, Tel : 41-075-24307
Malbunerhof, Tel: 41-075-22944
Montana, Tel: 41-075-27333.

# LITHUANIA

Baltic Sea · Klaipėda · Šiauliai · Panevėžys · Utena · Tauragė · Kaunas · VILNIUS · Marijampolė

150 km

## Economy

**Overview:** Since independence in September 1991, Lithuania has made steady progress in developing a market economy. Over 40% of state property has been privatized and trade is diversifying with a gradual shift away from the former Soviet Union to Western markets. Nevertheless, the process has been painful with industrial output in 1993 less than half the 1991 level. Inflation, while lower than in most ex-Soviet states, has exceeded rates in the other Baltic states. Full monetary stability and economic recovery are likely to be impeded by periodic government backtracking on key elements of its reform and stabilization program as it seeks to ease the economic pain of restructuring. Recovery will build on Lithuanian's strategic location with its ice-free port at Klaipeda and its rail and highway hub in Vilnius connecting it with Eastern Europe, Belarus, Russia, and Ukraine, and on its agriculture potential, highly skilled labor force, and diversified industrial sector. Lacking important natural resources, it will remain dependent on imports of fuels and raw materials.

**National product:** GDP—purchasing power equivalent—$12.4 billion (1993 estimate from the UN International Comparison Program, as extended to 1991 and published in the World Bank's World Development Report 1993; and as extrapolated to 1993 using official Lithuanian statistics, which are very uncertain because of major economic changes since 1990)

**National product real growth rate:** -10% (1993 est.)

**National product per capita:** $3,240 (1993 est.)

**Inflation rate (consumer prices):** 188% (1993)

**Unemployment rate:** 1.8% (July 1993)

**Budget:**
*revenues:* $258.5 million
*expenditures:* $270.2 million, including capital expenditures of $NA (1992 est.)

**Exports:** $NA
*commodities:* electronics 18%, petroleum products 5%, food 10%, chemicals 6% (1989)
*partners:* Russia 40%, Ukraine 16%, other FSU countries 32%, West 12%

**Imports:** $NA
*commodities:* oil 24%, machinery 14%, chemicals 8%, grain NA% (1989)
*partners:* Russia 62%, Belarus 18%, other FSU countries 10%, West 10%

**External debt:** $NA

**Industrial production:** growth rate -52% (1992)

**Electricity:**
*capacity:* 5,925,000 kW
*production:* 25 billion kWh
*consumption per capita:* 6,600 kWh (1992)

**Industries:** employs 42% of the labor force; accounts for 23% of GOP shares in the total production of the former USSR are: metal-cutting machine tools 6.6%; electric motors 4.6%; television sets 6.2%; refrigerators and freezers 5.4%; other branches: petroleum refining, shipbuilding (small ships), furniture making, textiles, food processing, fertilizers,

agricultural machinery, optical equipment, electronic components, computers, and amber
**Agriculture:** employs around 18% of labor force; accounts for 25% of GDP; sugar, grain, potatoes, sugar beets, vegetables, meat, milk, dairy products, eggs, fish; most developed are the livestock and dairy branches, which depend on imported grain; net exporter of meat, milk, and eggs
**Illicit drugs:** transshipment point for illicit drugs from Central and Southwest Asia and Latin America to Western Europe; limited producer of illicit opium; mostly for domestic consumption
**Economic aid:**
*recipient:* US commitments, including Ex-Im (1992), $10 million; Western (non-US) countries, ODA and OOF bilateral commitments (1970-86), $NA million; Communist countries (1971-86), $NA million
**Currency:** introduced the convertible litas in June 1993
**Exchange rates:** litai per US$1—4 (fixed rate 1 May 1994); 3.9 (late January 1994)
**Fiscal year:** calendar year

## Communications

**Railroads:** 2,000 km (1,524-mm gauge); 120 km electrified
**Highways:**
*total:* 44,200 km
*paved:* 35,500 km
*unpaved:* earth 8,700 km (1990)
**Inland waterways:** 600 km perennially navigable
**Pipelines:** crude oil 105 km, natural gas 760 km (1992)
**Ports:** coastal—Klaipeda; inland—Kaunas
**Merchant marine:** 44 ships (1,000 GRT or over) totaling 276,265 GRT/323,505 DWT, cargo 29, railcar carrier 3, roll-on/roll-off cargo 1, combination bulk 11
**Airports:**
*total:* 96
*usable:* 18
*with permanent-surface runways:* 12
*with runways over 3,659 m:* 0
*with runways 2,440-3,659 m:* 5

*with runways 1,060-2,439 m:* 11
*note:* a C-130 can land on a 1,060-m airstrip
**Telecommunications:** Lithuania ranks among the most modern of the former Soviet republics in respect to its telecommunications system; telephone subscriber circuits 900,000; subscriber density 240 per 1,000 persons; land lines or microwave to former USSR republics; international connections no longer depend on the Moscow gateway switch, but are established by satellite through Oslo from Vilnius and through Copenhagen from Kaunas; 2 satellite earth stations—1 EUTELSAT and 1 INTELSAT; an NMT-450 analog cellular network operates in Vilnius and other cities and is linked internationally through Copenhagen by EUTELSAT; international electronic mail is available; broadcast stations —13 AM, 26 FM, 1 SW, 1 LW, 3 TV

## Defense Forces

**Branches:** Ground Forces, Navy, Air Force, Security Forces (internal and border troops), National Guard (Skat)
**Manpower availability:** males age 15-49 941,273; fit for military service 744,867; reach military age (18) annually 27,375 (1994 est.)
**Defense expenditures:** exchange rate conversion—$NA, 5.5% of GDP (1993 est.)

## Geography

**Location:** Eastern Europe, bordering the Baltic Sea, between Sweden and Russia
**Map references:** Asia, Europe, Standard Time Zones of the World
**Area:**
*total area:* 65,200 sq km
*land area:* 65,200 sq km
*comparative area:* slightly larger than West Virginia
**Land boundaries:** total 1,273 km, Belarus 502 km, Latvia 453 km, Poland 91 km, Russia (Kaliningrad) 227 km
**Coastline:** 108 km
**Maritime claims:**
*territorial sea:* 12 nm

**International disputes:** dispute with Russia (Kaliningrad Oblast) over the position of the Nemunas (Nemen) River border presently located on the Lithuanian bank and not in midriver as by international standards
**Climate:** maritime; wet, moderate winters and summers
**Terrain:** lowland, many scattered small lakes, fertile soil
**Natural resources:** peat
**Land use:**
*arable land:* 49.1%
*permanent crops:* 0%
*meadows and pastures:* 22.2%
*forest and woodland:* 16.3%
*other:* 12.4%
**Irrigated land:** 430 sq km (1990)
**Environment:**
*current issues:* contamination of soil and groundwater with petroleum products and chemicals at military bases
*natural hazards:* NA
*international agreements:* party to—Ship Pollution; signed, but not ratified— Biodiversity, Climate Change

---

## People

**Population:** 3,848,389 (July 1994 est.)
**Population growth rate:** 0.74% (1994 est.)
**Birth rate:** 14.71 births/1,000 population (1994 est.)
**Death rate:** 10.95 deaths/1,000 population (1994 est.)
**Net migration rate:** 3.62 migrant(s)/1,000 population (1994 est.)
**Infant mortality rate:** 16.7 deaths/1,000 live births (1994 est.)
**Life expectancy at birth:**
*total population:* 71.24 years
*male:* 66.53 years
*female:* 76.19 years (1994 est.)
**Total fertility rate:** 2.01 children born/ woman (1994 est.)
**Nationality:**
*noun:* Lithuanian(s)
*adjective:* Lithuanian
**Ethnic divisions:** Lithuanian 80.1%, Russian 8.6%, Polish 7.7%, Byelorussian 1.5%, other 2.1%

**Religions:** Roman Catholic, Lutheran, other
**Languages:** Lithuanian (official), Polish, Russian
**Literacy:** age 9-49 can read and write (1989)
*total population:* 98%
*male:* 99%
*female:* 98%
**Labor force:** 1.836 million
*by occupation:* industry and construction 42%, agriculture and forestry 18%, other 40% (1990)

---

## Government

**Names:**
*conventional long form:* Republic of Lithuania
*conventional short form:* Lithuania
*local long form:* Lietuvos Respublika
*local short form:* Lietuva
*former:* Lithuanian Soviet Socialist Republic
**Digraph:** LH
**Type:** republic
**Capital:** Vilnius
**Administrative divisions:** 44 regions (rajonai, singular—rajonas) and 11 municipalities*: Akmenes Rajonas, Alytaus Rajonas, Alytus*, Anyksciu Rajonas, Birsionas*, Birzu Rajonas, Druskininkai*, Ignalinos Rajonas, Jonavos Rajonas, Joniskio Rajonas, Jurbarko Rajonas, Kaisiadoriu Rajonas, Marijampoles Rajonas, Kaunas*, Kauno Rajonas, Kedainiu Rajonas, Kelmes Rajonas, Klaipeda*, Klaipedos Rajonas, Kretingos Ragonas, Kupiskio Rajonas, Lazdiju Rajonas, Marijampole*, Mazeikiu Ragonas, Moletu Rajonas, Neringa* Pakruojo Rajonas, Palanga*, Panevezio Rajonas, Panevezys*, Pasvalio Rajonas, Plunges Rajonas, Prienu Rajonas, Radviliskio Rajonas, Raseiniu Rajonas, Rokiskio Rajonas, Sakiu Rajonas, Salcininky Rajonas, Siauliai*, Siauliu Rajonas, Silales Rajonas, Siltues Rajonas, Sirvinty Rajonas, Skuodo Rajonas, Svencioniu Rajonas, Taurages Rajonas, Telsiu Rajonas, Traky Rajonas, Ukmerges Rajonas, Utenos Rajonas, Varenos Rajonas, Vilkaviskio Rajonas, Vilniaus Rajonas, Vilnius*, Zarasu Rajonas
**Independence:** 6 September 1991 (from Soviet Union)

**National holiday:** Independence Day, 16 February (1918)
**Constitution:** adopted 25 October 1992
**Legal system:** based on civil law system; no judicial review of legislative acts
**Suffrage:** 18 years of age; universal
**Executive branch:**
*chief of state:* President Algirdas Mykolas BRAZAUSKAS (since 25 November 1992; elected acting president by Parliament 25 November 1992 and elected by direct vote 15 February 1993); election last held 14 February 1993 (next to be held NA 1997); results— Algirdas BRAZAUSKAS was elected; note— on 25 November 1992 BRAZAUSKAS was elected chairman of Parliament and, as such, acting president of the Republic; he was confirmed in office by direct balloting 15 February 1993
*head of government:* Premier Adolfas SLEZEVICIUS (since 10 March 1993)
*cabinet:* Council of Ministers; appointed by the president on the nomination of the prime minister
**Legislative branch:** unicameral
*Seimas (parliament):* elections last held 26 October and 25 November 1992 (next to be held NA); results—LDDP 51%; seats—(141 total) LDDP 73, Conservative Party 30, LKDP 17, LTS 8, Farmers' Union 4, LLS 4, Center Union 2, others 3
**Judicial branch:** Supreme Court, Court of Appeals
**Political parties and leaders:** Christian Democratic Party (LKDP), Povilas KATILIUS, chairman; Democratic Labor Party of Lithuania (LDDP), Adolfas SLEZEVICIUS, chairman; Lithuanian Nationalist Union (LTS), Rimantas SMETONA, chairman; Lithuanian Social Democratic Party (LSDP), Aloyzas SAKALAS, chairman; Farmers' Union, Jonas CIULEVICIUS, chairman; Center Union, Romualdas OZOLAS, chairman; Conservative Party, Vytautas LANDSBERGIS, chairman; Lithuanian Polish Union (LLS), Rytardas MACIKIANEC, chairman
**Other political or pressure groups:** Homeland Union; Lithuanian Future Forum; Farmers Union

**Member of:** BIS, CBSS, CCC, CE, CSCE, EBRD, ECE, FAO, IBRD, ICAO, ILO, IMF, INTELSAT (nonsignatory user), INTERPOL, IOC, ISO (correspondent), ITU, LORCS, NACC, UN, UNCTAD, UNESCO, UNIDO, UPU, WHO, WIPO, WMO
**Diplomatic representation in US:**
*chief of mission:* Ambassador Alfonsas EIDINTAS
*chancery:* 2622 16th Street NW, Washington, DC 20009
*telephone:* (202) 234-5860, 2639
*FAX:* (202) 328-0466
*consulate(s) general:* New York
**US diplomatic representation:**
*chief of mission:* Ambassador Darryl N. JOHNSON
*embassy:* Akmenu 6, Vilnius 232600
*mailing address:* APO AE 09723
*telephone:* 370-2-223-031
*FAX:* 370-2-222-779
**Flag:** three equal horizontal bands of yellow (top), green, and red

---

**U.S. Government Contacts:**

**U.S. Trade Desk:** (202) 482-4915

# LUXEMBOURG

## Economy

**Overview:** The stable, prosperous economy features moderate growth, low inflation, and negligible unemployment. Agriculture is based on small but highly productive family-owned farms. The industrial sector, until recently dominated by steel, has become increasingly more diversified, particularly toward high-technology firms. During the past decade, growth in the financial sector has more than compensated for the decline in steel. Services, especially banking, account for a growing proportion of the economy. Luxembourg participates in an economic union with Belgium on trade and most financial matters, is also closely connected economically to the Netherlands, and as a member of the 12-member European Union enjoys the advantages of the open European market.
**National product:** GDP—purchasing power equivalent—$8.7 billion (1993)
**National product real growth rate:** 1% (1993)
**National product per capita:** $22,600 (1993)
**Inflation rate (consumer prices):** 3.6% (1992)

**Unemployment rate:** 5.1% (March 1994)
**Budget:**
*revenues:* $3.5 billion
*expenditures:* $3.5 billion, including capital expenditures of $NA (1992 est.)
**Exports:** $6.4 billion (f.o.b., 1991 est.)
*commodities:* finished steel products, chemicals, rubber products, glass, aluminum, other industrial products
*partners:* EC 76%, US 5%
**Imports:** $8.3 billion (c.i.f., 1991 est.)
*commodities:* minerals, metals, foodstuffs, quality consumer goods
*partners:* Belgium 37%, FRG 31%, France 12%, US 2%
**External debt:** $131.6 million (1989 est.)
**Industrial production:** growth rate -0.5% (1990); accounts for 25% of GDP
**Electricity:**
*capacity:* 1,238,750 kW
*production:* 1.375 billion kWh
*consumption per capita:* 3,450 kWh (1990)
**Industries:** banking, iron and steel, food processing, chemicals, metal products, engineering, tires, glass, aluminum
**Agriculture:** accounts for less than 3% of GDP (including forestry); principal products— barley, oats, potatoes, wheat, fruits, wine grapes; cattle raising widespread
**Economic aid:** none
**Currency:** 1 Luxembourg franc (LuxF) = 100 centimes
**Exchange rates:** Luxembourg francs (LuxF) per US$1—36.242 (January 1994), 34.597 (1993), 32.150 (1992), 34.148 (1991), 33.418 (1990), 39.404 (1989); note—the Luxembourg franc is at par with the Belgian franc, which circulates freely in Luxembourg
**Fiscal year:** calendar year

## Communications

**Railroads:** Luxembourg National Railways (CFL) operates 272 km 1,435-mm standard gauge; 178 km double track; 197 km electrified

**Highways:**

*total:* 5,108 km

*paved:* 4,995 km (including 80 km of limited access divided highway)

*unpaved:* gravel 57 km; earth 56 km

**Inland waterways:** 37 km; Moselle River

**Pipelines:** petroleum products 48 km

**Ports:** Mertert (river port)

**Merchant marine:** 50 ships (1,000 GRT or over) totaling 1,477,998 GRT/2,424,994 DWT, cargo 2, container 4, roll-on/roll-off cargo 4, oil tanker 5, chemical tanker 4, combination ore/oil 2, liquefied gas 9, passenger 2, bulk 8, combination bulk 6, refrigerated cargo 4

**Airports:**

*total:* 2

*usable:* 2

*with permanent-surface runways:* 1

*with runways over 3,659 m:* 1

*with runways 2,440-3,659 m:* 0

*with runways 1,220-2,439 m:* 0

**Telecommunications:** highly developed, completely automated and efficient system, mainly buried cables; 230,000 telephones; broadcast stations—2 AM, 3 FM, 3 TV; 3 channels leased on TAT-6 coaxial submarine cable; 1 direct-broadcast satellite earth station; nationwide mobile phone system

---

**Defense Forces**

**Branches:** Army, National Gendarmerie

**Manpower availability:** males age 15-49 103,872; fit for military service 86,026; reach military age (19) annually 2,235 (1994 est.)

**Defense expenditures:** exchange rate conversion—$100 million, 1.2% of GDP (1992)

---

**Geography**

**Location:** Western Europe, between Belgium and Germany

**Map references:** Europe, Standard Time Zones of the World

**Area:**

*total area:* 2,586 sq km

*land area:* 2,586 sq km

*comparative area:* slightly smaller than Rhode Island

**Land boundaries:** total 359 km, Belgium 148 km, France 73 km, Germany 138 km

**Coastline:** 0 km (landlocked)

**Maritime claims:** none; landlocked

**International disputes:** none

**Climate:** modified continental with mild winters, cool summers

**Terrain:** mostly gently rolling uplands with broad, shallow valleys; uplands to slightly mountainous in the north; steep slope down to Moselle floodplain in the southeast

**Natural resources:** iron ore (no longer exploited)

**Land use:**

*arable land:* 24%

*permanent crops:* 1%

*meadows and pastures:* 20%

*forest and woodland:* 21%

*other:* 34%

**Irrigated land:** NA sq km

**Environment:**

*current issues:* deforestation

*natural hazards:* NA

*international agreements:* party to—Air Pollution, Air Pollution-Nitrogen Oxides, Air Pollution-Sulphur, Air Pollution-Volatile Organic Compounds, Endangered Species, Hazardous Wastes, Marine Dumping, Nuclear Test Ban, Ozone Layer Protection, Ship Pollution, Tropical Timber; signed, but not ratified—Biodiversity, Climate Change, Environmental Modification, Law of the Sea

**Note:** landlocked

---

**People**

**Population:** 401,900 (July 1994 est.)

**Population growth rate:** 0.8% (1994 est.)

**Birth rate:** 12.81 births/1,000 population (1994 est.)

**Death rate:** 9.47 deaths/1,000 population (1994 est.)

**Net migration rate:** 4.7 migrant(s)/1,000 population (1994 est.)

**Infant mortality rate:** 6.8 deaths/1,000 live births (1994 est.)

**Life expectancy at birth:**

*total population:* 76.69 years

*male:* 73.01 years
*female:* 80.52 years (1994 est.)
**Total fertility rate:** 1.64 children born/
woman (1994 est.)
**Nationality:**
*noun:* Luxembourger(s)
*adjective:* Luxembourg
**Ethnic divisions:** Celtic base (with French
and German blend), Portuguese, Italian, and
European (guest and worker residents)
**Religions:** Roman Catholic 97%, Protestant
and Jewish 3%
**Languages:** Luxembourgisch, German,
French, English
**Literacy:** age 15 and over can read and write
(1980 est.)
*total population:* 100%
*male:* 100%
*female:* 100%
**Labor force:** 177,300 (one-third of labor
force is foreign workers, mostly from Portugal,
Italy, France, Belgium, and Germany)
*by occupation:* services 65%, industry 31.6%,
agriculture 3.4% (1988)

## Government

**Names:**
*conventional long form:* Grand Duchy of
Luxembourg
*conventional short form:* Luxembourg
*local long form:* Grand-Duche de
Luxembourg
*local short form:* Luxembourg
**Digraph:** LU
**Type:** constitutional monarchy
**Capital:** Luxembourg
**Administrative divisions:** 3 districts;
Diekirch, Grevenmacher, Luxembourg
**Independence:** 1839
**National holiday:** National Day, 23 June
(1921) (public celebration of the Grand Duke's
birthday)
**Constitution:** 17 October 1868, occasional
revisions
**Legal system:** based on civil law system;
accepts compulsory ICJ jurisdiction
**Suffrage:** 18 years of age; universal and
compulsory

**Executive branch:**
*chief of state:* Grand Duke JEAN (since 12
November 1964); Heir Apparent Prince
HENRI (son of Grand Duke Jean, born 16
April 1955)
*head of government:* Prime Minister Jacques
SANTER (since 21 July 1984); Vice Prime
Minister Jacques F. POOS (since 21 July 1984)
*cabinet:* Council of Ministers; appointed by
the sovereign
**Legislative branch:** unicameral
*Chamber of Deputies (Chambre des Deputes):*
elections last held on 18 June 1989 (next to be
held by June 1994); results—CSV 31.7%,
LSAP 27.2%, DP 16.2%, Greens 8.4%, PAC
7.3%, KPL 5.1%, other 4.1%; seats—(60 total)
CSV 22, LSAP 18, DP 11, Greens 4, PAC 4,
KPL 1
*note:* the Council of State (Conseil d'Etat) is an
advisory body whose views are considered by
the Chamber of Deputies
**Judicial branch:** Superior Court of Justice
(Cour Superieure de Justice)
**Political parties and leaders:** Christian
Social Party (CSV), Jacques SANTER;
Socialist Workers Party (LSAP), Jacques
POOS; Liberal (DP), Colette FLESCH;
Communist (KPL), Andre HOFFMANN;
Green Alternative (GAP), Jean HUSS
**Other political or pressure groups:** group
of steel companies representing iron and steel
industry; Centrale Paysanne representing
agricultural producers; Christian and Socialist
labor unions; Federation of Industrialists;
Artisans and Shopkeepers Federation
**Member of:** ACCT, Australia Group,
Benelux, CCC, CE, COCOM, CSCE, EBRD,
EC, ECE, EIB, FAO, GATT, IAEA, IBRD,
ICAO, ICC, ICFTU, IDA, IEA, IFAD, IFC,
ILO, IMF, IMO, INTELSAT, INTERPOL,
IOC, IOM, ITU, LORCS, MTCR, NACC,
NATO, NEA, NSG, OECD, PCA, UN,
UNCTAD, UNESCO, UNIDO, UNPROFOR,
UPU, WCL, WEU, WHO, WIPO, WMO, ZC
**Diplomatic representation in US:**
*chief of mission:* Ambassador Alphonse
BERNS
*chancery:* 2200 Massachusetts Avenue NW,
Washington, DC 20008

*telephone:* (202) 265-4171
*FAX:* (202) 328-8270
*consulate(s) general:* New York and San Francisco
**US diplomatic representation:**
*chief of mission:* Ambassador Edward M. ROWELL
*embassy:* 22 Boulevard Emmanuel-Servais, 2535 Luxembourg City
*mailing address:* PSC 11, Luxembourg City; APO AE 09132-5380
*telephone:* [352] 460123
*FAX:* [352] 461401
**Flag:** three equal horizontal bands of red (top), white, and light blue; similar to the flag of the Netherlands, which uses a darker blue and is shorter; design was based on the flag of France

---

**U.S. Government Contacts:**

**U.S. Trade Desk**: (202) 482-5401

---

**Travel:**

**International Hotels in Country:**
Luxembourg City:
Le Royal, Tel: 352/41616, Fax: 352/225948
Cravat, Tel: 352/221975, Fax: 352/226711.

# MALTA

## Economy

**Overview:** Significant resources are limestone, a favorable geographic location, and a productive labor force. Malta produces only about 20% of its food needs, has limited freshwater supplies, and has no domestic energy sources. Consequently, the economy is highly dependent on foreign trade and services. Manufacturing and tourism are the largest contributors to the economy. Manufacturing accounts for about 27% of GDP, with the electronics and textile industries major contributors and the state-owned Malta drydocks which employs about 4,300 people. In 1992, about 1,000,000 tourists visited the island. Per capita GDP at $6,600 places Malta in the middle-income range of the world's nations.

**National product:** GDP—exchange rate conversion—$2.4 billion (1992 est.)

**National product real growth rate:** 4.5% (1992)

**National product per capita:** $6,600 (1992)

**Inflation rate (consumer prices):** 1.64% (1992)

**Unemployment rate:** 4% (1992)

**Budget:**
*revenues:* $1.2 billion
*expenditures:* $1.2 billion, including capital expenditures of $182 million (FY94 est.)

**Exports:** $1.3 billion (f.o.b., 1992)
*commodities:* machinery and transport equipment, clothing and footware, printed matter
*partners:* Italy 30%, Germany 22%, UK 11%

**Imports:** $1.93 million (f.o.b., 1992)
*commodities:* food, petroleum, machinery and semimanufactured goods
*partners:* Italy 30%, UK 16%, Germany 13%, US 4%

**External debt:** $118 million (1990)

**Industrial production:** growth rate 5.4% (1992); accounts for 27% of GDP

**Electricity:**
*capacity:* 328,000 kW
*production:* 1.11 billion kWh
*consumption per capita:* 3,000 kWh (1992)

**Industries:** tourism, electronics, ship repair yard, construction, food manufacturing, textiles, footwear, clothing, beverages, tobacco

**Agriculture:** accounts for 3% of GDP and 2% of the work force (1992); overall, 20% self-sufficient; main products—potatoes, cauliflower, grapes, wheat, barley, tomatoes, citrus, cut flowers, green peppers, hogs, poultry, eggs; generally adequate supplies of vegetables, poultry, milk, pork products; seasonal or periodic shortages in grain, animal fodder, fruits, other basic foodstuffs

**Illicit drugs:** transshipment point for hashish from North Africa to Western Europe

**Economic aid:**
*recipient:* US commitments, including Ex-Im (FY70-81), $172 million; Western (non-US) countries, ODA and OOF bilateral commitments (1970-89), $336 million; OPEC bilateral aid (1979-89), $76 million; Communist countries (1970-88), $48 million

**Currency:** 1 Maltese lira (LM) = 100 cents

**Exchange rates:** Maltese liri (LM) per US$1—0.3951 (January 1994), 0.3821 (1993),

0.3178 (1992), 0.3226 (1991), 0.3172 (1990), 0.3483 (1989)
**Fiscal year:** 1 April—31 March

**Defense expenditures:** exchange rate conversion—$21.9 million, 1.3% of GDP (1989 est.)

## Communications

**Highways:**
*total:* 1,291 km
*paved:* asphalt 1,179 km
*unpaved:* gravel, crushed stone 77 km; earth 35 km
**Ports:** Valletta, Marsaxlokk
**Merchant marine:** 897 ships (1,000 GRT or over) totaling 13,959,195 GRT/24,038,587 DWT, passenger 6, short-sea passenger 19, cargo 296, container 26, passenger-cargo 3, roll-on/roll-off cargo 20, vehicle carrier 9, barge carrier 3, refrigerated cargo 17, chemical tanker 25, combination ore/oil 18, specialized tanker 5, liquefied gas 2, oil tanker 157, bulk 259, combination bulk 28, multifunction large load carrier 3, railcar carrier 1
*note:* a flag of convenience registry; China owns 11 ships, Russia owns 42 ships, Cuba owns 10, Vietnam owns 6, Croatia owns 63, Romania owns 4
**Airports:**
*total:* 1
*usable:* 1
*with permanent-surface runways:* 1
*with runways over 3,659 m:* 0
*with runways 2,440-3,659 m:* 1
*with runways 1,220-2,439 m:* 0
**Telecommunications:** automatic system satisfies normal requirements; 153,000 telephones; excellent service by broadcast stations—8 AM, 4 FM, and 2 TV; submarine cable and microwave radio relay between islands; international service by 1 submarine cable and 1 Atlantic Ocean INTELSAT earth station

## Defense Forces

**Branches:** Armed Forces, Maltese Police Force
**Manpower availability:** males age 15-49 98,241; fit for military service 78,071

## Geography

**Location:** Southern Europe, in the central Mediterranean Sea, 93 km south of Sicily (Italy), 290 km north of Libya
**Map references:** Europe, Standard Time Zones of the World
**Area:**
*total area:* 320 sq km
*land area:* 320 sq km
*comparative area:* slightly less than twice the size of Washington, DC
**Land boundaries:** 0 km
**Coastline:** 140 km
**Maritime claims:**
*contiguous zone:* 24 nm
*continental shelf:* 200-m depth or to depth of exploitation
*exclusive fishing zone:* 25 nm
*territorial sea:* 12 nm
**International disputes:** none
**Climate:** Mediterranean with mild, rainy winters and hot, dry summers
**Terrain:** mostly low, rocky, flat to dissected plains; many coastal cliffs
**Natural resources:** limestone, salt
**Land use:**
*arable land:* 38%
*permanent crops:* 3%
*meadows and pastures:* 0%
*forest and woodland:* 0%
*other:* 59%
**Irrigated land:** 10 sq km (1989)
**Environment:**
*current issues:* fresh water very scarce; increasing reliance on desalination
*natural hazards:* NA
*international agreements:* party to—Climate Change, Endangered Species, Law of the Sea, Marine Dumping, Nuclear Test Ban, Ozone Layer Protection, Ship Pollution, Wetlands; signed, but not ratified—Biodiversity
**Note:** the country comprises an archipelago, with only the 3 largest islands (Malta, Gozo, and Comino) being inhabited; numerous bays provide good harbors

## People

**Population:** 366,767 (July 1994 est.)
**Population growth rate:** 0.79% (1994 est.)
**Birth rate:** 13.56 births/1,000 population (1994 est.)
**Death rate:** 7.45 deaths/1,000 population (1994 est.)
**Net migration rate:** 1.84 migrant(s)/1,000 population (1994 est.)
**Infant mortality rate:** 7.9 deaths/1,000 live births (1994 est.)
**Life expectancy at birth:**
*total population:* 76.77 years
*male:* 74.53 years
*female:* 79.18 years (1994 est.)
**Total fertility rate:** 1.94 children born/woman (1994 est.)
**Nationality:**
*noun:* Maltese (singular and plural)
*adjective:* Maltese
**Ethnic divisions:** Arab, Sicilian, Norman, Spanish, Italian, English
**Religions:** Roman Catholic 98%
**Languages:** Maltese (official), English (official)
**Literacy:** age 15 and over can read and write (1985)
*total population:* 84%
*male:* 86%
*female:* 82%
**Labor force:** 127,200
*by occupation:* government (excluding job corps) 37%, services 26%, manufacturing 22%, training programs 9%, construction 4%, agriculture 2% (1990)

## Government

**Names:**
*conventional long form:* Republic of Malta
*conventional short form:* Malta
**Digraph:** MT
**Type:** parliamentary democracy
**Capital:** Valletta
**Administrative divisions:** none (administration directly from Valletta)
**Independence:** 21 September 1964 (from UK)

**National holiday:** Independence Day, 21 September (1964)
**Constitution:** 1964 constitution substantially amended on 13 December 1974
**Legal system:** based on English common law and Roman civil law; has accepted compulsory ICJ jurisdiction, with reservations
**Suffrage:** 18 years of age; universal
**Executive branch:**
*chief of state:* President Ugo MIFSUD BONNICI (since 4 April 1994)
*head of government:* Prime Minister Dr. Edward (Eddie) FENECH ADAMI (since 12 May 1987); Deputy Prime Minister Dr. Guido DE MARCO (since 14 May 1987)
*cabinet:* Cabinet; appointed by the president on advice of the prime minister
**Legislative branch:** unicameral
*House of Representatives:* elections last held on 22 February 1992 (next to be held by February 1997); results—NP 51.8%, MLP 46.5%; seats—(usually 65 total) MLP 36, NP 29; note—additional seats are given to the party with the largest popular vote to ensure a legislative majority; current total 69 (MLP 33, NP 36 after adjustment)
**Judicial branch:** Constitutional Court, Court of Appeal
**Political parties and leaders:** Nationalist Party (NP), Edward FENECH ADAMI; Malta Labor Party (MLP), Alfred SANT
**Member of:** C, CCC, CE, CSCE, EBRD, ECE, FAO, G-77, GATT, IBRD, ICAO, ICFTU, IFAD, ILO, IMF, IMO, INMARSAT, INTELSAT (nonsignatory user), INTERPOL, IOC, IOM (observer), ISO (correspondent), ITU, NAM, PCA, UN, UNCTAD, UNESCO, UNIDO, UPU, WCL, WHO, WIPO, WMO, WTO
**Diplomatic representation in US:**
*chief of mission:* Ambassador Albert BORG OLIVIER DE PUGET
*chancery:* 2017 Connecticut Avenue NW, Washington, DC 20008
*telephone:* (202) 462-3611 or 3612
*FAX:* (202) 387-5470
*consulate(s):* New York
**US diplomatic representation:**
*chief of mission:* (vacant); Charge d'Affaires William A. MOFFITT (new ambassador

nominated, but not confirmed)
*embassy:* 2nd Floor, Development House,
Saint Anne Street, Floriana, Valletta
*mailing address:* P. O. Box 535, Valletta
*telephone:* [356] 235960
*FAX:* [356] 243229
**Flag:** two equal vertical bands of white (hoist side) and red; in the upper hoist-side corner is a representation of the George Cross, edged in red

## U.S. Government contacts:

**U.S. Trade Desk**: (202) 482-3748

## Malta Government Contacts:

**Malta Development Corporation**
P.O. Box 571, Valletta, CMR 01, Malta
Tel: 356-448944
Fax: 356-448966

**Minister for Economic Services**
The Hon. George Bonello du Puis, LL.D., M.P.
Auberge d'Aragon, Valletta
Tel: 356-245391/5
Fax: 356-443595

**Minister of Finance**
St. Calcidonius Square, Floriana
Tel: 232646, 246309
Fax: 224667

**Malta International Business Authority**
Palazzo Spinola, St. Julians
Malta

## Consultants:

**Coopers and Lybrand**
P.O. Box 61
167 Merchants Street
Valletta
Malta
Tel: 234504
Fax: 624768

# MONACO

1 km

Monte Carlo
Casino

Mediterranean
Sea

Palace

## Economy

**Overview:** Monaco, situated on the French Mediterranean coast, is a popular resort, attracting tourists to its casino and pleasant climate. The Principality has successfully sought to diversify into services and small, high-value-added, nonpolluting industries. The state has no income tax and low business taxes and thrives as a tax haven both for individuals who have established residence and for foreign companies that have set up businesses and offices. About 50% of Monaco's annual revenue comes from value-added taxes on hotels, banks, and the industrial sector; about 25% of revenue comes from tourism. Living standards are high, that is, roughly comparable to those in prosperous French metropolitan suburbs.

**National product:** GDP—exchange rate conversion—$475 million (1991 est.)

**National product real growth rate:** NA%

**National product per capita:** $16,000 (1991 est.)

**Inflation rate (consumer prices):** NA%

**Unemployment rate:** NEGL%

**Budget:**

*revenues:* $424 million

*expenditures:* $376 million, including capital expenditures of $NA (1991 est.)

**Exports:** $NA; full customs integration with France, which collects and rebates Monacan trade duties; also participates in EU market system through customs union with France

**Imports:** $NA; full customs integration with France, which collects and rebates Monacan trade duties; also participates in EU market system through customs union with France

**External debt:** $NA

**Industrial production:** growth rate NA%

**Electricity:**

*capacity:* 10,000 kW standby; power imported from France

*production:* NA

*consumption per capita:* NA (1992)

**Agriculture:** none

**Economic aid:** $NA

**Currency:** 1 French franc (F) = 100 centimes

**Exchange rates:** French francs (F) per US$1—5.9205 (January 1994), 5.6632 (1993), 5.2938 (1992), 5.6421 (1991), 5.4453 (1990), 6.3801 (1989)

**Fiscal year:** calendar year

## Communications

**Railroads:** 1.6 km 1.435-meter gauge

**Highways:** none; city streets

**Ports:** Monaco

**Merchant marine:** 1 oil tanker (1,000 GRT or over) totaling 3,268 GRT/4,959 DWT

**Airports:** 1 usable airfield with permanent-surface runways

**Telecommunications:** served by cable into the French communications system; automatic telephone system; 38,200 telephones; broadcast stations—3 AM, 4 FM, 5 TV; no communication satellite earth stations

## Defense Forces

**Note:** defense is the responsibility of France

## Geography

**Location:** Western Europe, bordering the Mediterranean Sea, in southern France near the border with Italy
**Map references:** Europe, Standard Time Zones of the World
**Area:**
*total area:* 1.9 sq km
*land area:* 1.9 sq km
*comparative area:* about three times the size of The Mall in Washington, DC
**Land boundaries:** total 4.4 km, France 4.4 km
**Coastline:** 4.1 km
**Maritime claims:**
*territorial sea:* 12 nm
**International disputes:** none
**Climate:** Mediterranean with mild, wet winters and hot, dry summers
**Terrain:** hilly, rugged, rocky
**Natural resources:** none
**Land use:**
*arable land:* 0%
*permanent crops:* 0%
*meadows and pastures:* 0%
*forest and woodland:* 0%
*other:* 100%
**Irrigated land:** NA sq km
**Environment:**
*current issues:* NA
*natural hazards:* NA
*international agreements:* party to—Biodiversity, Climate Change, Hazardous Wastes, Marine Dumping, Ozone Layer Protection, Ship Pollution, Whaling; signed, but not ratified—Law of the Sea
**Note:** second smallest independent state in world (after Holy See); almost entirely urban

## People

**Population:** 31,278 (July 1994 est.)
**Population growth rate:** 0.81% (1994 est.)
**Birth rate:** 10.71 births/1,000 population (1994 est.)
**Death rate:** 12.21 deaths/1,000 population (1994 est.)
**Net migration rate:** 9.59 migrant(s)/1,000 population (1994 est.)
**Infant mortality rate:** 7.2 deaths/1,000 live births (1994 est.)
**Life expectancy at birth:**
*total population:* 77.69 years
*male:* 73.94 years
*female:* 81.64 years (1994 est.)
**Total fertility rate:** 1.7 children born/woman (1994 est.)
**Nationality:**
*noun:* Monacan(s) or Monegasque(s)
*adjective:* Monacan or Monegasque
**Ethnic divisions:** French 47%, Monegasque 16%, Italian 16%, other 21%
**Religions:** Roman Catholic 95%
**Languages:** French (official), English, Italian, Monegasque
**Literacy:**
*total population:* NA%
*male:* NA%
*female:* NA%
**Labor force:** NA

## Government

**Names:**
*conventional long form:* Principality of Monaco
*conventional short form:* Monaco
*local long form:* Principaute de Monaco
*local short form:* Monaco
**Digraph:** MN
**Type:** constitutional monarchy
**Capital:** Monaco
**Administrative divisions:** 4 quarters (quartiers, singular—quartier); Fontvieille, La Condamine, Monaco-Ville, Monte-Carlo
**Independence:** 1419 (rule by the House of Grimaldi)
**National holiday:** National Day, 19 November
**Constitution:** 17 December 1962
**Legal system:** based on French law; has not accepted compulsory ICJ jurisdiction
**Suffrage:** 25 years of age; universal
**Executive branch:**
*chief of state:* Prince RAINIER III (since NA November 1949); Heir Apparent Prince

ALBERT Alexandre Louis Pierre (born 14 March 1958)
*head of government:* Minister of State Jacques DUPONT (since NA 1991)
*cabinet:* Council of Government; under the authority of the Prince
**Legislative branch:** unicameral
*National Council (Conseil National):*
elections last held on 24 January 1988 (next to be held NA); results—percent of vote by party NA; seats—(18 total) UND 18
**Judicial branch:** Supreme Tribunal (Tribunal Supreme)
**Political parties and leaders:** National and Democratic Union (UND); Democratic Union Movement (MUD): Monaco Action; Monegasque Socialist Party (PSM)
**Member of:** ACCT, CSCE, ECE, IAEA, ICAO, IMF (observer), IMO, INMARSAT, INTELSAT, INTERPOL, IOC, ITU, LORCS, UN, UNCTAD, UNESCO, UPU, WHO, WIPO
**Diplomatic representation in US:**
*honorary consulate(s) general:* Boston, Chicago, Los Angeles, New Orleans, New York, San Francisco, San Juan (Puerto Rico)
*honorary consulate(s):* Dallas, Palm Beach, Philadelphia, and Washington
**US diplomatic representation:** no mission in Monaco, but the US Consul General in Marseille, France, is accredited to Monaco
**Flag:** two equal horizontal bands of red (top) and white; similar to the flag of Indonesia which is longer and the flag of Poland which is white (top) and red

# NETHERLANDS

## Economy

**Overview:** This highly developed and affluent economy is based on private enterprise. The government makes its presence felt, however, through many regulations, permit requirements, and welfare programs affecting most aspects of economic activity. The trade and financial services sector contributes over 50% of GDP. Industrial activity provides about 25% of GDP and is led by the food-processing, oil-refining, and metalworking industries. The highly mechanized agricultural sector employs only 5% of the labor force, but provides large surpluses for export and the domestic food-processing industry. Rising unemployment and a sizable budget deficit are currently the most serious economic problems. Many of the economic issues of the 1990s will reflect the course of European economic integration.
**National product:** GDP—purchasing power equivalent—$262.8 billion (1993)
**National product real growth rate:** -0.2% (1993)
**National product per capita:** $17,200 (1993)
**Inflation rate (consumer prices):** 3.5% (1992 est.)

**Unemployment rate:** 9.1% (March 1994)
**Budget:**
*revenues:* $109.9 billion
*expenditures:* $122.1 billion, including capital expenditures of $NA (1992 est.)
**Exports:** $139 billion (f.o.b., 1992)
*commodities:* metal products, chemicals, processed food and tobacco, agricultural products
*partners:* EC 77% (Germany 27%, Belgium-Luxembourg 15%, UK 10%), US 4% (1991)
**Imports:** $130.3 billion (f.o.b., 1992)
*commodities:* raw materials and semifinished products, consumer goods, transportation equipment, crude oil, food products
*partners:* EC 64% (Germany 26%, Belgium-Luxembourg 14%, UK 8%), US 8% (1991)
**External debt:** $0
**Industrial production:** growth rate -1.5% (1993 est.); accounts for 25% of GDP
**Electricity:**
*capacity:* 22,216,000 kW
*production:* 63.5 billion kWh
*consumption per capita:* 4,200 kWh (1992)
**Industries:** agroindustries, metal and engineering products, electrical machinery and equipment, chemicals, petroleum, fishing, construction, microelectronics
**Agriculture:** accounts for 4.6% of GDP; animal production predominates; crops—grains, potatoes, sugar beets, fruits, vegetables; shortages of grain, fats, and oils
**Illicit drugs:** gateway for cocaine, heroin, and hashish entering Europe; European producer of illicit amphetamines and other synthetic drugs
**Economic aid:**
*donor:* ODA and OOF commitments (1970-89), $19.4 billion
**Currency:** 1 Netherlands guilder, gulden, or florin (f.) = 100 cents
**Exchange rates:** Netherlands guilders, gulden, or florins (f.) per US$1—1.9508 (January 1994), 1.8573 (1993), 1.7585 (1992) 1.8697 (1991), 1.8209 (1990), 2.1207 (1989)
**Fiscal year:** calendar year

## Communications

**Railroads:** 2,828 km 1.435-meter standard gauge operated by Netherlands Railways (NS) (includes 1,957 km electrified and 1,800 km double track)

**Highways:**
*total:* 104,590 km
*paved:* 92,525 km (including 2,185 km of expressway)
*unpaved:* gravel, crushed stone 12,065 km (1990)

**Inland waterways:** 6,340 km, of which 35% is usable by craft of 1,000 metric ton capacity or larger

**Pipelines:** crude oil 418 km; petroleum products 965 km; natural gas 10,230 km

**Ports:** coastal—Amsterdam, Delfzijl, Den Helder, Dordrecht, Eemshaven, Ijmuiden, Rotterdam, Scheveningen, Terneuzen, Vlissingen; inland—29 ports

**Merchant marine:** 324 ships (1,000 GRT or over) totaling 2,507,112 GRT/3,208,838 DWT, short-sea passenger 3, cargo 180, refrigerated cargo 20, container 32, roll-on/roll-off cargo 15, livestock carrier 1, multifunction large-load carrier 4, oil tanker 27, chemical tanker 21, liquefied gas 12, specialized tanker 2, bulk 3, combination bulk 3, railcar carrier 1
*note:* many Dutch-owned ships are also registered on the captive Netherlands Antilles register

**Airports:**
*total:* 28
*usable:* 28
*with permanent-surface runways:* 19
*with runways over 3,659 m:* 0
*with runways 2,440-3,659 m:* 10
*with runways 1,220-2,439 m:* 7

**Telecommunications:** highly developed, well maintained, and integrated; extensive redundant system of multiconductor cables, supplemented by microwave radio relay microwave links; 9,418,000 telephones; broadcast stations—3 (3 relays) AM, 12 (39 repeaters) FM, 8 (7 repeaters) TV; 5 submarine cables; 1 communication satellite earth station operating in INTELSAT (1 Indian Ocean and 2 Atlantic Ocean antenna) and EUTELSAT systems; nationwide mobile phone system

## Defense Forces

**Branches:** Royal Netherlands Army, Royal Netherlands Navy (including Naval Air Service and Marine Corps), Royal Netherlands Air Force, Royal Constabulary

**Manpower availability:** males age 15-49 4,180,745; fit for military service 3,667,212; reach military age (20) annually 98,479 (1994 est.)

**Defense expenditures:** exchange rate conversion—$7.8 billion, 3% of GDP (1992)

## Geography

**Location:** Western Europe, bordering the North Sea, between Belgium and Germany

**Map references:** Europe, Standard Time Zones of the World

**Area:**
*total area:* 37,330 sq km
*land area:* 33,920 sq km
*comparative area:* slightly less than twice the size of New Jersey

**Land boundaries:** total 1,027 km, Belgium 450 km, Germany 577 km

**Coastline:** 451 km

**Maritime claims:**
*continental shelf:* not specified
*exclusive fishing zone:* 200 nm
*territorial sea:* 12 nm

**International disputes:** none

**Climate:** temperate; marine; cool summers and mild winters

**Terrain:** mostly coastal lowland and reclaimed land (polders); some hills in southeast

**Natural resources:** natural gas, petroleum, fertile soil

**Land use:**
*arable land:* 26%
*permanent crops:* 1%
*meadows and pastures:* 32%
*forest and woodland:* 9%
*other:* 32%

**Irrigated land:** 5,500 sq km (1989 est.)
**Environment:**
*current issues:* water pollution in the form of heavy metals, organic compounds, and nutrients such as nitrates and phosphates; air pollution from vehicles and refining activities; acid rain
*natural hazards:* the extensive system of dikes and dams, protects nearly one-half of the total area from being flooded
*international agreements:* party to—Air Pollution, Air Pollution-Nitrogen Oxides, Air Pollution-Sulphur, Air Pollution-Volatile Organic Compounds, Antarctic-Environmental Protocol, Antarctic Treaty, Climate Change, Endangered Species, Environmental Modification, Hazardous Wastes, Marine Dumping, Marine Life Conservation, Nuclear Test Ban, Ozone Layer Protection, Ship Pollution, Tropical Timber, Wetlands, Whaling; signed, but not ratified—Biodiversity, Law of the Sea
**Note:** located at mouths of three major European rivers (Rhine, Maas or Meuse, Schelde)

# People

**Population:** 15,367,928 (July 1994 est.)
**Population growth rate:** 0.58% (1994 est.)
**Birth rate:** 12.62 births/1,000 population (1994 est.)
**Death rate:** 8.5 deaths/1,000 population (1994 est.)
**Net migration rate:** 1.68 migrant(s)/1,000 population (1994 est.)
**Infant mortality rate:** 6.1 deaths/1,000 live births (1994 est.)
**Life expectancy at birth:**
*total population:* 77.75 years
*male:* 74.69 years
*female:* 80.97 years (1994 est.)
**Total fertility rate:** 1.58 children born/woman (1994 est.)
**Nationality:**
*noun:* Dutchman(men), Dutchwoman(women)
*adjective:* Dutch
**Ethnic divisions:** Dutch 96%, Moroccans, Turks, and other 4% (1988)

**Religions:** Roman Catholic 34%, Protestant 25%, Muslim 3%, other 2%, unaffiliated 36% (1991)
**Languages:** Dutch
**Literacy:** age 15 and over can read and write (1979 est.)
*total population:* 99%
*male:* NA%
*female:* NA%
**Labor force:** 6.7 million (1991)
*by occupation:* services 50.1%, manufacturing and construction 28.2%, government 15.9%, agriculture 5.8% (1986)

# Government

**Names:**
*conventional long form:* Kingdom of the Netherlands
*conventional short form:* Netherlands
*local long form:* Koninkrijk de Nederlanden
*local short form:* Nederland
**Digraph:** NL
**Type:** constitutional monarchy
**Capital:** Amsterdam; The Hague is the seat of government
**Administrative divisions:** 12 provinces (provincien, singular—provincie); Drenthe, Flevoland, Friesland, Gelderland, Groningen, Limburg, Noord-Brabant, Noord-Holland, Overijssel, Utrecht, Zeeland, Zuid-Holland

**Dependent areas:** Aruba, Netherlands Antilles
**Independence:** 1579 (from Spain)
**National holiday:** Queen's Day, 30 April (1938)
**Constitution:** 17 February 1983
**Legal system:** civil law system incorporating French penal theory; judicial review in the Supreme Court of legislation of lower order rather than Acts of the States General; accepts compulsory ICJ jurisdiction, with reservations
**Suffrage:** 18 years of age; universal
**Executive branch:**
*chief of state:* Queen BEATRIX Wilhelmina Armgard (since 30 April 1980); Heir Apparent WILLEM-ALEXANDER, Prince of Orange, son of Queen Beatrix (born 27 April 1967)
*head of government:* Prime Minister

RUDOLPHUS (Ruud) F. M. LUBBERS (since 4 November 1982); Vice Prime Minister Willem (Wim) KOK (since 2 November 1989)—resigned after 3 May 1994 parliamentary elections; no new government has been formed to date
*cabinet:* Ministry of General Affairs; appointed by the prime minister
**Legislative branch:** bicameral legislature (Staten Generaal)
*First Chamber (Eerste Kamer):* elections last held on 9 June 1991 (next to be held 9 June 1995); results—elected by the country's 12 provincial councils; seats—(75 total) percent of seats by party NA
*Second Chamber (Tweede Kamer):* elections last held on 3 May 1994 (next to be held in May 1999); results—PvdA 24.3%, CDA 22.3%, VVD 20.4%, D'66 16.5%, other 16.5%; seats—(150 total) PvdA 37, CDA 34, VVD 31, D'66 24, other 24
**Judicial branch:** Supreme Court (De Hoge Raad)
**Political parties and leaders:** Christian Democratic Appeal (CDA), Elco BRINKMAN; Labor (PvdA), Wim KOK; Liberal (VVD), Frits BOLKESTEIN; Democrats '66 (D'66), Hans van MIERLO; a host of minor parties
**Other political or pressure groups:** large multinational firms; Federation of Netherlands Trade Union Movement (comprising Socialist and Catholic trade unions) and a Protestant trade union; Federation of Catholic and Protestant Employers Associations; the nondenominational Federation of Netherlands Enterprises; and Interchurch Peace Council (IKV)
**Member of:** AfDB, AG (observer), AsDB, Australia Group, Benelux, BIS, CCC, CE, CERN, COCOM, CSCE, EBRD, EC, ECE, ECLAC, EIB, ESA, ESCAP, FAO, G-10, GATT, IADB, IAEA, IBRD, ICAO, ICC, ICFTU, IDA, IEA, IFAD, IFC, ILO, IMF, IMO, INMARSAT, INTELSAT, INTERPOL, IOC, IOM, ISO, ITU, LORCS, MTCR, NACC, NAM (guest), NATO, NEA, NSG, OAS (observer), OECD, PCA, UN, UNAVEM II, UNCTAD, UNESCO, UNHCR, UNIDO, UNOMUR, UNPROFOR, UNTAC, UNTSO, UPU, WCL, WEU, WHO, WIPO, WMO, WTO, ZC
**Diplomatic representation in US:**
*chief of mission:* Ambassador Adriaan Pieter Roetert JACOBOVITS DE SZEGED
*chancery:* 4200 Linnean Avenue NW, Washington, DC 20008
*telephone:* (202) 244-5300
*FAX:* (202) 362-3430
*consulate(s) general:* Chicago, Houston, Los Angeles, Manila (Trust Territories of the Pacific Islands), New York
**US diplomatic representation:**
*chief of mission:* Ambassador Kirk Terry DORNBUSH
*embassy:* Lange Voorhout 102, 2514 EJ The Hague
*mailing address:* PSC 71, Box 1000, the Hague; APO AE 09715
*telephone:* [31] (70) 310-9209
*FAX:* [31] (70) 361-4688
*consulate(s) general:* Amsterdam
**Flag:** three equal horizontal bands of red (top), white, and blue; similar to the flag of Luxembourg, which uses a lighter blue and is longer

---

**U.S. Government Contacts:**

**U.S. Trade Desk:** (202) 482-3039

**American Embassy Commercial Section**
Lange Voorhout 102
The Hague, the Netherlands
APO AE 09715
Tel: 31-70-310-9417
Fax: 31-70-363-29-85

**American Consulate General - Amsterdam Commercial Section**
Museumplein 19
Amsterdam, the Netherlands
APO AE 09715
Tel: 31-20-664-8111

---

**Netherlands Government Contacts:**

**Embassy of the Netherlands Commercial Section**
4200 Linnean Avenue, N.W.

Washington, DC 20008
Tel: (202) 244-5300

---

**Chambers of Commerce & Organizations:**

**The American Chamber of Commerce in the Netherlands**
Carnegieplein 5
2517 KJ The Hague, the Netherlands
Tel: 21-70-65-98-08
Fax: 31-70-64-69-92

---

**Legal Services:**

**Nauta Dutilh**
Advocaten en Notarissen
Gebouw Vierlander
Fellenoord 19
P.O. Box 6019
NL-5612 AA Eindhoven 5600 HA, The Netherlands
Tel: (31-40) 656500
Fax: (31-40) 461375

**Parramore Advocaten**
Burg. Stramanweg 102
1101 AA Amsterdam, The Netherlands
Tel: 31-20-6963211
Fax: 31-20-6968581
*International Business Law, General International Trade Law, Corporate Law, International Tax Law, Lititgation.*

**Van Benthem & Keulen**
Euclideslaan 51
3584 BM Utrecht, The Netherlands
Tel: 31-30-528-528
Fax: 31-30-528-500
*General Civil Practice, Corporate Labour, Health Care, Real Esate and Administrative, Insolvency, Intellectual Property, Insurance and Liability, EEC Antitrust, Family, Criminal.*

---

**Travel:**

**International Airlines to Country:**
Continental, Northwest, United

**International Hotels in Country**
Amsterdam:
Amstel Inter-Continental, Tel: 3120/6226060, Fax: 3120/6225808
Amsterdam Hilton, Tel: 3120/6780780, Fax: 3120/6626688
Hotel de l'Europe, Tel: 3120/6234836, Fax: 3120/6242962.

# NORWAY

400 km
Hammerfest
Barents Sea
Vardø
Tromsø
Bodø
Narvik
Norwegian Sea
Mo
Trondheim
Ålesund
Bergen
Hamar
North Sea
OSLO
Stavanger

## Economy

**Overview:** Norway has a mixed economy involving a combination of free market activity and government intervention. The government controls key areas, such as the vital petroleum sector (through large-scale state enterprises) and extensively subsidizes agriculture, fishing, and areas with sparse resources. Norway also maintains an extensive welfare system that helps propel public sector expenditures to slightly more than 50% of the GDP and results in one of the highest average tax burdens in the world (54%). A small country with a high dependence on international trade, Norway is basically an exporter of raw materials and semiprocessed goods, with an abundance of small- and medium-sized firms, and is ranked among the major shipping nations. The country is richly endowed with natural resources—petroleum, hydropower, fish, forests, and minerals—and is highly dependent on its oil sector to keep its economy afloat. Although one of the government's main priorities is to reduce this dependency, this situation is not likely to improve for years to come. The government also hopes to reduce

unemployment and strengthen and diversify the economy through tax reform and a series of expansionary budgets. The budget deficit is expected to hit a record 8% of GDP because of welfare spending and bail-outs of the banking system. Unemployment continues at record levels of over 10%—including those in job programs—because of the weakness of the economy outside the oil sector. Economic growth was only 1.6% in 1993, while inflation was a moderate 2.3%. Oslo, a member of the European Free Trade Area, has applied for membership in the European Union and continues to deregulate and harmonize with EU regulations. Membership is expected in early 1995.

**National product:** GDP—purchasing power equivalent—$89.5 billion (1993)

**National product real growth rate:** 1.6% (1993)

**National product per capita:** $20,800 (1993)

**Inflation rate (consumer prices):** 2.3% (1993 est.)

**Unemployment rate:** 5.5% (excluding people in job-training programs) (1993 est.)

**Budget:**
*revenues:* $45.3 billion
*expenditures:* $51.8 billion, including capital expenditures of $NA (1993)

**Exports:** $32.1 billion (f.o.b., 1993)
*commodities:* petroleum and petroleum products 40%, metals and products 10.6%, fish and fish products 6.9%, chemicals 6.4%, natural gas 6.0%, ships 5.4%
*partners:* EC 66.3%, Nordic countries 16.3%, developing countries 8.4%, US 6.0%, Japan 1.8% (1993)

**Imports:** $24.8 billion (c.i.f., 1993)
*commodities:* machinery and equipment 38.9%, chemicals and other industrial inputs 26.6%, manufactured consumer goods 17.8%, foodstuffs 6.4%
*partners:* EC 48.6%, Nordic countries 25.1%, developing countries 9.6%, US 8.1%, Japan 8.0% (1993)

**External debt:** $6.5 billion (1992 est.)
**Industrial production:** growth rate 6.2% (1992); accounts for 14% of GDP
**Electricity:**
*capacity:* 26,900,000 kW
*production:* 111 billion kWh
*consumption per capita:* 25,850 kWh (1992)
**Industries:** petroleum and gas, food processing, shipbuilding, pulp and paper products, metals, chemicals, timber, mining, textiles, fishing
**Agriculture:** accounts for 3% of GDP and about 6% of labor force; among world's top 10 fishing nations; livestock output exceeds value of crops; over half of food needs imported; fish catch of 1.76 million metric tons in 1989
**Illicit drugs:** transshipment point for drugs shipped via the CIS and Baltic states for the European market
**Economic aid:**
*donor:* ODA and OOF commitments (1970-89), $4.4 billion
**Currency:** 1 Norwegian krone (NKr) = 100 oere
**Exchange rates:** Norwegian kroner (NKr) per US$1—7.4840 (January 1994), 7.0941 (1993), 6.2145 (1992), 6.4829 (1991), 6.2597 (1990), 6.9045 (1989)
**Fiscal year:** calendar year

## Communications

**Railroads:** 4,223 km 1.435-meter standard gauge; Norwegian State Railways (NSB) operates 4,219 km (2,450 km electrified and 96 km double track); 4 km other
**Highways:**
*total:* 88,800 km
*paved:* 38,580 km
*unpaved:* gravel, crushed stone, earth 50,220 km
**Inland waterways:** 1,577 km along west coast; 2.4 m draft vessels maximum
**Pipelines:** refined products 53 km
**Ports:** Oslo, Bergen, Fredrikstad, Kristiansand, Stavanger, Trondheim
**Merchant marine:** 764 ships (1,000 GRT or over) totaling 20,793,968 GRT/35,409,472 DWT, passenger 13, short-sea passenger 21, cargo 92, passenger-cargo 2, refrigerated cargo

13, container 17, roll-on/roll-off cargo 54, vehicle carrier 28, railcar carrier 1, oil tanker 162, chemical tanker 85, liquefied gas 81, combination ore/oil 28, bulk 159, combination bulk 8
*note:* the government has created a captive register, the Norwegian International Ship Register (NIS), as a subset of the Norwegian register; ships on the NIS enjoy many benefits of flags of convenience and do not have to be crewed by Norwegians; the majority of ships (761) under the Norwegian flag are now registered with the NIS
**Airports:**
*total:* 103
*usable:* 102
*with permanent-surface runways:* 65
*with runways over 3,659 m:* 0
*with runways 2,440-3,659 m:* 13
*with runways 1,220-2,439 m:* 15
**Telecommunications:** high-quality domestic and international telephone, telegraph, and telex services; 2 buried coaxial cable systems; 3,102,000 telephones; broadcast stations—46 AM, 350 private and 143 government FM, 54 (2,100 repeaters) TV; 4 coaxial submarine cables; 3 communications satellite earth stations operating in the EUTELSAT, INTELSAT (1 Atlantic Ocean), MARISAT, and domestic systems

## Defense Forces

**Branches:** Norwegian Army, Royal Norwegian Navy, Royal Norwegian Air Force, Home Guard
**Manpower availability:** males age 15-49 1,119,405; fit for military service 932,438; reach military age (20) annually 30,557 (1994 est.)
**Defense expenditures:** exchange rate conversion—$3.8 billion, 3.4% of GDP (1992)

## Geography

**Location:** Nordic State, Northern Europe, bordering the North Atlantic Ocean, west of Sweden
**Map references:** Arctic Region, Europe, Standard Time Zones of the World

**Area:**
*total area:* 324,220 sq km
*land area:* 307,860 sq km
*comparative area:* slightly larger than New Mexico
**Land boundaries:** total 2,515 km, Finland 729 km, Sweden 1,619 km, Russia 167 km
**Coastline:** 21,925 km (includes mainland 3,419 km, large islands 2,413 km, long fjords, numerous small islands, and minor indentations 16,093 km)
**Maritime claims:**
*contiguous zone:* 10 nm
*continental shelf:* to depth of exploitation
*exclusive economic zone:* 200 nm
*territorial sea:* 4 nm
**International disputes:** territorial claim in Antarctica (Queen Maud Land); dispute between Denmark and Norway over maritime boundary in Arctic Ocean between Greenland and Jan Mayen has been settled by the International Court of Justice; maritime boundary dispute with Russia over portion of Barents Sea
**Climate:** temperate along coast, modified by North Atlantic Current; colder interior; rainy year-round on west coast
**Terrain:** glaciated; mostly high plateaus and rugged mountains broken by fertile valleys; small, scattered plains; coastline deeply indented by fjords; arctic tundra in north
**Natural resources:** petroleum, copper, natural gas, pyrites, nickel, iron ore, zinc, lead, fish, timber, hydropower
**Land use:**
*arable land:* 3%
*permanent crops:* 0%
*meadows and pastures:* 0%
*forest and woodland:* 27%
*other:* 70%
**Irrigated land:** 950 sq km (1989)
**Environment:**
*current issues:* water pollution; acid rain damaging forests and adversely affecting lakes, threatening fish stocks; air pollution from vehicle emissions
*natural hazards:* NA
*international agreements:* party to—Air Pollution, Air Pollution-Nitrogen Oxides, Air Pollution-Sulphur, Air Pollution-Volatile Organic Compounds, Antarctic-Environmental Protocol, Antarctic Treaty, Biodiversity, Climate Change, Endangered Species, Environmental Modification, Hazardous Wastes, Marine Dumping, Nuclear Test Ban, Ozone Layer Protection, Ship Pollution, Tropical Timber, Wetlands, Whaling; signed, but not ratified—Law of the Sea
**Note:** about two-thirds mountains; some 50,000 islands off its much indented coastline; strategic location adjacent to sea lanes and air routes in North Atlantic; one of most rugged and longest coastlines in world; Norway and Turkey only NATO members having a land boundary with Russia

---

**People**

**Population:** 4,314,604 (July 1994 est.)
**Population growth rate:** 0.39% (1994 est.)
**Birth rate:** 13.32 births/1,000 population (1994 est.)
**Death rate:** 10.44 deaths/1,000 population (1994 est.)
**Net migration rate:** 1.01 migrant(s)/1,000 population (1994 est.)
**Infant mortality rate:** 6.3 deaths/1,000 live births (1994 est.)
**Life expectancy at birth:**
*total population:* 77.38 years
*male:* 74.02 years
*female:* 80.94 years (1994 est.)
**Total fertility rate:** 1.81 children orn/woman (1994 est.)
**Nationality:**
*noun:* Norwegian(s)
*adjective:* Norwegian
**Ethnic divisions:** Germanic (Nordic, Alpine, Baltic), Lapps (Sami) 20,000
**Religions:** Evangelical Lutheran 87.8% (state church), other Protestant and Roman Catholic 3.8%, none 3.2%, unknown 5.2% (1980)
**Languages:** Norwegian (official)
*note:* small Lapp- and Finnish-speaking minorities
**Literacy:** age 15 and over can read and write (1976 est.)
*total population:* 99%
*male:* NA%
*female:* NA%

**Labor force:** 2.004 million (1992)
*by occupation:* services 39.1%, commerce 17.6%, mining, oil, and manufacturing 16.0%, banking and financial services 7.6%, transportation and communications 7.8%, construction 6.1%, agriculture, forestry, and fishing 5.5% (1989)

## Government

**Names:**
*conventional long form:* Kingdom of Norway
*conventional short form:* Norway
*local long form:* Kongeriket Norge
*local short form:* Norge
**Digraph:** NO
**Type:** constitutional monarchy
**Capital:** Oslo
**Administrative divisions:** 19 provinces (fylker, singular—fylke); Akershus, Aust-Agder, Buskerud, Finnmark, Hedmark, Hordaland, More og Romsdal, Nordland, Nord-Trondelag, Oppland, Oslo, Ostfold, Rogaland, Sogn og Fjordane, Sor-Trondelag, Telemark, Troms, Vest-Agder, Vestfold
**Dependent areas:** Bouvet Island, Jan Mayen, Svalbard
**Independence:** 26 October 1905 (from Sweden)
**National holiday:** Constitution Day, 17 May (1814)
**Constitution:** 17 May 1814, modified in 1884
**Legal system:** mixture of customary law, civil law system, and common law traditions; Supreme Court renders advisory opinions to legislature when asked; accepts compulsory ICJ jurisdiction, with reservations
**Suffrage:** 18 years of age; universal
**Executive branch:**
*chief of state:* King HARALD V (since 17 January 1991); Heir Apparent Crown Prince HAAKON MAGNUS (born 20 July 1973)
*head of government:* Prime Minister Gro Harlem BRUNDTLAND (since 3 November 1990)
*cabinet:* State Council; appointed by the king in accordance with the will of the Storting
**Legislative branch:** unicameral Parliament (Storting)

*Storting:* elections last held on 13 September 1993 (next to be held September 1997); results—Labor 37.1%, Center Party 18.5%, Conservatives 15.6%, Christian Peoples' 8.4%, Socialist Left 7.9%, Progress 6%, Left Party 3.6%, Red Electoral Alliance 1.2%; seats—(165 total) Labor 67, Center Party 32, Consevatives 18, Christian Peoples' 13, Socialist Left 13, Progress 10, Left Party 1, Red Electoral Alliance 1, unawarded 10
*Lagting:* Storting elects one-fourth of its member to upper house
**Judicial branch:** Supreme Court (Hoyesterett)
**Political parties and leaders:** Labor Party, Thorbjorn JAGLUND; Conservative Party, Jan PETERSEN; Center Party, Anne ENGER LAHNSTEIN; Christian People's Party, Kjell Magne BONDEVIK; Socialist Left, Eric SOLHEIM; Norwegian Communist, Ingre IVERSEN; Progress Party, Carl I. HAGEN; Liberal, Odd Einar DORUM; Finnmark List, leader NA; Left Party; Red Electoral Alliance
**Member of:** AfDB, AsDB, Australia Group, BIS, CBSS, CCC, CE, CERN, COCOM, CSCE, EBRD, ECE, EFTA, ESA, FAO, GATT, IADB, IAEA, IBRD, ICAO, ICC, ICFTU, IDA, IEA, IFAD, IFC, ILO, IMF, IMO, INMARSAT, INTELSAT, INTERPOL, IOC, IOM, ISO, ITU, LORCS, MTCR, NACC, NAM (guest), NATO, NC, NEA, NIB, NSG, OECD, ONUSAL, PCA, UN, UNAVEM II, UNCTAD, UNESCO, UNHCR, UNIDO, UNIFIL, UNIKOM, UNMOGIP, UNOSOM, UNPROFOR, UNTAC, UNTSO, UPU, WEU (associate), WHO, WIPO, WMO, ZC
**Diplomatic representation in US:**
*chief of mission:* Ambassador Kjeld VIBE
*chancery:* 2720 34th Street NW, Washington, DC 20008
*telephone:* (202) 333-6000
*FAX:* (202) 337-0870
*consulate(s) general:* Houston, Los Angeles, Minneapolis, New York, and San Francisco
*consulate(s):* Miami
**US diplomatic representation:**
*chief of mission:* Ambassador Thomas A. LOFTUS
*embassy:* Drammensveien 18, 0244 Oslo 2
*mailing address:* PSC 69, Box 1000, APO AE 09707

*telephone:* [47] 22-44-85-50
*FAX:* [47] 22-43-07-77
**Flag:** red with a blue cross outlined in white that extends to the edges of the flag; the vertical part of the cross is shifted to the hoist side in the style of the Dannebrog (Danish flag)

## U.S. Government Contacts:

**U.S. Trade Desk**: (202) 482-4414

**American Embassy Commercial Section**
Drammensveien 18
Oslo 2, Norway
APO AE 09707
Tel: 47-2-44-85-50
Fax: 47-2-55-88-03

## Norway Government Contacts:

**Embassy of Norway Commercial Section**
2720 34th Street, N.W.
Washington DC20008
Tel: (202) 333-6000

## Chambers of Commerce & Organizations:

**The American Club in Oslo**
Ing. Hoels Vei 13, P.O. Box 56
N-1346, Gjettum, Norway
Tel: (47) 67-54-6880
Fax: (47) 67-54-6930

## Legal Services:

**Advokatfirma Engelschion & Co. Da**
Akersgt. 65 B
P.O. Box 8333 Hammersborg
0129 Oslo 1, Norway
Tel: 47-22-36-36-30
Fax: 47-22-36-36-80
*General Business and Civil Law, Corporate, Commercial, Industrial, Tax and International Law, Computer, Technology. General Law.*

**Forenede Advokater Johansen og Unhjem Johansen A/S**
Keysersgt. 4
N-0165 Oslo, Norway

Tel: 47-22-112670
Fax: 47-22-201849
*General Civil Practice, Corporation, Taxation, Trade, Divorce, Inheritance.*

## Travel:

**International Airlines to Country:**
Continental

**International Hotels in Country:**
Oslo:
Grand, Tel: 47/22429390, Fax: 47/22421225
Holmenkollen Park Rica, Tel: 47/22922000, Fax: 47/22141692.

# POLAND

Boundary representation is
not necessarily authoritative

## Economy

**Overview:** Poland is continuing the difficult transition to a market economy that began on 1 January 1990, when the new democratic government instituted "shock therapy" by decontrolling prices, slashing subsidies, and drastically reducing import barriers. The economy contracted sharply in 1990 and 1991, but in 1992 real GDP grew 1% despite a severe drought. Real GDP expanded about 4% in 1993, the highest rate in Europe except for Albania. About half of GDP now comes from the private sector even though privatization of the large state-owned enterprises is proceeding slowly and most industry remains in state hands. The pattern of industrial production is changing rapidly; output of textiles and construction materials is well above 1990 levels, while output of basic metals remains depressed. Inflation, which had exceeded 50% monthly in late 1989, was down to about 37% for all of 1993, as the government held the budget deficit below 3% of GDP. Unemployment has risen steadily, however, to about 16%. The trade deficit is also a problem, in part due to recession in Western Europe,

Poland's main customer. The new government elected in September 1993 is politically to the left of its predecessor but is continuing the reform process.

**National product:** GDP—purchasing power equivalent—$180.4 billion (1993 est.)

**National product real growth rate:** 4.1% (1993 est.)

**National product per capita:** $4,680 (1993 est.)

**Inflation rate (consumer prices):** 37% (1993)

**Unemployment rate:** 15.7% (December 1993)

**Budget:**
*revenues:* $24.3 billion
*expenditures:* $27.1 billion, including capital expenditures of $1.5 billion (1993 est.)

**Exports:** $13.5 billion (f.o.b., 1993 est.)
*commodities:* machinery 24%, metals 17%, chemicals 12%, fuels and power 11%, food 10% (1992)
*partners:* Germany 31.4%, Netherlands 6.0%, Italy 5.6%, Russia 5.5% (1992)

**Imports:** $15.6 billion (f.o.b., 1993 est.)
*commodities:* fuels and power 17%, machinery 36%, chemicals 17%, food 8% (1992)
*partners:* Germany 23.9%, Russia 8.5%, Italy 6.9%, UK 6.7% (1992)

**External debt:** $47 billion (1993); note—Poland's Western government creditors promised in 1991 to forgive 30% of Warsaw's $35 billion official debt immediately and to forgive another 20% in 1994; foreign banks agreed in early 1994 to forgive 45% of their $12 billion debt claim

**Industrial production:** growth rate 7% (1993)

**Electricity:**
*capacity:* 31,530,000 kW
*production:* 137 billion kWh
*consumption per capita:* 3,570 kWh (1992)

**Industries:** machine building, iron and steel, extractive industries, chemicals, shipbuilding, food processing, glass, beverages, textiles

**Agriculture:** accounts for 7% of GDP and a much larger share of labor force; 75% of output from private farms. 25% from state farms; productivity remains low by European standards; leading European producer of rye, rapeseed, and potatoes; wide variety of other crops and livestock; major exporter of pork products; normally self-sufficient in food

**Illicit drugs:** illicit producers of opium for domestic consumption and amphetamines for the international market; transshipment point for Asian and Latin American illicit drugs to Western Europe

**Economic aid:**

*donor:* bilateral aid to non-Communist less developed countries (1954-89), $2.2 billion

*recipient:* Western governments and institutions have pledged $8 billion in grants and loans since 1989, but most of the money has not been disbursed

**Currency:** 1 zloty (Zl) = 100 groszy

**Exchange rates:** zlotych (Zl) per US$1— 21,080 (January 1994), 18,115 (1993), 13,626 (1992), 10,576 (1991), 9,500 (1990), 1,439.18 (1989)

**Fiscal year:** calendar year

## Communications

**Railroads:** 26,250 km total; 23,857 km 1.435-meter gauge, 397 km 1.520-meter gauge, 1,996 km narrow gauge; 8,987 km double track; 11,510 km electrified; government owned (1991)

**Highways:**

*total:* 360,629 km (excluding farm, factory and forest roads)

*paved:* 220,000 km (220 km of which are limited access expressways)

*unpaved:* 140,629 km (1988)

**Inland waterways:** 3,997 km navigable rivers and canals (1991)

**Pipelines:** natural gas 4,600 km, crude oil 1,986 km, petroleum products 360 km (1992)

**Ports:** Gdansk, Gdynia, Szczecin, Swinoujscie; principal inland ports are Gliwice on Kanal Gliwicki, Wrocaw on the Oder, and Warsaw on the Vistula

**Merchant marine:** 173 ships (1,000 GRT or over) totaling 2,327.855 GRT/3,458,445 DWT, short-sea passenger 5, cargo 57, roll-on/roll-off cargo 8, container 8, oil tanker 1, chemical tanker 4, bulk 89, passenger 1

*note:* Poland owns 3 ships operating under Liberian registry

**Airports:**

*total:* 209

*usable:* 167

*with permanent-surface runways:* 70

*with runway over 3,659 m:* 1

*with runways 2,440-3,659 m:* 47

*with runways 1,060-2,439 m:* 78

*note:* a C-130 can land on a 1,060-m airstrip

**Telecommunications:** severely underdeveloped and outmoded system; cable, open wire and microwave; phone density is 10.5 phones per 100 residents (October 1990); 3.6 million telephone subscribers; exchanges are 86% automatic (1991); broadcast stations—27 AM, 27 FM, 40 (5 Soviet repeaters) TV; 9.6 million TVs; 1 satellite earth station using INTELSAT, EUTELSAT, INMARSAT and Intersputnik

## Defense Forces

**Branches:** Army, Navy, Air and Air Defense Force

**Manpower availability:** males age 15-49 10,046,993; fit for military service 7,856,680; reach military age (19) annually 316,339 (1994 est.)

**Defense expenditures:** 30.8 trillion zlotych, 1.8% of GNP (1993 est.); note—conversion of defense expenditures into US dollars using the current exchange rate could produce misleading results

## Geography

**Location:** Central Europe, between Germany and Belarus

**Map references:** Asia, Ethnic Groups in Eastern Europe, Europe, Standard Time Zones of the World

**Area:**

*total area:* 312,680 sq km

*land area:* 304,510 sq km
*comparative area:* slightly smaller than New Mexico
**Land boundaries:** total 3,114 km, Belarus 605 km, Czech Republic 658 km, Germany 456 km, Lithuania 91 km, Russia (Kaliningrad Oblast) 432 km, Slovakia 444 km, Ukraine 428 km
**Coastline:** 491 km
**Maritime claims:**
*exclusive economic zone:* 200 nm
*territorial sea:* 12 nm
**International disputes:** none
**Climate:** temperate with cold, cloudy, moderately severe winters with frequent precipitation; mild summers with frequent showers and thundershowers
**Terrain:** mostly flat plain; mountains along southern border
**Natural resources:** coal, sulfur, copper, natural gas, silver, lead, salt
**Land use:**
*arable land:* 46%
*permanent crops:* 1%
*meadows and pastures:* 13%
*forest and woodland:* 28%
*other:* 12%
**Irrigated land:** 1,000 sq km (1989 est.)
**Environment:**
*current issues:* forest damage due to air pollution; improper means for disposal of large amounts of hazardous and industrial waste; severe water pollution from industrial and municipal sources; severe air pollution results from emissions of sulfur dioxide from coal-fired power plants
*natural hazards:* NA
*international agreements:* party to—Air Pollution, Antarctic Treaty, Endangered Species, Environmental Modification, Hazardous Wastes, Marine Dumping, Nuclear Test Ban, Ozone Layer Protection, Ship Pollution, Wetlands; signed, but not ratified— Air Pollution-Nitrogen Oxides, Antarctic-Environmental Protocol, Biodiversity, Climate Change, Law of the Sea
**Note:** historically, an area of conflict because of flat terrain and the lack of natural barriers on the North European Plain

## People

**Population:** 38,654,561 (July 1994 est.)
**Population growth rate:** 0.35% (1994 est.)
**Birth rate:** 13.44 births/1,000 population (1994 est.)
**Death rate:** 9.4 deaths/1,000 population (1994 est.)
**Net migration rate:** -0.52 migrant(s)/1,000 population (1994 est.)
**Infant mortality rate:** 13.1 deaths/1,000 live births (1994 est.)
**Life expectancy at birth:**
*total population:* 72.66 years
*male:* 68.64 years
*female:* 76.91 years (1994 est.)
**Total fertility rate:** 1.94 children born/ woman (1994 est.)
**Nationality:**
*noun:* Pole(s)
*adjective:* Polish
**Ethnic divisions:** Polish 97.6%, German 1.3%, Ukrainian 0.6%, Byelorussian 0.5% (1990 est.)
**Religions:** Roman Catholic 95% (about 75% practicing), Eastern Orthodox, Protestant, and other 5%
**Languages:** Polish
**Literacy:** age 15 and over can read and write (1978)
*total population:* 98%
*male:* 99%
*female:* 98%
**Labor force:** 17.329 million
*by occupation:* industry and construction 32.0%, agriculture 27.6%, trade, transport, and communications 14.7%, government and other 24.6% (1992)

## Government

**Names:**
*conventional long form:* Republic of Poland
*conventional short form:* Poland
*local long form:* Rzeczpospolita Polska
*local short form:* Polska
**Digraph:** PL
**Type:** democratic state
**Capital:** Warsaw

**Administrative divisions:** 49 provinces
(wojewodztwa, singular—wojewodztwo);
Biala Podlaska, Bialystok, Bielsko Biala,
Bydgoszcz, Chelm, Ciechanow, Czestochowa,
Elblag, Gdansk, Gorzow, Jelenia Gora, Kalisz,
Katowice, Kielce, Konin, Koszalin, Krakow,
Krosno, Legnica, Leszno, Lodz, Lomza,
Lublin, Nowy Sacz, Olsztyn, Opole, Ostroleka,
Pila, Piotrkow, Plock, Poznan, Przemysl,
Radom, Rzeszow, Siedlce, Sieradz,
Skierniewice, Slupsk, Suwalki, Szczecin,
Tarnobrzeg, Tarnow, Torun, Walbrzych,
Warszawa, Wloclawek, Wroclaw, Zamosc,
Zielona Gora
**Independence:** 11 November 1918
(independent republic proclaimed)
**National holiday:** Constitution Day, 3 May
(1791)
**Constitution:** interim "small constitution"
came into effect in December 1992 replacing
the Communist-imposed Constitution of 22
July 1952; new democratic Constitution being
drafted
**Legal system:** mixture of Continental
(Napoleonic) civil law and holdover
Communist legal theory; changes being
gradually introduced as part of broader
democratization process; limited judicial
review of legislative acts; has not accepted
compulsory ICJ jurisdiction
**Suffrage:** 18 years of age; universal
**Executive branch:**
*chief of state:* President Lech WALESA (since
22 December 1990); election first round held
25 November 1990, second round held 9
December 1990 (next to be held NA November
1995); results—second round Lech WALESA
74.7%, Stanislaw TYMINSKI 25.3%
*head of government:* Prime Minister
Waldemar PAWLAK (since 26 October 1993)
*cabinet:* Council of Ministers; responsible to
the president and the Sejm
**Legislative branch:** bicameral National
Assembly (Zgromadzenie Narodowe)
*Senate (Senat):* elections last held 19
September 1993 (next to be held no later than
NA October 1997); seats—(100 total)
*post-Solidarity bloc:* UW 6, NSZZ 12,
BBWR 2
*non-Communist, non-Solidarity:*

independents 7, unaffiliated 1, vacant 1 (to be
filled in a 19 June election)
*Communist origin or linked:* PSL 34, SLD 37
*Diet (Sejm):* elections last held 19 September
1993 (next to be held no later than NA October
1997); seats—(460 total)
*post-Solidarity bloc:* UW 74, UP 41,
BBWR 16
*non-Communist, non-Solidarity:* KPN 22
*Communist origin or linked:* SLD 171,
PSL 132
*note:* 4 seats were won by ethnic Germans
**Judicial branch:** Supreme Court
**Political parties and leaders:**
*post-Solidarity parties:* Freedom Union (WD;
UD and Liberal Democratic Congress merged
to form Freedom Union), Tadeusz
MAZOWIECKI; Christian-National Union
(ZCHN), Wieslaw CHRZANOWSKI;
Centrum (PC), Jaroslaw KACZYNSKI;
Peasant Alliance (PL), Gabriel JANOWSKI;
Solidarity Trade Union (NSZZ), Marian
KRZAKLEWSKI; Union of Labor (UP),
Ryszard BUGAJ; Christian-Democratic Party
(PCHD), Pawel LACZKOWSKI;
Conservative Party, Alexander HALL;
Nonparty Bloc for the Support of the Reforms
(BBWR)
*non-Communist, non-Solidarity:*
Confederation for an Independent Poland
(KPN), Leszek MOCZULSKI; Polish
Economic Program (PPG), Janusz
REWINSKI; Christian Democrats (CHD),
Andrzej OWSINSKI; German Minority (MN),
Henryk KROL; Union of Real Politics (UPR),
Janusz KORWIN-MIKKE; Democratic Party
(SD), Antoni MACKIEWICZ; Party X,
Stanislaw Tyminski
*Communist origin or linked:* Social
Democracy (SDRP, party of Poland),
Aleksander KWASNIEWSKI; Polish
Peasants' Party (PSL), Waldemar PAWLAK;
Democratic Left Alliance, Aleksander
KWASNIEWSKI
**Other political or pressure groups:**
powerful Roman Catholic Church; Solidarity
(trade union); All Poland Trade Union Alliance
(OPZZ), populist program
**Member of:** BIS, BSEC (observer), CBSS,
CCC, CE, CEI, CERN, COCOM

(cooperating), CSCE, EBRD, ECE, FAO, GATT, IAEA, IBRD, ICAO, ICFTU, IDA, IFC, ILO, IMF, IMO, INMARSAT, INTELSAT (nonsignatory user), INTERPOL, IOC, IOM, ISO, ITU, LORCS, MINURSO, NACC, NAM (guest), NSG, OAS (observer), PCA, UN, UNCTAD, UNESCO, UNDOF, UNIDO, UNIFIL, UNIKOM, UNOMIG, UNPROFOR, UNTAC, UPU, WCL, WFTU, WHO, WIPO, WMO, WTO, ZC

**Diplomatic representation in US:**
*chief of mission:* Ambassador Jerzy KOZMINSKI
*chancery:* 2640 16th Street NW, Washington, DC 20009
*telephone:* (202) 234-3800 through 3802
*FAX:* (202) 328-6271
*consulate(s) general:* Chicago, Los Angeles, and New York

**US diplomatic representation:**
*chief of mission:* Ambassador Nicholas A. REY
*embassy:* Aleje Ujazdowskie 29/31, Warsaw
*mailing address:* American Embassy Warsaw, Unit 1340, or APO AE 09213-1340
*telephone:* [48] (2) 628-3041
*FAX:* [48] (2) 628-8298
*consulate(s) general:* Krakow, Poznan

**Flag:** two equal horizontal bands of white (top) and red; similar to the flags of Indonesia and Monaco which are red (top) and white

**U.S. Government Contacts:**

**U.S. Trade Desk**: (202) 482-4915

**American Embassy Commercial Section**
Ulica Wiejska 20
Warsaw, Poland
APO AE 09213 (WAW)
Tel: 48-22-21-45-15
Fax: 48-22-21-63-27

**Poland Government Contacts:**

**Ministry of Foreign Economic Relations**
Pl. Trzech Krzyzy 5
00-950 Warszawa
Tel: 693-50-00

**Ploand Foreign Investment Agency (PAIZ)**
Al. Roz 2
00-556 Warszawa, Poland
Tel: 48 2 621-6261
Fax: 48-2 621-8427

**Chambers of Commerce & Organizations:**

**American Chamber of Commerce in Poland**
Swietokrzyska 36 m 6, Entrance 1
00-116 Warsaw, Poland
Tel: (48 22) 209-867, 209-962     Ext. 222, 223
Fax: (48 22) 622-5525

**Travel:**

**International Hotels in Country:**
Warsaw:
Bristol, Tel: 4822 02/625-25-25, Fax: 4822 02/625-25-77
Marriott, Tel: 4822 02/630-63-06, Fax: 4822 022/30-52-39
Holiday Inn, Tel: 4822/20-03-41, Fax: 4822/30-05-69.

# PORTUGAL

125 km

North
Atlantic
Ocean

Braga
Porto
Covilhã
Coimbra
Portalegre
LISBON
Beja
Faro

Azores and Madeira
Islands are not shown

## Economy

**Overview:** Portugal's economy registered only 1.1% growth in 1992 and contracted by 0.4% in 1993, in contrast to the 4.5% average of the fast-paced 1986-90 period. Recession in the European Union, which accounts for 75% of Portugal's international trade, is the key factor in the downturn. The government's long-run economic goal is the modernization of Portuguese markets, industry, infrastructure, and workforce in order to catch up with productivity and income levels of the more advanced EU countries. Per capita income now equals only 55% of the EU average. The government's medium-term economic objective is to be in the first tier of EU countries eligible to join the economic and monetary union (EMU) as early as 1997. Economic policy in 1993 focused on reducing inflationary pressures by lowering the fiscal deficit, maintaining a stable escudo, moderating wage increases, and encouraging increased competition. Resumption of growth in the short run depends on the revival of growth in Europe as a whole, not a likely prospect in the immediate future.

**National product:** GDP—purchasing power equivalent—$91.5 billion (1993)
**National product real growth rate:** -0.4% (1993)
**National product per capita:** $8,700 (1993)
**Inflation rate (consumer prices):** 7% (1993 est.)
**Unemployment rate:** 7% (1993 est.)
**Budget:**
*revenues:* $27.3 billion
*expenditures:* $33.2 billion, including capital expenditures of $4.5 billion (1991 est.)
**Exports:** $17.5 billion (f.o.b., 1993 est.)
*commodities:* cotton textiles, cork and paper products, canned fish, wine, timber and timber products, resin, machinery, appliances
*partners:* EC 75.4%, other developed countries 12.4%, US 3.8% (1992)
**Imports:** $28 billion (c.i.f., 1993 est.)
*commodities:* machinery and transport equipment, agricultural products, chemicals, petroleum, textiles
*partners:* EC 72%, other developed countries 10.9% less developed countries 12.9%, US 3.4%
**External debt:** $20 billion (1993 est.)
**Industrial production:** growth rate 9.1% (1990); accounts for 40% of GDP
**Electricity:**
*capacity:* 6,624,000 kW
*production:* 26.4 billion kWh
*consumption per capita:* 2,520 kWh (1992)
**Industries:** textiles and footwear; wood pulp, paper, and cork; metalworking; oil refining; chemicals; fish canning; wine; tourism
**Agriculture:** accounts for 6.1% of GDP and 20% of labor force; small, inefficient farms; imports more than half of food needs; major crops—grain, potatoes, olives, grapes; livestock sector—sheep, cattle, goats, poultry, meat, dairy products
**Illicit drugs:** increasingly important gateway country for Latin American cocaine entering the European market; transshipment point for hashish from North Africa to Europe

**Economic aid:**
*recipient:* US commitments, including Ex-Im (FY70-89), $1.8 billion
Western (non-US) countries, ODA and OOF bilateral commitments (1970-89), $1.2 billion
**Currency:** 1 Portuguese escudo (Esc) = 100 centavos
**Exchange rates:** Portuguese escudos (Esc) per US$1—176.16 (January 1994), 160.80 (1993), 135.00 (1992), 144.48 (1991), 142.55 (1990), 157.46 (1989)
**Fiscal year:** calendar year

## Communications

**Railroads:** 3,625 km total; state-owned Portuguese Railroad Co. (CP) operates 2,858 km 1.665-meter gauge (434 km electrified and 426 km double track), 755 km 1.000-meter gauge; 12 km (1.435-meter gauge) electrified, double track, privately owned
**Highways:**
*total:* 73,661 km
*paved and gravel:* 61,599 km (including 453 km of expressways)
*unpaved:* earth 12,062 km
**Inland waterways:** 820 km navigable; relatively unimportant to national economy, used by shallow-draft craft limited to 300-metric-ton cargo capacity
**Pipelines:** crude oil 11 km; petroleum products 58 km
**Ports:** Leixoes, Lisbon, Porto, Ponta Delgada (Azores), Velas (Azores), Setubal, Sines
**Merchant marine:** 61 ships (1,000 GRT or over) totaling 962,293 GRT/1,779,855 DWT, short-sea passenger 2, cargo 25, refrigerated cargo 3, container 3, roll-on/roll-off cargo 1, oil tanker 18, chemical tanker 4, bulk 3, liquified gas 2
*note:* Portugal has created a captive register on Madeira (MAR) for Portuguese-owned ships that will have the taxation and crewing benefits of a flag of convenience; although only one ship currently is known to fly the Portuguese flag on the MAR register, it is likely that a majority of Portuguese flag ships will transfer to this subregister in a few years

**Airports:**
*total:* 65
*usable:* 63
*with permanent-surface runways:* 37
*with runways over 3,659 m:* 2
*with runways 2,440-3,659 m:* 10
*with runways 1,220-2,439 m:* 11
**Telecommunications:** generally adequate integrated network of coaxial cables, open wire and microwave radio relay; 2,690,000 telephones; broadcast stations—57 AM, 66 (22 repeaters) FM, 66 (23 repeaters) TV; 6 submarine cables; 3 INTELSAT earth stations (2 Atlantic Ocean, 1 Indian Ocean), EUTELSAT, domestic satellite systems (mainland and Azores); tropospheric link to Azores

## Defense Forces

**Branches:** Army, Navy (including Marines), Air Force, National Republican Guard, Fiscal Guard, Public Security Police
**Manpower availability:** males age 15-49 2,723,987; fit for military service 2,207,637; reach military age (20) annually 89,380 (1994 est.)
**Defense expenditures:** exchange rate conversion—$2.4 billion, 2.9% of GDP (1992)

## Geography

**Location:** Southwestern Europe, bordering the North Atlantic Ocean west of Spain
**Map references:** Africa, Europe, Standard Time Zones of the World
**Area:**
*total area:* 92,080 sq km
*land area:* 91,640 sq km
*comparative area:* slightly smaller than Indiana
*note:* includes Azores and Madeira Islands
**Land boundaries:** total 1,214 km, Spain 1,214 km
**Coastline:** 1,793 km
**Maritime claims:**
*continental shelf:* 200-m depth or to depth of exploitation

*exclusive economic zone:* 200 nm
*territorial sea:* 12 nm
**International disputes:** sovereignty over Timor Timur (East Timor Province) disputed with Indonesia
**Climate:** maritime temperate; cool and rainy in north, warmer and drier in south
**Terrain:** mountainous north of the Tagus, rolling plains in south
**Natural resources:** fish, forests (cork), tungsten, iron ore, uranium ore, marble
**Land use:**
*arable land:* 32%
*permanent crops:* 6%
*meadows and pastures:* 6%
*forest and woodland:* 40%
*other:* 16%
**Irrigated land:** 6,340 sq km (1989 est.)
**Environment:**
*current issues:* soil erosion; air pollution caused by industrial and vehicle emissions; water pollution, especially in coastal areas
*natural hazards:* Azores subject to severe earthquakes
*international agreements:* party to—Air Pollution, Biodiversity, Climate Change, Endangered Species, Hazardous Wastes, Marine Dumping, Marine Life Conservation, Ozone Layer Protection, Ship Pollution, Tropical Timber, Wetlands; signed, but not ratified—Air Pollution-Volatile Organic Compounds, Environmental Modification, Law of the Sea, Nuclear Test Ban
**Note:** Azores and Madeira Islands occupy strategic locations along western sea approaches to Strait of Gibraltar

## People

**Population:** 10,524,210 (July 1994 est.)
**Population growth rate:** 0.36% (1994 est.)
**Birth rate:** 11.66 births/1,000 population (1994 est.)
**Death rate:** 9.7 deaths/1,000 population (1994 est.)
**Net migration rate:** 1.67 migrant(s)/1,000 population (1994 est.)
**Infant mortality rate:** 9.5 deaths/1,000 live births (1994 est.)

**Life expectancy at birth:**
*total population:* 75.2 years
*male:* 71.77 years
*female:* 78.86 years (1994 est.)
**Total fertility rate:** 1.46 children born/woman (1994 est.)
**Nationality:**
*noun:* Portuguese (singular and plural)
*adjective:* Portuguese
**Ethnic divisions:** homogeneous Mediterranean stock in mainland, Azores, Madeira Islands; citizens of black African descent who immigrated to mainland during decolonization number less than 100,000
**Religions:** Roman Catholic 97%, Protestant denominations 1%, other 2%
**Languages:** Portuguese
**Literacy:** age 15 and over can read and write (1990 est.)
*total population:* 85%
*male:* 89%
*female:* 82%
**Labor force:** 4,605,700
*by occupation:* services 45%, industry 35%, agriculture 20% (1988)

## Government

**Names:**
*conventional long form:* Portuguese Republic
*conventional short form:* Portugal
*local long form:* Republica Portuguesa
*local short form:* Portugal
**Digraph:** PO
**Type:** republic
**Capital:** Lisbon
**Administrative divisions:** 18 districts (distritos, singular—distrito) and 2 autonomous regions* (regioes autonomas, singular—regiao autonoma); Aveiro, Acores (Azores)*, Beja, Braga, Braganca, Castelo Branco, Coimbra, Evora, Faro, Guarda, Leiria, Lisboa, Madeira*, Portalegre, Porto, Santarem, Setubal, Viana do Castelo, Vila Real, Viseu
**Dependent areas:** Macau (scheduled to become a Special Administrative Region of China on 20 December 1999)
**Independence:** 1140 (independent republic proclaimed 5 October 1910)

**National holiday:** Day of Portugal, 10 June (1580)

**Constitution:** 25 April 1976, revised 30 October 1982 and 1 June 1989

**Legal system:** civil law system; the Constitutional Tribunal reviews the constitutionality of legislation; accepts compulsory ICJ jurisdiction, with reservations

**Suffrage:** 18 years of age; universal

**Executive branch:**

*chief of state:* President Dr. Mario Alberto Nobre Lopes SOARES (since 9 March 1986); election last held 13 February 1991 (next to be held NA February 1996); results—Dr. Mario Lopes SOARES 70%, Basilio HORTA 14%, Carlos CARVALHAS 13%, Carlos MARQUES 3%

*head of government:* Prime Minister Anibal CAVACO SILVA (since 6 November 1985)

*Council of State:* acts as a consultative body to the president

*cabinet:* Council of Ministers; appointed by the president on recommendation of the prime minister

**Legislative branch:** unicameral

*Assembly of the Republic (Assembleia da Republica):* elections last held 6 October 1991 (next to be held NA October 1995); results— PSD 50.4%, PS 29.3%, CDU 8.8%, Center Democrats 4.4%, National Solidarity Party 1.7%, PRD 0.6%, other 4.8%; seats—(230 total) PSD 136, PS 71, CDU 17, Center Democrats 5, National Solidarity Party 1

**Judicial branch:** Supreme Tribunal of Justice (Supremo Tribunal de Justica)

**Political parties and leaders:** Social Democratic Party (PSD), Anibal CAVACO Silva; Portuguese Socialist Party (PS), Antonio GUTERRES; Party of Democratic Renewal (PRD), Pedro CANAVARRO; Portuguese Communist Party (PCP), Carlos CARVALHAS; Social Democratic Center (CDS), Manuel MONTEIRO; National Solidarity Party (PSN), Manuel SERGIO; Center Democratic Party (CDS); United Democratic Coalition (CDU; Communists)

**Member of:** AfDB, Australian Group, BIS, CCC, CE, CERN, COCOM, CSCE, EBRD, EC, ECE, ECLAC, EIB, FAO, GATT, IADB, IAEA, IBRD, ICAO, ICC, ICFTU, IDA, IEA, IFAD, IFC, ILO, IMF, IMO, INMARSAT, INTELSAT, INTERPOL, IOC, IOM, ISO, ITU, LAIA (observer), LORCS, MTCR, NACC, NAM (guest), NATO, NEA, NSG, OAS (observer), OECD, PCA, UN, UNCTAD, UNESCO, UNIDO, UNOMOZ, UNPROFOR, UPU, WCL, WEU, WHO, WIPO, WMO, WTO, ZC

**Diplomatic representation in US:**

*chief of mission:* Ambassador Francisco Jose Laco Treichler KNOPFLI

*chancery:* 2125 Kalorama Road NW, Washington, DC 20008

*telephone:* (202) 328-8610

*FAX:* (202) 462-3726

*consulate(s) general:* Boston, New York, Newark (New Jersey), and San Francisco

*consulate(s):* Los Angeles, New Bedford (Massachusetts), and Providence (Rhode Island)

**US diplomatic representation:**

*chief of mission:* (vacant); Charge d'Affaires Sharon P. WILKINSON

*embassy:* Avenida das Forcas Armadas, 1600 Lisbon

*mailing address:* PSC 83, Lisbon; APO AE 09726

*telephone:* [351] (1) 726-6600 or 6659, 8670, 8880

*FAX:* [351] (1) 726-9109

*consulate(s):* Ponta Delgada (Azores)

**Flag:** two vertical bands of green (hoist side, two-fifths) and red (three-fifths) with the Portuguese coat of arms centered on the dividing line

---

**U.S. Government Contacts:**

**U.S. Trade Desk**: (202) 482-4508

**American Embassy Commercial Section**
Avenida das Forcas Armadas
1600 Lisbon, Protugal
APO AE 09726
Tel: 351-1-726-6600
Fax: 351-1-726-8914

## Portugal Government contacts:

**Embassy of Portugal Commercial Section**
1914 Connecticut Avenue, N.W.
Washington, DC 20008
Tel: (202) 328-8610

## Chamber of Commerce & Organizations:

**American Chamber of Commerce in Portugal**
Rue de D. Esafania 155, 5 Esq.
Lisbon 1000, Portugal
Tel: 351-1-572-561

## Legal Services:

**Noronha-Advogados**
Praca Marques de Pombal, 16A - 5' Piso
1200 Lisbon, Portugal
Tel: 351-01-355-7435
        351-01-355-7650
Fax: 351-01-355-7854
*Practice limited to Portuguese, Brazilian, European Community and International Law.*

## Travel:

**International Airlines to Country:**
TWA

**International Hotels in Country:**
Lisbon:
Liboa Sheraton and Towers, Tel: 351 01/575757, Fax: 351 01/547164
Meridien Lisboa, Tel: 351 01/690400, Fax: 351 01/693231
Ritz Lisboa, Tel: 351 01/692020, Fax: 351 01/691783.

# SAN MARINO

## Economy

**Overview:** The tourist sector contributes over 50% of GDP. In 1991 more than 3.1 million tourists visited San Marino, 2.7 million of whom were Italians. The key industries are wearing apparel, electronics, and ceramics. Main agricultural products are wine and cheeses. The per capita level of output and standard of living are comparable to those of Italy.

**National product:** GDP—purchasing power equivalent—$370 million (1992 est.)

**National product real growth rate:** NA%

**National product per capita:** $16,000 (1992 est.)

**Inflation rate (consumer prices):** 6.2% (1992 est.)

**Unemployment rate:** 3% (1991)

**Budget:**
*revenues:* $275 million
*expenditures:* $275 million, including capital expenditures of $NA (1992 est.)

**Exports:** trade data are included with the statistics for Italy; commodity trade consists primarily of exchanging building stone, lime, wood, chestnuts, wheat, wine, baked goods, hides, and ceramics for a wide variety of consumer manufactures

**Imports:** see exports

**External debt:** $NA

**Industrial production:** growth rate NA%; accounts for 42% of workforce

**Electricity:** supplied by Italy

**Industries:** wine, olive oil, cement, leather, textile, tourism

**Agriculture:** employs 3% of labor force; products—wheat, grapes, maize, olives, meat, cheese, hides; small numbers of cattle, pigs, horses; depends on Italy for food imports

**Economic aid:** $NA

**Currency:** 1 Italian lire (Lit) = 100 centesimi; note—also mints its own coins

**Exchange rates:** Italian lire (Lit) per US$1—1,700.2 (January 1994), 1,573.7 (1993), 1,232.4 (1992), 1,240.6 (1991), 1,198.1 (1990), 1,372.1 (1989)

**Fiscal year:** calendar year

## Communications

**Highways:**
*total:* 104 km
*paved:* NA
*unpaved:* NA

**Telecommunications:** automatic telephone system completely integrated into Italian system; 11,700 telephones; broadcast services from Italy; microwave and cable links into Italian networks; no communication satellite facilities

## Defense Forces

**Branches:** public security or police force

**Defense expenditures:** $3.7 million (1992 est.), 1% of GDP

## Geography

**Location:** Southern Europe, an enclave in central Italy

**Map references:** Europe, Standard Time Zones of the World
**Area:**
*total area:* 60 sq km
*land area:* 60 sq km
*comparative area:* about 0.3 times the size of Washington, DC
**Land boundaries:** total 39 km, Italy 39 km
**Coastline:** 0 km (landlocked)
**Maritime claims:** none; landlocked
**International disputes:** none
**Climate:** Mediterranean; mild to cool winters; warm, sunny summers
**Terrain:** rugged mountains
**Natural resources:** building stone
**Land use:**
*arable land:* 17%
*permanent crops:* 0%
*meadows and pastures:* 0%
*forest and woodland:* 0%
*other:* 83%
**Irrigated land:** NA sq km
**Environment:**
*international agreements:* NA
*current issues:* NA
*natural hazards:* signed, but not ratified—Air Pollution, Biodiversity, Climate Change
**Note:** landlocked; smallest independent state in Europe after the Holy See and Monaco; dominated by the Apennines

---

**People**

**Population:** 24,091 (July 1994 est.)
**Population growth rate:** 0.96% (1994 est.)
**Birth rate:** 11.17 births/1,000 population (1994 est.)
**Death rate:** 7.39 deaths/1,000 population (1994 est.)
**Net migration rate:** 5.77 migrant(s)/1,000 population (1994 est.)
**Infant mortality rate:** 5.6 deaths/1,000 live births (1994 est.)

**Life expectancy at birth:**
*total population:* 81.23 years
*male:* 77.17 years
*female:* 85.28 years (1994 est.)
**Total fertility rate:** 1.53 children born/woman (1994 est.)

**Nationality:**
*noun:* Sammarinese (singular and plural)
*adjective:* Sammarinese
**Ethnic divisions:** Sammarinese, Italian
**Religions:** Roman Catholic
**Languages:** Italian
**Literacy:** age 14 and over can read and write (1976)
*total population:* 96%
*male:* 96%
*female:* 95%
**Labor force:** 4,300 (est.)
*by occupation:* NA

---

**Government**

**Names:**
*conventional long form:* Republic of San Marino
*conventional short form:* San Marino
*local long form:* Repubblica di San Marino
*local short form:* San Marino
**Digraph:** SM
**Type:** republic
**Capital:** San Marino
**Administrative divisions:** 9 municipalities (castelli, singular—castello); Acquaviva, Borgo Maggiore, Chiesanuova, Domagnano, Faetano, Fiorentino, Monte Giardino, San Marino, Serravalle
**Independence:** 301 AD (by tradition)
**National holiday:** Anniversary of the Foundation of the Republic, 3 September
**Constitution:** 8 October 1600; electoral law of 1926 serves some of the functions of a constitution
**Legal system:** based on civil law system with Italian law influences; has not accepted compulsory ICJ jurisdiction
**Suffrage:** 18 years of age; universal
**Executive branch:**
*co-chiefs of state:* Captain Regent Alberto CECCHETTI and Captain Regent Fausto MULARONI (for the period 1 April 1994-30 September 1994) real executive power is wielded by the secretary of state for foreign affairs and the secretary of state for internal affairs
*head of government:* Secretary of State

Gabriele GATTI (since July 1986)
*cabinet:* Congress of State; elected by the
Council for the duration of its term
**Legislative branch:** unicameral
*Great and General Council:* (Consiglio
Grande e Generale) elections last held 30 May
1993 (next to be held by NA May 1998);
results—DCS 41.4%, PSS 23.7%, PDP 18.6%,
ADP 7.7%, MD 5.3%, RC 3.3%; seats—(60
total) DCS 26, PSS 14, PDP 11, ADP 4, MD 3,
RC 2
**Judicial branch:** Council of Twelve
(Consiglio dei XII)
**Political parties and leaders:** Christian
Democratic Party (DCS), Pier Marino
MENICUCCI, Luigi LONFERNINI;
Democratic Progressive Party (PDP) formerly
San Marino Communist Party (PSS), Stefano
MACINA; San Marino Socialist Party (PSS),
Dr. Emma ROSSI, Antonio Lazzaro
VOLPINARI; Democratic Movement (MD),
Emilio Della BALDA; Popular Democratic
Alliance (ADP); Communist Refoundation
(RC), Guiseppe AMICHI, Renato FABBRI
**Member of:** CE, CSCE, ECE, ICAO, ICFTU,
ILO, IMF, IOC, IOM (observer), ITU,
LORCS, NAM (guest), UN, UNCTAD,
UNESCO, UPU, WHO, WIPO, WTO
**Diplomatic representation in US:**
*honorary consulate(s) general:* Washington
and New York
*honorary consulate(s):* Detroit
**US diplomatic representation:** no mission in
San Marino, but the Consul General in
Florence (Italy) is accredited to San Marino
**Flag:** two equal horizontal bands of white
(top) and light blue with the national coat of
arms superimposed in the center; the coat of
arms has a shield (featuring three towers on
three peaks) flanked by a wreath, below a
crown and above a scroll bearing the word
LIBERTAS (Liberty)

# SERBIA AND MOTENEGRO

Serbia and Montenegro have asserted the formation of a joint independent state, but this entity has not been formally recognized as a state by the United States.

**Note:** Serbia and Montenegro have asserted the formation of a joint independent state, but this entity has not been formally recognized as a state by the US; the US view is that the Socialist Federal Republic of Yugoslavia (SFRY) has dissolved and that none of the successor republics represents its continuation

## Economy

**Overview:** The swift collapse of the Yugoslav federation has been followed by bloody ethnic warfare, the destabilization of republic boundaries, and the breakup of important interrepublic trade flows. Serbia and Montenegro faces major economic problems; output has dropped sharply, particularly in 1993. First, like the other former Yugoslav republics, it depended on its sister republics for large amounts of foodstuffs, energy supplies, and manufactures. Wide varieties in climate, mineral resources, and levels of technology among the republics accentuate this interdependence, as did the communist practice of concentrating much industrial output in a small number of giant plants. The breakup of many of the trade links, the sharp drop in output as industrial plants lost suppliers and markets, and the destruction of physical assets in the fighting all have contributed to the economic difficulties of the republics. One singular factor in the economic situation of Serbia and Montenegro is the continuation in office of a communist government that is primarily interested in political and military mastery, not economic reform. A further complication is the imposition of economic sanctions by the UN.

**National product:** GDP—exchange rate conversion—$10 billion (1993 est.)

**National product real growth rate:** NA%

**National product per capita:** $1,000 (1993 est.)

**Inflation rate (consumer prices):** hyperinflation (1993)

**Unemployment rate:** more than 60% (1993 est.)

**Budget:**
*revenues:* $NA
*expenditures:* $NA, including capital expenditures of $NA

**Exports:** $4.4 billion (f.o.b., 1990)
*commodities:* machinery and transport equipment 29%, manufactured goods 28.5%, miscellaneous manufactured articles 13.5%, chemicals 11%, food and live animals 9%, raw materials 6%, fuels and lubricants 2%, beverages and tobacco 1%
*partners:* prior to the imposition of sanctions by the UN Security Council trade partners were principally the other former Yugoslav republics; Italy, Germany, other EC, the FSU countries, East European countries, US

**Imports:** $6.4 billion (c.i.f., 1990)
*commodities:* machinery and transport equipment 26%, fuels and lubricants 18%, manufactured goods 16%, chemicals 12.5%, food and live animals 11%, miscellaneous manufactured items 8%, raw materials, including coking coal for the steel industry 7%, beverages, tobacco, and edible oils 1.5%

*partners:* prior to the imposition of sanctions by the UN Security Council the trade partners were principally the other former Yugoslav republics; the FSU countries, EC countries (mainly Italy and Germany), East European countries, US

**External debt:** $4.2 billion (1993 est.)

**Industrial production:** growth rate -42% (1993 est.)

**Electricity:**
*capacity:* 8,850,000 kW
*production:* 42 billion kWh
*consumption per capita:* 3,950 kWh (1992)

**Industries:** machine building (aircraft, trucks, and automobiles; armored vehicles and weapons; electrical equipment; agricultural machinery), metallurgy (steel, aluminum, copper, lead, zinc, chromium, antimony, bismuth, cadmium), mining (coal, bauxite, nonferrous ore, iron ore, limestone), consumer goods (textiles, footwear, foodstuffs, appliances), electronics, petroleum products, chemicals, and pharmaceuticals

**Agriculture:** the fertile plains of Vojvodina produce 80% of the cereal production of the former Yugoslavia and most of the cotton, oilseeds, and chicory; Vojvodina also produces fodder crops to support intensive beef and dairy production; Serbia proper, although hilly, has a well-distributed rainfall and a long growing season; produces fruit, grapes, and cereals; in this area, livestock production (sheep and cattle) and dairy farming prosper; Kosovo produces fruits, vegetables, tobacco, and a small amount of cereals; the mountainous pastures of Kosovo and Montenegro support sheep and goat husbandry; Montenegro has only a small agriculture sector, mostly near the coast where a Mediterranean climate permits the culture of olives, citrus, grapes, and rice

**Illicit drugs:** NA

**Economic aid:** $NA

**Currency:** 1 Yugoslav New Dinar (YD) = 100 paras

**Exchange rates:** Yugoslav New Dinars (YD) per US $1—1,100,000 (15 June 1993), 28.230 (December 1991), 15.162 (1990), 15.528 (1989), 0.701 (1988), 0.176 (1987)

**Fiscal year:** calendar year

## Communications

**Railroads:** NA

**Highways:**
*total:* 46,019 km
*paved:* 26,949 km
*unpaved:* gravel 10,373 km; earth 8,697 km (1990)

**Inland waterways:** NA km

**Pipelines:** crude oil 415 km, petroleum products 130 km, natural gas 2,110 km

**Ports:** coastal—Bar; inland—Belgrade

**Merchant marine:**
*Montenegro:* 42 ships (1,000 GRT or over) totaling 804,156 GRT/1,368,813 DWT (controlled by Montenegrin beneficial owners) cargo 16, container 5, bulk 19, passenger ship 1, combination ore/oil 1
*note:* most under Maltese flag
*Serbia:* total 3 (1,000 GRT or over) totaling 246,631 GRT/451,843 DWT (controlled by Serbian beneficial owners)
bulk 2, conbination tanker/ore carrier 1
*note:* all under the flag of Saint Vincent and the Grenadines; no ships remain under Yugoslav flag

**Airports:**
*total:* 55
*usable:* 51
*with permanent-surface runways:* 18
*with runways over 3,659 m:* 0
*with runways 2,440-3,659 m:* 7
*with runways 1,220-2,439 m:* 11

**Telecommunications:** 700,000 telephones; broadcast stations—26 AM, 9 FM, 18 TV; 2,015,000 radios; 1,000,000 TVs; satellite ground stations—1 Atlantic Ocean INTELSAT

## Defense Forces

**Branches:** People's Army—Ground Forces (internal and border troops), Naval Forces, Air and Air Defense Forces, Frontier Guard, Territorial Defense Force, Civil Defense

**Manpower availability:**
*Montenegro:* males age 15-49 179,868; fit for military service 146,158; reach military age (19) annually 5,399 (1994 est.)

*Serbia:* males age 15-49 2,546,717; fit for military service 2,048,921; reach military age (19) annually 80,937 (1994 est.)
**Defense expenditures:** 245 billion dinars, 4%-6% of GDP (1992 est.); note—conversion of defense expenditures into US dollars using the prevailing exchange rate could produce misleading results

## Geography

**Location:** Balkan State, Southeastern Europe, bordering the Adriatic Sea, between Bosnia and Herzegovina and Bulgaria
**Map references:** Ethnic Groups in Eastern Europe, Europe, Standard Time Zones of the World
**Area:**
*total area:* 102,350 sq km
*land area:* 102,136 sq km
*comparative area:* slightly larger than Kentucky
*note:* Serbia has a total area and a land area of 88,412 sq km making it slightly larger than Maine; Montenegro has a total area of 13,938 sq km and a land area of 13,724 sq km making it slightly larger than Connecticut
**Land boundaries:** total 2,246 km, Albania 287 km (114 km with Serbia; 173 km with Motenegro), Bosnia and Herzegovina 527 km (312 km with Serbia; 215 km with Montenegro), Bulgaria 318 km, Croatia (north) 241 km, Croatia (south) 25 km, Hungary 151 km, The Former Yugoslav Republic of Macedonia 221 km, Romania 476 km
*note:* the internal boundary between Montenegro and Serbia is 211 km
**Coastline:** 199 km (Montenegro 199 km, Serbia 0 km)
**Maritime claims:**
*territorial sea:* 12 nm
**International disputes:** Sandzak region bordering northern Montenegro and southeastern Serbia—Muslims seeking autonomy; disputes with Bosnia and Herzegovina and Croatia over Serbian populated areas; Albanian majority in Kosovo seeks independence from Serbian Republic

**Climate:** in the north, continental climate (cold winter and hot, humid summers with well distributed rainfall); central portion, continental and Mediterranean climate; to the south, Adriatic climate along the coast, hot, dry summers and autumns and relatively cold winters with heavy snowfall inland
**Terrain:** extremely varied; to the north, rich fertile plains; to the east, limestone ranges and basins; to the southeast, ancient mountain and hills; to the southwest, extremely high shoreline with no islands off the coast; home of largest lake in former Yugoslavia, Lake Scutari
**Natural resources:** oil, gas, coal, antimony, copper, lead, zinc, nickel, gold, pyrite, chrome
**Land use:**
*arable land:* 30%
*permanent crops:* 5%
*meadows and pastures:* 20%
*forest and woodland:* 25%
*other:* 20%
**Irrigated land:** NA sq km
**Environment:**
*current issues:* coastal water pollution from sewage outlets, especially in tourist-related areas such as Kotor; air pollution around Belgrade and other industrial cities; water pollution from industrial wastes dumped into the Sava which flows into the Danube
*natural hazards:* subject to destructive earthquakes
*international agreements:* NA
**Note:** controls one of the major land routes from Western Europe to Turkey and the Near East; strategic location along the Adriatic coast

## People

**Population:**
*total:* 10,759,897 (July 1994 est.)
*Montenegro:* 666,583 (July 1994 est.)
*Serbia:* 10,093,314 (July 1994 est.)
**Population growth rate:**
*Montenegro:* 0.79% (1994 est.)
*Serbia:* 0.54% (1994 est.)
**Birth rate:**
*Montenegro:* 13.72 births/1,000 population (1994 est.)
*Serbia:* 14.35 births/1,000 population (1994 est.)
**Death rate:**

*Montenegro:* 5.84 deaths/1,000 population (1994 est.)
*Serbia:* 8.94 deaths/1,000 population (1994 est.)
**Net migration rate:**
*Montenegro:* 0 migrant(s)/1,000 population (1994 est.)
*Serbia:* 0 migrant(s)/1,000 population (1994 est.)
**Infant mortality rate:**
*Montenegro:* 10.8 deaths/1,000 live births (1994 est.)
*Serbia:* 21.4 deaths/1,000 live births (1994 est.)

**Life expectancy at birth:**
*Montenegro:*
*total population:* 79.44 years
*male:* 76.57 years
*female:* 82.5 years (1994 est.)
*Serbia:*
*total population:* 73.39 years
*male:* 70.9 years
*female:* 76.07 years (1994 est.)
**Total fertility rate:**
*Montenegro:* 1.74 children born/woman (1994 est.)
*Serbia:* 2.06 children born/woman (1994 est.)
**Nationality:**
*noun:* Serb(s) and Montenegrin(s)
*adjective:* Serbian and Montenegrin
**Ethnic divisions:** Serbs 63%, Albanians 14%, Montenegrins 6%, Hungarians 4%, other 13%
**Religions:** Orthodox 65%, Muslim 19%, Roman Catholic 4%, Protestant 1%, other 11%
**Languages:** Serbo-Croatian 95%, Albanian 5%
**Literacy:**
*total population:* NA%
*male:* NA%
*female:* NA%
**Labor force:** 2,640,909
*by occupation:* industry, mining 40%, agriculture 5% (1990)

---

**Government**

**Names:**
*conventional long form:* none
*conventional short form:* Serbia and

Montenegro
*local long form:* none
*local short form:* Srbija-Crna Gora
**Digraph:**
*Serbia:* SR
*Montenegro:* MW
**Type:** republic
**Capital:** Belgrade
**Administrative divisions:** 2 republics (pokajine, singular—pokajina); and 2 autonomous provinces*: Kosovo*, Montenegro, Serbia, Vojvodina*
**Independence:** 11 April 1992 (Federal Republic of Yugoslavia formed as self-proclaimed successor to the Socialist Federal Republic of Yugoslavia—SFRY)
**National holiday:** NA
**Constitution:** 27 April 1992
**Legal system:** based on civil law system
**Suffrage:** 16 years of age, if employed; 18 years of age, universal
**Executive branch:**
*chief of state:* Zoran LILIC (since 25 June 1993); note—Slobodan MILOSEVIC is president of Serbia (since 9 December 1990); Momir BULATOVIC is president of Montenegro (since 23 December 1990); Federal Assembly elected Zoran LILIC on 25 June 1993
*head of government:* Prime Minister Radoje KONTIC (since 29 December 1992); Deputy Prime Ministers Jovan ZEBIC (since NA March 1993), Asim TELACEVIC (since NA March 1993), Zeljko SIMIC (since NA 1993)
*cabinet:* Federal Executive Council
**Legislative branch:** bicameral Federal Assembly
*Chamber of Republics:* elections last held 31 May 1992 (next to be held NA 1996); results—percent of vote by party NA; seats—(40 total; 20 Serbian, 20 Montenegrin)
*Chamber of Citizens:* elections last held 31 May 1992 (next to be held NA 1996); results—percent of votes by party NA; seats—(138 total; 108 Serbian, 30 Montenegrin) SPS 73, SRS 33, DPSCG 23, SK-PJ 2, DZVM 2, independents 2, vacant 3
**Judicial branch:** Savezni Sud (Federal Court), Constitutional Court

**Political parties and leaders:** Serbian
Socialist Party (SPS; former Communist
Party), Slobodan MILOSEVIC; Serbian
Radical Party (SRS), Vojislav SESELJ;
Serbian Renewal Movement (SPO), Vuk
DRASKOVIC, president; Democratic Party
(DS), Zoran DJINDJIC; Democratic Party of
Serbia, Vojlslav KOSTUNICA; Democratic
Party of Socialists (DPSCG), Momir
BULATOVIC, president; People's Party of
Montenegro (NS), Novak KILIBARDA;
Liberal Alliance of Montenegro, Slavko
PEROVIC; Democratic Community of
Vojvodina Hungarians (DZVM), Agoston
ANDRAS; League of Communists-Movement
for Yugoslavia (SK-PJ), Dragan
ATANASOVSKI; Democratic Alliance of
Kosovo (LDK), Dr. Ibrahim RUGOVA,
president

**Other political or pressure groups:** Serbian
Democratic Movement (DEPOS; coalition of
opposition parties)

**Diplomatic representation in US:** US and
Serbia and Montenegro do not maintain full
diplomatic relations; the Embassy of the
former Socialist Federal Republic of
Yugoslavia continues to function in the US

**US diplomatic representation:**
*chief of mission:* (vacant); Charge d'Affaires
Rudolf V. PERINA
*embassy:* address NA, Belgrade
*mailing address:* American Embassy Box
5070, Unit 25402, APO AE 09213-5070
*telephone:* [38] (11) 645-655
*FAX:* [38] (1) 645-221

**Flag:** three equal horizontal bands of blue
(top), white, and red

# SLOVAKIA

150 km

## Economy

**Overview:** The dissolution of Czechoslovakia into two independent states—the Czech Republic and Slovakia—on 1 January 1993 has complicated the task of moving toward a more open and decentralized economy. The old Czechoslovakia, even though highly industrialized by East European standards, suffered from an aging capital plant, lagging technology, and a deficiency in energy and many raw materials. In January 1991, approximately one year after the end of communist control of Eastern Europe, the Czech and Slovak Federal Republic launched a sweeping program to convert its almost entirely state-owned and controlled economy to a market system. In 1991-92 these measures resulted in privatization of some medium- and small-scale economic activity and the setting of more than 90% of prices by the market—but at a cost in inflation, unemployment, and lower output. For Czechoslovakia as a whole inflation in 1991 was roughly 50% and output fell 15%. In 1992 in Slovakia, inflation slowed to an estimated 8.7% and the estimated fall in GDP was a more moderate 7%. In 1993 GDP fell roughly 5%, with the disruptions from the separation from the Czech lands probably accounting for half the decline; exports to the Czech Republic fell about 35%. Bratislava adopted an austerity program in June and devalued its currency 10% in July. In 1993, inflation rose an estimated 23%, unemployment topped 14%, and the budget deficit exceeded the IMF target of $485 million by over $200 million. By yearend 1993 Bratislava estimated that 29% of GDP was being produced in the private sector. The forecast for 1994 is gloomy; Bratislava optimistically projects no growth in GDP, 17% unemployment, a $425 million budget deficit, and 12% inflation. At best, if Slovakia stays on track with the IMF, GDP could fall by only 2-3% in 1994 and unemployment could be held under 18%, but a currency devaluation will likely drive inflation above 15%.

**National product:** GDP—purchasing power equivalent—$31 billion (1993 est.)

**National product real growth rate:** -5% (1993 est.)

**National product per capita:** $5,800 (1993 est.)

**Inflation rate (consumer prices):** 23% (1993 est.)

**Unemployment rate:** 14.4% (1993 est.)

**Budget:**
*revenues:* $4.5 billion
*expenditures:* $5.2 billion, including capital expenditures of $NA (1993 est.)

**Exports:** $5.13 billion (f.o.b., 1993 est.)
*commodities:* machinery and transport equipment; chemicals; fuels, minerals, and metals; agricultural products
*partners:* Czech Republic, CIS republics, Germany, Poland, Austria, Hungary, Italy, France, US, UK

**Imports:** $5.95 billion (f.o.b., 1993 est.)
*commodities:* machinery and transport equipment; fuels and lubricants; manufactured goods; raw materials; chemicals; agricultural products

*partners:* Czech Republic, CIS republics, Germany, Austria, Poland, Switzerland, Hungary, UK, Italy
**External debt:** $3.2 billion hard currency indebtedness (31 December 1993)
**Industrial production:** growth rate -13.5% (December 1993 over December 1992)
**Electricity:**
*capacity:* 6,800,000 kW
*production:* 24 billion kWh
*consumption per capita:* 4,550 kWh (1992)
**Industries:** brown coal mining, chemicals, metal-working, consumer appliances, fertilizer, plastics, armaments
**Agriculture:** largely self-sufficient in food production; diversified crop and livestock production, including grains, potatoes, sugar beets, hops, fruit, hogs, cattle, and poultry; exporter of forest products
**Illicit drugs:** transshipment point for Southwest Asian heroin bound for Western Europe
**Economic aid:**
*donor:* the former Czechoslovakia was a donor—$4.2 billion in bilateral aid to non-Communist less developed countries (1954-89)
**Currency:** 1 koruna (Sk) = 100 halierov
**Exchange rates:** koruny (Sk) per US$1—32.9 (December 1993), 28.59 (December 1992), 28.26 (1992), 29.53 (1991), 17.95 (1990), 15.05 (1989); note—values before 1993 reflect Czechoslovak exchange rate
**Fiscal year:** calendar year

---

**Communications**

**Railroads:** 3,669 km total (1990)
**Highways:**
*total:* 17,650 km (1990)
*paved:* NA
*unpaved:* NA
**Inland waterways:** NA km
**Pipelines:** natural gas 2,700 km; petroleum products NA km
**Ports:** maritime outlets are in Poland (Gdynia, Gdansk, Szczecin), Croatia (Rijeka), Slovenia (Koper), Germany (Hamburg, Rostock); principal river ports are Komarno on the Danube and Bratislava on the Danube
**Merchant marine:** 19 ships (1,000 GRT or over) totaling 309,502 GRT/521,997 DWT, bulk 13, cargo 6; note—most under the flag of Saint Vincent and the Grenadines
**Airports:**
*total:* 46
*usable:* 32
*with permanent-surface runways:* 7
*with runways over 3,659 m:* 0
*with runways 2,440-3,659 m:* 6
*with runways 1,060-2,439 m:* 18
*note:* a C-130 can land on a 1,060-m airstrip
**Telecommunications:** NA

---

**Defense Forces**

**Branches:** Army, Air and Air Defense Forces, Civil Defense, Railroad Units
**Manpower availability:** males age 15-49 1,426,290; fit for military service 1,095,604; reach military age (18) annually 48,695 (1994 est.)
**Defense expenditures:** 8.2 billion koruny, NA% of GDP (1993 est.); note—conversion of defense expenditures into US dollars using the current exchange rate could produce misleading results

---

**Geography**

**Location:** Central Europe, between Hungary and Poland
**Map references:** Ethnic Groups in Eastern Europe, Europe, Standard Time Zones of the World
**Area:**
*total area:* 48,845 sq km
*land area:* 48,800 sq km
*comparative area:* about twice the size of New Hampshire
**Land boundaries:** total 1,355 km, Austria 91 km, Czech Republic 215 km, Hungary 515 km, Poland 444 km, Ukraine 90 km
**Coastline:** 0 km (landlocked)
**Maritime claims:** none; landlocked
**International disputes:** Gabcikovo Dam dispute with Hungary; unresolved property

issues with Czech Republic over redistribution of former Czechoslovak federal property
**Climate:** temperate; cool summers; cold, cloudy, humid winters
**Terrain:** rugged mountains in the central and northern part and lowlands in the south
**Natural resources:** brown coal and lignite; small amounts of iron ore, copper and manganese ore; salt
**Land use:**
*arable land:* NA%
*permanent crops:* NA%
*meadows and pastures:* NA%
*forest and woodland:* NA%
*other:* NA%
**Irrigated land:** NA sq km
**Environment:**
*current issues:* acid rain damaging forests
*natural hazards:* NA
*international agreements:* party to—Air Pollution, Air Pollution-Nitrogen Oxides, Air Pollution-Sulphur, Antarctic Treaty, Environmental Modification, Hazardous Wastes, Law of the Sea, Nuclear Test Ban, Ozone Layer Protection; signed, but not ratified—Antarctic-Environmental Protocol, Biodiversity, Climate Change
**Note:** landlocked

## People

**Population:** 5,403,505 (July 1994 est.)
**Population growth rate:** 0.53% (1994 est.)
**Birth rate:** 14.55 births/1,000 population (1994 est.)
**Death rate:** 9.28 deaths/1,000 population (1994 est.)
**Net migration rate:** 0 migrant(s)/1,000 population (1994 est.)
**Infant mortality rate:** 10.4 deaths/1,000 live births (1994 est.)
**Life expectancy at birth:**
*total population:* 72.81 years
*male:* 68.66 years
*female:* 77.2 years (1994 est.)
**Total fertility rate:** 1.96 children born/woman (1994 est.)
**Nationality:**
*noun:* Slovak(s)
*adjective:* Slovak

**Ethnic divisions:** Slovak 85.6%, Hungarian 10.8%, Gypsy 1.5% (the 1992 census figures underreport the Gypsy/Romany community, which could reach 500,000 or more), Czech 1.1%, Ruthenian 15,000, Ukrainian 13,000, Moravian 6,000, German 5,000, Polish 3,000
**Religions:** Roman Catholic 60.3%, atheist 9.7%, Protestant 8.4%, Orthodox 4.1%, other 17.5%
**Languages:** Slovak (official), Hungarian
**Literacy:**
*total population:* NA%
*male:* NA%
*female:* NA%
**Labor force:** 2.484 million
*by occupation:* industry 33.2%, agriculture 12.2%, construction 10.3%, communication and other 44.3% (1990)

## Government

**Names:**
*conventional long form:* Slovak Republic
*conventional short form:* Slovakia
*local long form:* Slovenska Republika
*local short form:* Slovensko
**Digraph:** LO
**Type:** parliamentary democracy
**Capital:** Bratislava
**Administrative divisions:** 4 departments (kraje, singular—Kraj) Bratislava, Zapadoslovensky, Stredoslovensky, Vychodoslovensky
**Independence:** 1 January 1993 (from Czechoslovakia)
**National holiday:** Anniversary of Slovak National Uprising, August 29 (1944)
**Constitution:** ratified 1 September 1992; fully effective 1 January 1993
**Legal system:** civil law system based on Austro-Hungarian codes; has not accepted compulsory ICJ jurisdiction; legal code modified to comply with the obligations of Conference on Security and Cooperation in Europe (CSCE) and to expunge Marxist-Leninist legal theory
**Suffrage:** 18 years of age; universal
**Executive branch:**
*chief of state:* President Michal KOVAC (since 8 February 1993); election last held 8

February 1993 (next to be held NA 1998);
results—Michal KOVAC elected by the
National Council
*head of government:* Prime Minister Jozef
MORAVCIK (since 16 March 1994)
*cabinet:* Cabinet; appointed by the president
on recommendation of the prime minister
**Legislative branch:** unicameral
*National Council (Narodni Rada):* elections
last held 5-6 June 1992 (next to be held 31
September-1 October 1994); results—percent
of vote by party NA; seats—(150 total)
Movement for a Democratic Slovakia 55, Party
of the Democratic Left 28, Christian
Democratic Movement 18, Slovak National
Party 9, National Democratic Party 5,
Hungarian Christian Democratic Movement/
Coexistence 14, Democratic Union of Slovakia
16, independents 5
**Judicial branch:** Supreme Court
**Political parties and leaders:** Movement for
a Democratic Slovakia, Vladimir MECIAR,
chairman; Party of the Democratic Left, Peter
WEISS, chairman; Christian Democratic
Movement, Jan CARNOGURSKY; Slovak
National Party, Jan SLOTA, chairman;
Hungarian Christian Democratic Movement,
Vojtech BUGAR; National Democratic Party-
New Alternative, Ludovit CERNAK,
chairman; Democratic Union of Slovakia,
Jozef MORAVCIK, chairman; Coexistence
Movement, Miklos DURAY, chairman
**Other political or pressure groups:** Green
Party; Social Democratic Party in Slovakia;
Freedom Party; Slovak Christian Union;
Hungarian Civic Party
**Member of:** BIS, CCC, CE (guest), CEI,
CERN, COCOM (cooperating), CSCE, EBRD,
ECE, FAO, GATT, IAEA, IBRD, ICAO,
ICFTU, IDA, IFC, ILO, IMF, IMO,
INMARSAT, INTELSAT (nonsignatory user),
INTERPOL, IOC, IOM (observer), ISO, ITU,
LORCS, NACC, NSG, PCA, UN (as of 8
January 1993), UNAVEM II, UNCTAD,
UNESCO, UNIDO, UNOMUR, UNPROFOR,
UPU, WFTU, WHO, WIPO, WMO, WTO, ZC
**Diplomatic representation in US:**
*chief of mission:* Ambassador-designate
Bravislav LICHARDUS

*chancery:* (temporary) Suite 330, 2201
Wisconsin Avenue NW, Washington, DC
20007
*telephone:* (202) 965-5161
*FAX:* (202) 965-5166
**US diplomatic representation:**
*chief of mission:* Ambassdor Theodore
RUSSELL
*embassy:* Hviezdoslavovo Namesite 4, 81102
Bratislava
*mailing address:* use embassy street address
*telephone:* [42] (7) 330-861
*FAX:* [42] (7) 335-439
**Flag:** three equal horizontal bands of white
(top), blue, and red superimposed with the
Slovak cross in a shield centered on the hoist
side; the cross is white centered on a
background of red and blue

---

**U.S. Government Contacts:**

**U.S. Trade Desk**: (202) 482-4915

---

**Chambers of Commerce &
Organizations:**

**American Chamber of Commerce in the
Slovak Republic**
Mileticova 23, Suite 307
821 08 Bratislova, Slovak Republic
Phone/Fax: (427) 214-730

---

**Travel:**

**International Hotels in Country:**
Bratislava:
Danube, Tel: 427/340833, Fax: 427/314311
Forum Bratislava, Tel: 427/348111, Fax:
427/314645.

# SLOVENIA

**75 km**

## Economy

**Overview:** Slovenia was by far the most prosperous of the former Yugoslav republics, with a per capita income more than twice the Yugoslav average, indeed not far below the levels in neighboring Austria and Italy. Because of its strong ties to Western Europe and the small scale of damage during its brief fight for independence from Yugoslavia, Slovenia has the brightest prospects among the former Yugoslav republics for economic recovery over the next few years. The dissolution of Yugoslavia, however, has led to severe short-term dislocations in production, employment, and trade ties. For example, overall industrial production has fallen 26% since 1990; particularly hard hit have been the iron and steel, machine-building, chemical, and textile industries. Meanwhile, the continued fighting in other former Yugoslav republics has led to further destruction of long-established trade channels and to an influx of tens of thousands of Croatian and Bosnian refugees. The key program for breaking up and privatizing major industrial firms was

established in late 1992. Despite slow progress in privatization Slovenia has reasonable prospects for an upturn in 1994. Bright spots for encouraging Western investors are Slovenia's comparatively well-educated work force, its developed infrastructure, and its Western business attitudes, but instability in Croatia is a deterrent. Slovenia in absolute terms is a small economy, and a little Western investment would go a long way.

**National product:** GDP—purchasing power equivalent—$15 billion (1993 est.)

**National product real growth rate:** 0% (1993 est.)

**National product per capita:** $7,600 (1993 est.)

**Inflation rate (consumer prices):** 22.9% (1993)

**Unemployment rate:** 15.5% (1993)

**Budget:**
*revenues:* $NA
*expenditures:* $NA, including capital expenditures of $NA

**Exports:** $5.1 billion (f.o.b., 1993)
*commodities:* machinery and transport equipment 38%, other manufactured goods 44%, chemicals 9%, food and live animals 4.6%, raw materials 3%, beverages and tobacco less than 1% (1992)
*partners:* Germany 27%, Croatia 14%, Italy 13%, France 9% (1992)

**Imports:** $5.3 billion (c.i.f., 1993)
*commodities:* machinery and transport equipment 35%, other manufactured goods 26.7%, chemicals 14.5%, raw materials 9.4%, fuels and lubricants 7%, food and live animals 6% (1992)
*partners:* Germany 23%, Croatia 14%, Italy 14%, France 8%, Austria 8% (1992)

**External debt:** $1.9 billion

**Industrial production:** growth rate -2.8% (1993); accounts for 30% of GDP

**Electricity:**
*capacity:* 2,900,000 kW
*production:* 10 billion kWh
*consumption per capita:* 5,090 kWh (1992)

**Industries:** ferrous metallurgy and rolling mill products, aluminum reduction and rolled products, lead and zinc smelting, electronics (including military electronics), trucks, electric power equipment, wood products, textiles, chemicals, machine tools

**Agriculture:** accounts for 5% of GDP; dominated by stock breeding (sheep and cattle) and dairy farming; main crops—potatoes, hops, hemp, flax; an export surplus in these commodities; Slovenia must import many other agricultural products and has a negative overall trade balance in this sector

**Illicit drugs:** NA

**Economic aid:** $NA

**Currency:** 1 tolar (SIT) = 100 stotins

**Exchange rates:** tolars (SIT) per US$1—112 (June 1993), 28 (January 1992)

**Fiscal year:** calendar year

---

### Communications

**Railroads:** 1,200 km, 1.435 m gauge (1991)

**Highways:**
*total:* 14,553 km
*paved:* 10,525 km
*unpaved:* gravel 4,028 km

**Inland waterways:** NA

**Pipelines:** crude oil 290 km, natural gas 305 km

**Ports:** coastal—Koper

**Merchant marine:** 19 ships (1,000 GRT or over) totaling 309,502 GRT/521,997 DWT controlled by Slovenian owners, bulk 13, cargo 6
*note:* most under the flag of Saint Vincent and the Grenadines; no ships remain under the Slovenian flag

**Airports:**
*total:* 14
*usable:* 13
*with permanent-surface runways:* 6
*with runways over 3,659 m:* 0
*with runways 2,440-3,659 m:* 2
*with runways 1,220-2,439 m:* 2

**Telecommunications:** 130,000 telephones; broadcast stations—6 AM, 5 FM, 7 TV; 370,000 radios; 330,000 TVs

---

### Defense Forces

**Branches:** Slovene Defense Forces

**Manpower availability:** males age 15-49 513,885; fit for military service 411,619; reach military age (19) annually 15,157 (1994 est.)

**Defense expenditures:** 13.5 billion tolars, 4.5% of GDP (1993); note—conversion of the military budget into US dollars using the current exchange rate could produce misleading results

---

### Geography

**Location:** Balkan State, Southeastern Europe, bordering the Adriatic Sea, between Austria and Croatia

**Map references:** Ethnic Groups in Eastern Europe, Europe, Standard Time Zones of the World

**Area:**
*total area:* 20,296 sq km
*land area:* 20,296 sq km
*comparative area:* slightly larger than New Jersey

**Land boundaries:** total 1,045 km, Austria 262 km, Croatia 501 km, Italy 199 km, Hungary 83 km

**Coastline:** 32 km

**Maritime claims:**
*continental shelf:* 200-m depth or to depth of exploitation
*territorial sea:* 12 nm

**International disputes:** dispute with Croatia over fishing rights in the Adriatic and over some border areas; the border issue is currently under negotiation

**Climate:** Mediterranean climate on the coast, continental climate with mild to hot summers and cold winters in the plateaus and valleys to the east

**Terrain:** a short coastal strip on the Adriatic, an alpine mountain region adjacent to Italy, mixed mountain and valleys with numerous rivers to the east

**Natural resources:** lignite coal, lead, zinc, mercury, uranium, silver

**Land use:**
*arable land:* 10%

*permanent crops:* 2%
*meadows and pastures:* 20%
*forest and woodland:* 45%
*other:* 23%
**Irrigated land:** NA sq km
**Environment:**
*current issues:* Sava River polluted with domestic and industrial waste; heavy metals and toxic chemicals along coastal waters; forest damage near Koper from air pollution originating at metallurgical and chemical plants
*natural hazards:* subject to flooding and earthquakes
*international agreements:* party to—Air Pollution, Hazardous Wastes, Marine Dumping, Nuclear Test Ban, Ozone Layer Protection, Ship Pollution; signed, but not ratified—Biodiversity, Climate Change

---

**People**

**Population:** 1,972,227 (July 1994 est.)
**Population growth rate:** 0.23% (1994 est.)
**Birth rate:** 11.81 births/1,000 population (1994 est.)
**Death rate:** 9.5 deaths/1,000 population (1994 est.)
**Net migration rate:** 0 migrant(s)/1,000 population (1994 est.)
**Infant mortality rate:** 8.1 deaths/1,000 live births (1994 est.)
**Life expectancy at birth:**
*total population:* 74.36 years
*male:* 70.49 years
*female:* 78.44 years (1994 est.)
**Total fertility rate:** 1.67 children born/woman (1994 est.)
**Nationality:**
*noun:* Slovene(s)
*adjective:* Slovenian
**Ethnic divisions:** Slovene 91%, Croat 3%, Serb 2%, Muslim 1%, other 3%
**Religions:** Roman Catholic 96% (including 2% Uniate), Muslim 1%, other 3%
**Languages:** Slovenian 91%, Serbo-Croatian 7%, other 2%
**Literacy:**
*total population:* NA%
*male:* NA%

*female:* NA%
**Labor force:** 786,036
*by occupation:* agriculture 2%, manufacturing and mining 46%

---

**Government**

**Names:**
*conventional long form:* Republic of Slovenia
*conventional short form:* Slovenia
*local long form:* Republika Slovenije
*local short form:* Slovenija
**Digraph:** SI
**Type:** emerging democracy
**Capital:** Ljubljana
**Administrative divisions:** 60 provinces (pokajine, singular—pokajina) Ajdovscina, Brezice, Celje, Cerknica, Crnomelj, Dravograd, Gornja Radgona, Grosuplje, Hrastnik Lasko, Idrija, Ilirska Bistrica, Izola, Jesenice, Kamnik, Kocevje, Koper, Kranj, Krsko, Lenart, Lendava, Litija, Ljubljana-Bezigrad, Ljubljana-Center. Ljubljana-Moste-Polje, Ljubljana-Siska, Ljubljana-Vic-Rudnik, Ljutomer, Logatec, Maribor, Metlika, Mozirje, Murska Sobota, Nova Gorica, Novo Mesto, Ormoz, Pesnica, Piran, Postojna, Ptuj, Radlje Ob Dravi, Radovljica, Ravne Na Koroskem, Ribnica, Ruse, Sentjur Pri Celju, Sevnica, Sezana, Skofja Loka, Slovenj Gradec, Slovenska Bistrica, Slovenske Konjice, Smarje Pri Jelsah, Tolmin, Trbovlje, Trebnje, Trzic, Velenje, Vrhnika, Zagorje Ob Savi, Zalec
**Independence:** 25 June 1991 (from Yugoslavia)
**National holiday:** Statehood Day, 25 June (1991)
**Constitution:** adopted 23 December 1991, effective 23 December 1991
**Legal system:** based on civil law system
**Suffrage:** 16 years of age, if employed; 18 years of age, universal
**Executive branch:**
*chief of state:* President Milan KUCAN (since 22 April 1990); election last held 6 December 1992 (next to be held NA 1996); results—Milan KUCAN reelected by direct popular vote
*head of government:* Prime Minister Janez DRNOVSEK (since 14 May 1992); Deputy

Prime Minister Lojze PETERLE (since NA)
*cabinet:* Council of Ministers
**Legislative branch:** bicameral National
Assembly
*State Assembly:* elections last held 6 December
1992 (next to be held NA 1996); results—
percent of vote by party NA; seats—(total 90)
LDS 22, SKD 15, United List (former
Communists and allies) 14, Slovene National
Party 12, SLS 10, Democratic Party 6, ZS 5,
SDSS 4, Hungarian minority 1, Italian
minority 1
*State Council:* will become operational after
next election in 1996; in the election of 6
December 1992 40 members were elected to
represent local and socioeconomic interests
**Judicial branch:** Supreme Court,
Constitutional Court
**Political parties and leaders:** Slovene
Christian Democrats (SKD), Lozje PETERLE,
chairman; Liberal Democratic (LDS), Janez
DRNOVSEK, chairman; Social-Democratic
Party of Slovenia (SDSS), Joze PUCNIK,
chairman; Socialist Party of Slovenia (SSS),
Viktor ZAKELJ, chairman; Greens of Slovenia
(ZS), Dusan PLUT, chairman; National
Democratic, Rajko PIRNAT, chairman;
Democratic Peoples Party, Marjan
PODOBNIK, chairman; Reformed Socialists
(former Communist Party), Ciril RIBICIC,
chairman; United List (former Communists
and allies); Slovene National Party, leader NA;
Democratic Party, Igor BAVCAR; Slovene
People's Party (SLS), Ivan OMAN
*note:* parties have changed as of the December
1992 elections
**Other political or pressure groups:** none
**Member of:** CCC, CE, CEI, CSCE, EBRD,
ECE, IAEA, IBRD, ICAO, IDA, IFC, ILO,
IMF, IMO, INTELSAT (nonsignatory user),
INTERPOL, IOC, IOM (observer), ITU,
NAM (guest), UN, UNCTAD, UNESCO,
UNIDO, UPU, WHO, WIPO, WMO
**Diplomatic representation in US:**
*chief of mission:* Ambassador Ernest PETRIC
*chancery:* 1525 New Hampshir Avenue NW,
Washington, DC, 20036
*telephone:* (202) 667-5363
*consulate(s) general:* New York

**US diplomatic representation:**
*chief of mission:* Ambassador E. Allan
WENDT
*embassy:* P.O. Box 254, Prazakova 4, 61000
Ljubljana
*mailing address:* use embassy street address
*telephone:* [386] (61) 301-427/472/485
*FAX:* [386] (61) 301-401
**Flag:** three equal horizontal bands of white
(top), blue, and red with the Slovenian seal (a
shield with the image of Triglav in white
against a blue background at the center,
beneath it are two wavy blue lines depicting
seas and rivers, and around it, there are three
six-sided stars arranged in an inverted
triangle); the seal is located in the upper hoist
side of the flag centered in the white and blue
bands

# SPAIN

Bay of Biscay
300 km

La Coruña · Bilbao · León · Zaragoza · Barcelona · Valladolid · Salamanca · MADRID · Valencia · Córdoba · Alicante · Sevilla · Málaga

Balearic Sea
Balearic Islands
Mediterranean Sea

North Atlantic Ocean
Strait of Gibraltar
Canary Islands. Ceuta. and Melilla are not shown.

## Economy

**Overview:** After the economic boom of 1986-90, the Spanish economy fell into recession along with the economies of other EU member states. Real GDP barely grew in 1992 and declined by approximately 1% in 1993. Unemployment, now nearly one-fourth of the workforce, and the sharp downturn in business investment have contributed to sagging domestic demand. Devaluation of the peseta since September 1992 has made Spanish exports more competitive, but an export-led recovery in 1994 will depend largely on economic recovery in Spain's major market—the other EU nations. A solid recovery will also require appropriate domestic policy actions, including controlling the budget deficit and wage increases, reforming labor market regulations, and possibly loosening monetary policy another notch. Foreign investors, principally from other EU countries, have invested over $60 billion in Spain since 1986. Despite the recession, inflation remained at about 5% in 1993. The main source of inflationary pressure is the fiscal deficit.

**National product:** GDP—purchasing power equivalent—$498 billion (1993)
**National product real growth rate:** -1% (1993)
**National product per capita:** $12,700 (1993)
**Inflation rate (consumer prices):** 4.5% (1993 est.)
**Unemployment rate:** 22% (yearend 1993)
**Budget:**
*revenues:* $97.7 billion
*expenditures:* $128 billion, including capital expenditures of $NA (1993 est.)
**Exports:** $72.8 billion (f.o.b., 1993)
*commodities:* cars and trucks, semifinished manufactured goods, foodstuffs, machinery
*partners:* EC 71.2%, US 4.8%, other developed countries 7.9% (1992)
**Imports:** $92.5 billion (c.i.f., 1993)
*commodities:* machinery, transport equipment, fuels, semifinished goods, foodstuffs, consumer goods, chemicals
*partners:* EC 60.7%, US 7.4%, other developed countries 11.5%, Middle East 5.9% (1992)
**External debt:** $90 billion (1993 est.)
**Industrial production:** growth rate -1.7% (1992)
**Electricity:**
*capacity:* 46,600,000 kW
*production:* 157 billion kWh
*consumption per capita:* 4,000 kWh (1992)
**Industries:** textiles and apparel (including footwear), food and beverages, metals and metal manufactures, chemicals, shipbuilding, automobiles, machine tools, tourism
**Agriculture:** accounts for about 5% of GDP and 14% of labor force; major products—grain, vegetables, olives, wine grapes, sugar beets, citrus fruit, beef, pork, poultry, dairy; largely self-sufficient in food; fish catch of 1.4 million metric tons is among top 20 nations
**Illicit drugs:** key European gateway country for Latin American cocaine and North African hashish entering the European market

**Economic aid:**
*recipient:* US commitments, including Ex-Im (FY70-87), $1.9 billion; Western (non-US) countries, ODA and OOF bilateral commitments (1970-79), $545 million
*note:* not currently a recipient
**Currency:** 1 peseta (Pta) = 100 centimos
**Exchange rates:** pesetas (Ptas) per US$1— 136.6 (May 1994), 127.26 (1993), 102.38 (1992), 103.91 (1991), 101.93 (1990), 118.38 (1989)
**Fiscal year:** calendar year

---

## Communications

**Railroads:** 15,430 km total; Spanish National Railways (RENFE) operates 12,691 km (all 1,668-mm gauge, 6,184 km electrified, and 2,295 km double track); FEVE (government-owned narrow-gauge railways) operates 1,821 km (predominantly 1,000-mm gauge, 441 km electrified); privately owned railways operate 918 km (predominantly 1,000-mm gauge, 512 km electrified, and 56 km double track)
**Highways:**
*total:* 318,022 km (1988)
*paved:* 178,092 km (including 2,142 km of expressways)
*unpaved:* 139,930 km
**Inland waterways:** 1,045 km, but of minor economic importance
**Pipelines:** crude oil 265 km, petroleum products 1,794 km, natural gas 1,666 km
**Ports:** Algeciras, Alicante, Almeria, Barcelona, Bilbao, Cadiz, Cartagena, Castellon de la Plana, Ceuta, El Ferrol del Caudillo, Puerto de Gijon, Huelva, La Coruna, Las Palmas (Canary Islands), Mahon, Malaga, Melilla, Rota, Santa Cruz de Tenerife, Sagunto, Tarragona, Valencia, Vigo, and 175 minor ports
**Merchant marine:** 192 ships (1,000 GRT or over) totaling 1,328,730 GRT/2,213,671 DWT, passenger 2, short-sea passenger 6, cargo 55, refrigerated cargo 12, container 11, roll-on/roll-off cargo 33, vehicle carrier 1, oil tanker 29, chemical tanker 14, liquefied gas 5, specialized tanker 3, bulk 21

**Airports:**
*total:* 105
*usable:* 99
*with permanent-surface runways:* 60
*with runways over 3,659 m:* 4
*with runways 2,440-3,659 m:* 22
*with runways 1,220-2,439 m:* 26
**Telecommunications:** generally adequate, modern facilities; 15,350,464 telephones; broadcast stations—190 AM, 406 (134 repeaters) FM, 100 (1,297 repeaters) TV; 22 coaxial submarine cables; 2 communications satellite earth stations operating in INTELSAT (Atlantic Ocean and Indian Ocean); MARECS, INMARSAT, and EUTELSAT systems; tropospheric links

---

## Defense Forces

**Branches:** Army, Navy, Air Force, Marines, Civil Guard, National Police, Coastal Civil Guard
**Manpower availability:** males age 15-49 10,377,990; fit for military service 8,396,405; reach military age (20) annually 337,764 (1994 est.)
**Defense expenditures:** exchange rate conversion—$5.8 billion, 1.26% of GDP (1994)

---

## Geography

**Location:** Southwestern Europe, bordering the North Atlantic Ocean and the Mediterranean Sea, between Portugal and France
**Map references:** Africa, Europe, Standard Time Zones of the World
**Area:**
*total area:* 504,750 sq km
*land area:* 499,400 sq km
*comparative area:* slightly more than twice the size of Oregon
*note:* includes Balearic Islands, Canary Islands, and five places of sovereignty (plazas de soberania) on and off the coast of Morocco—Ceuta, Mellila, Islas Chafarinas, Penon de Alhucemas, and Penon de Velez de la Gomera

**Land boundaries:** total 1,903.2 km, Andorra 65 km, France 623 km, Gibraltar 1.2 km, Portugal 1,214 km

**Coastline:** 4,964 km

**Maritime claims:**

*exclusive economic zone:* 200 nm

*territorial sea:* 12 nm

**International disputes:** Gibraltar question with UK; Spain controls five places of sovereignty (plazas de soberania) on and off the coast of Morocco—the coastal enclaves of Ceuta and Melilla, which Morocco contests, as well as the islands of Penon de Alhucemas, Penon de Velez de la Gomera, and Islas Chafarinas

**Climate:** temperate; clear, hot summers in interior, more moderate and cloudy along coast; cloudy, cold winters in interior, partly cloudy and cool along coast

**Terrain:** large, flat to dissected plateau surrounded by rugged hills; Pyrenees in north

**Natural resources:** coal, lignite, iron ore, uranium, mercury, pyrites, fluorspar, gypsum, zinc, lead, tungsten, copper, kaolin, potash, hydropower

**Land use:**

*arable land:* 31%

*permanent crops:* 10%

*meadows and pastures:* 21%

*forest and woodland:* 31%

*other:* 7%

**Irrigated land:** 33,600 sq km (1989 est.)

**Environment:**

*current issues:* pollution of the Mediterranean Sea from untreated sewage and effluents from the offshore production of oil and gas; air pollution; deforestation; desertification

*natural hazards:* NA

*international agreements:* party to—Air Pollution, Air Pollution-Volatile Organic Compounds, Antarctic-Environmental Protocol, Antarctic Treaty, Biodiversity, Climate Change, Endangered Species, Environmental Modification, Hazardous Wastes, Marine Dumping, Marine Life Conservation, Nuclear Test Ban, Ozone Layer Protection, Ship Pollution, Tropical Timber, Wetlands, Whaling; signed, but not ratified—Air Pollution-Nitrogen Oxides, Law of the Sea

**Note:** strategic location along approaches to Strait of Gibraltar

## People

**Population:** 39,302,665 (July 1994 est.)

**Population growth rate:** 0.25% (1994 est.)

**Birth rate:** 11.05 births/1,000 population (1994 est.)

**Death rate:** 8.82 deaths/1,000 population (1994 est.)

**Net migration rate:** 0.27 migrant(s)/1,000 population (1994 est.)

**Infant mortality rate:** 6.9 deaths/1,000 live births (1994 est.)

**Life expectancy at birth:**

*total population:* 77.71 years

*male:* 74.45 years

*female:* 81.21 years (1994 est.)

**Total fertility rate:** 1.4 children born/woman (1994 est.)

**Nationality:**

*noun:* Spaniard(s)

*adjective:* Spanish

**Ethnic divisions:** composite of Mediterranean and Nordic types

**Religions:** Roman Catholic 99%, other sects 1%

**Languages:** Castilian Spanish, Catalan 17%, Galician 7%, Basque 2%

**Literacy:** age 15 and over can read and write (1990 est.)

*total population:* 95%

*male:* 97%

*female:* 93%

**Labor force:** 14.621 million

*by occupation:* services 53%, industry 24%, agriculture 14%, construction 9% (1988)

## Government

**Names:**

*conventional long form:* Kingdom of Spain

*conventional short form:* Spain

*local short form:* Espana

**Digraph:** SP

**Type:** parliamentary monarchy

**Capital:** Madrid

**Administrative divisions:** 17 autonomous communities (comunidades autonomas, singular—comunidad autonoma); Andalucia, Aragon, Asturias, Canarias, Cantabria, Castilla-La Mancha, Castilla y Leon, Cataluna,

Communidad Valencia, Extremadura, Galicia, Islas Baleares, La Rioja, Madrid, Murcia, Navarra, Pais Vasco

*note:* there are five places of sovereignty on and off the coast of Morocco (Ceuta, Mellila, Islas Chafarinas, Penon de Alhucemas, and Penon de Velez de la Gomera) with administrative status unknown

**Independence:** 1492 (expulsion of the Moors and unification)

**National holiday:** National Day, 12 October

**Constitution:** 6 December 1978, effective 29 December 1978

**Legal system:** civil law system, with regional applications; does not accept compulsory ICJ jurisdiction

**Suffrage:** 18 years of age; universal

**Executive branch:**

*chief of state:* King JUAN CARLOS I (since 22 November 1975)

*head of government:* Prime Minister Felipe GONZALEZ Marquez (since 2 December 1982); Deputy Prime Minister Narcis SERRA y Serra (since 13 March 1991)

*cabinet:* Council of Ministers; designated by the prime minister

*Council of State:* is the supreme consultative organ of the government

**Legislative branch:** bicameral The General Courts or National Assembly (Las Cortes Generales)

*Senate (Senado):* elections last held 6 June 1993 (next to be held by NA June 1997); results—percent of vote by party NA; seats— (255 total) PSOE 117, PP 107, CiU 15, PNV 5, IU 2, other 9

*Congress of Deputies (Congreso de los Diputados):* elections last held 6 June 1993 (next to be held by NA June 1997); results— percent of vote by party NA; seats—(350 total) PSOE 159, PP 141, IU 18, CiU 17, PNV 5, CN 4, HB 2, other 4

**Judicial branch:** Supreme Court (Tribunal Supremo)

**Political parties and leaders:**

*principal national parties, from right to left:* Popular Party (PP), Jose Maria AZNAR; Social Democratic Center (CDS), Rafael Calvo ORTEGA; Spanish Socialist Workers Party (PSOE), Felipe GONZALEZ Marquez, secretary general; Socialist Democracy Party (DS), Ricardo Garcia DAMBORENEA; Spanish Communist Party (PCE), Julio ANGUITA; United Left (IU) a coalition of parties including the PCE, a branch of the PSOE, and other small parties, Julio ANGUITA

*chief regional parties:* Convergence and Unity (CiU), Jordi PUJOL Saley and Miguel ROCA in Catalonia; Basque Nationalist Party (PNV), Xabier ARZALLUS and Jose Antonio ARDANZA; Basque Solidarity (EA), Carlos GARAICOETXEA Urizza; Basque Popular Unity (HB), Jon IDIGORAS and Inaki ESNAOLA; Basque Socialist Party (PSE), coalition of the PSE, EE and PSOE, Jose Maria BANEGAS and Jon LARRINAGA; Andalusian Progress Party (PA), Pedro PACHECO; Canarian Coalition (CN), Dimas MARTIN; Catalan Republican Left, Angel COLOM; Galician Coalition, Senen BERNARDEZ; Aragonese Regionalist Party (PAR), Jose Maria MUR Bernad; Valencian Union (UV), Vicente GONZALEZ Lizondo, Manuel CAMPILLOS Martinez

**Other political or pressure groups:** on the extreme left, the Basque Fatherland and Liberty (ETA) and the First of October Antifascist Resistance Group (GRAPO) use terrorism to oppose the government; free labor unions (authorized in April 1977) include the Communist-dominated Workers Commissions (CCOO); the Socialist General Union of Workers (UGT), and the smaller independent Workers Syndical Union (USO); business and landowning interests; the Catholic Church; Opus Dei; university students

**Member of:** AG (observer), AsDB, Australian Group, BIS, CCC, CE, CERN, COCOM, CSCE, EBRD, AfDB, EC, ECE, ECLAC, EIB, ESA, FAO, G-8, GATT, IADB, IAEA, IBRD, ICAO, ICC, ICFTU, IDA, IEA, IFAD, IFC, ILO, IMF, IMO, INMARSAT, INTELSAT, INTERPOL, IOC, IOM (observer), ISO, ITU, LAIA (observer), LORCS, MTRC, NACC, NAM (guest), NATO, NEA, NSG, OAS (observer), OECD, ONUSAL, PCA, UN, UNAVEM II, UNCTAD, UNESCO, UNIDO, UNOMOZ, UNPROFOR, UPU, WCL, WEU, WHO, WIPO, WMO, WTO, ZC

**Diplomatic representation in US:**
*chief of mission:* Ambassador Jaime De
OJEDA y Eiseley
*chancery:* 2700 15th Street NW, Washington,
DC 20009
*telephone:* (202) 265-0190 or 0191
*consulate(s) general:* Boston, Chicago,
Houston, Los Angeles, Miami, New Orleans,
New York, San Francisco, and San Juan
(Puerto Rico)
**US diplomatic representation:**
*chief of mission:* Ambassador Richard N.
GARDNER
*embassy:* Serrano 75, 28006 Madrid
*mailing address:* APO AE 09642
*telephone:* [34] (1) 577-4000
*FAX:* [34] (1) 577-5735
*consulate(s) general:* Barcelona
*consulate(s):* Bilbao
**Flag:** three horizontal bands of red (top),
yellow (double width), and red with the
national coat of arms on the hoist side of the
yellow band; the coat of arms includes the
royal seal framed by the Pillars of Hercules,
which are the two promontories (Gibraltar and
Ceuta) on either side of the eastern end of the
Strait of Gibraltar

---

**U.S. Government Contacts:**

**U.S. Trade Desk:** (202) 482-4508

**American Embassy Commercial Section**
Serrano 75
Madrid, Spain
APO AE 09642
Tel: 34-1-577-4000
Fax: 34-1-575-8655

**American Consulate General - Barcelona
Commercial Section**
Via Layetana
Barcelona, Spain
Box 5
APO AE 09642
Tel: 34-3-319-9550
Fax: 34-3-319-5621

**US Foreign Commercial Service
American Embassy/Embajada de los EE.UU.**
Serrano, 75
28006 Madrid
Tel: 34-3-577-4000
Fax: 34-3-577-4000

**US Foreign Commercial Service
American Consulate/Consulado de los
EE.UU**
Paseo Reina Elisenda, 23
08034 Barcelona
Tel: 34 280 2227
Fax: 34 205 7705

---

**Spain Government Contacts:**

**Embassy of Spain Commercial Section**
2700 15th Street, N.W.
Washington, DC 20009
Tel: (202) 265-8600

---

**Chambers of Commerce &
Organizations:**

**American Chamber of Commerce in Spain**
Avenida Diagonal 477, Box 8
Barcelona 36, Spain
Tel: 34-3-319-9550
Fax: 34-3-321-8197

**American Chamber of Commerce
Camara de Comercio Americana**
Padre Damian, 23 (Eurobuilding)
28036 Madrid
Tel: 34 359 6559
Fax: 34 359 6520

---

**Legal Services:**

**Brugueras, Garcia-Bragado, Molinero y
Asociados**
Paseo de Garcia, 81
08008 Barcelona, Spain
Tel: 343-487-21-02
        343-215-05-62
Fax: 343-487-18-53
*International and Foreign Investments,
General Practice, Commercial, Financial,
Stock-Exchange, Corporation, Bankruptcy,
EEC's Law.*

**Travel:**

**International Airlines to Country:**
American, Continental, TWA, United

**International Hotels in Country:**
Madrid:
Palace, Tel: 341 91/521-2857, Fax: 341 91/420-2547
Ritz, Tel: 341 91/521-2857, Fax: 341 91/532-8776
Villamagna, Tel: 341 576-7500, Fax: 341 91/575-9504.

# SWEDEN

400 km

Kiruna
Tärnaby
Luleå
Umeå
Gulf of Bothnia
Sundsvall
Gävle
Uppsala
Karlstad
STOCKHOLM
Jönköping
Göteborg
Gotland
Kattegat
Öland
Baltic Sea
Malmö
Karlskrona

## Economy

**Overview:** Aided by a long period of peace and neutrality during World War I through World War II, Sweden has achieved an enviable standard of living under a mixed system of high-tech capitalism and extensive welfare benefits. It has a modern distribution system, excellent internal and external communications, and a skilled labor force. Timber, hydropower, and iron ore constitute the resource base of an economy that is heavily oriented toward foreign trade. Privately owned firms account for about 90% of industrial output, of which the engineering sector accounts for 50% of output and exports. In the last few years, however, this extraordinarily favorable picture has been clouded by inflation, growing unemployment, and a gradual loss of competitiveness in international markets. Although Prime Minister BILDT's center-right minority coalition had hoped to charge ahead with free-market-oriented reforms, a skyrocketing budget deficit—almost 14% of GDP in FY94 projections—and record unemployment have forestalled many of the plans. Unemployment in 1993 is estimated at around 8% with another 5% in job training. Continued heavy foreign exchange speculation forced the government to cooperate in late 1992 with the opposition Social Democrats on two crisis packages—one a severe austerity pact and the other a program to spur industrial competitiveness—which basically set economic policy through 1997. In November 1992, Sweden broke its tie to the EC's ECU, and the krona has since depreciated about 25% against the dollar. The government hopes the boost in export competitiveness from the depreciation will help lift Sweden out of its 3-year recession. To curb the budget deficit and bolster confidence in the economy, BILDT continues to propose cuts in welfare benefits, subsidies, defense, and foreign aid. Sweden continues to harmonize its economic policies with those of the EU in preparation for scheduled membership by early 1995, which will help to broaden European economic unity.
**National product:** GDP—purchasing power equivalent—$153.7 billion (1993)
**National product real growth rate:** -2.7% (1993)
**National product per capita:** $17,600 (1993)
**Inflation rate (consumer prices):** 4.4% (1993 est.)
**Unemployment rate:** 8.2% (1993 est.)
**Budget:**
*revenues:* $45.1 billion
*expenditures:* $73.1 billion, including capital expenditures of $NA (FY94)
**Exports:** $49.7 billion (f.o.b., 1993 est.)
*commodities:* machinery, motor vehicles, paper products, pulp and wood, iron and steel products, chemicals, petroleum and petroleum products
*partners:* EC 55.8% (Germany 15%, UK 9.7%, Denmark 7.2%, France 5.8%), EFTA 17.4% (Norway 8.4%, Finland 5.1%), US 8.2%, Central and Eastern Europe 2.5% (1992)
**Imports:** $42.3 billion (c.i.f., 1993 est.)
*commodities:* machinery, petroleum and

petroleum products, chemicals, motor vehicles, foodstuffs, iron and steel, clothing
*partners:* EC 53.6% (Germany 17.9%, UK 6.3%, Denmark 7.5%, France 4.9%), EFTA (Norway 6.6%, Finland 6%), US 8.4%, Central and Eastern Europe 3% (1992)
**External debt:** $19.5 billion (1992 est.)
**Industrial production:** growth rate 0.8% (1993 est.)
**Electricity:**
*capacity:* 39,716,000 kW
*production:* 142.5 billion kWh
*consumption per capita:* 16,560 kWh (1992)
**Industries:** iron and steel, precision equipment (bearings, radio and telephone parts, armaments), wood pulp and paper products, processed foods, motor vehicles
**Agriculture:** animal husbandry predominates, with milk and dairy products accounting for 37% of farm income; main crops—grains, sugar beets, potatoes; 100% self-sufficient in grains and potatoes; Sweden is about 50% self-sufficient in most products; farming accounted for 1.2% of GDP and 1.9% of jobs in 1990
**Illicit drugs:** transshipment point for narcotics shipped via the CIS and Baltic states for the European market
**Economic aid:**
*donor:* ODA and OOF commitments (1970-89), $10.3 billion
**Currency:** 1 Swedish krona (SKr) = 100 oere
**Exchange rates:** Swedish kronor (SKr) per US$1—8.1255 (January 1994), 7.834 (1993), 5.8238 (1992), 6.0475 (1991) 5.9188 (1990), 6.4469 (1989)
**Fiscal year:** 1 July—30 June

## Communications

**Railroads:** 12,084 km total; Swedish State Railways (SJ) 11,202 km—10,819 km 1.435-meter standard gauge, 6,955 km electrified and 1,152 km double track; 182 km 0.891-meter gauge; 117 km rail ferry service; privately-owned railways 882 km—511 km 1.435-meter standard gauge (332 km electrified) and 371 km 0.891-meter gauge (all electrified)

**Highways:**
*total:* 205,000 km
*paved:* 69,754 km (including 936 km of expressways)
*unpaved:* gravel 45,900 km; unimproved earth 38,060 km; NA 51,286 km (1990)
**Inland waterways:** 2,052 km navigable for small steamers and barges
**Pipelines:** natural gas 84 km
**Ports:** Gavle, Goteborg, Halmstad, Helsingborg, Kalmar, Malmo, Stockholm; numerous secondary and minor ports
**Merchant marine:** 161 ships (1,000 GRT or over) totaling 2,049,554 GRT/2,516,350 DWT, short-sea passenger 10, cargo 24, container 2, roll-on/roll-off cargo 39, vehicle carrier 13, railcar carrier 2, oil tanker 30, chemical tanker 25, specialized tanker 4, combination ore/oil 1, bulk 10, refrigerated cargo 1
**Airports:**
*total:* 252
*usable:* 248
*with permanent-surface runways:* 138
*with runways over 3,659 m:* 0
*with runways 2,440-3,659 m:* 11
*with runways 1,220-2,439 m:* 94
**Telecommunications:** excellent domestic and international facilities; 8,200,000 telephones; mainly coaxial and multiconductor cables carry long-distance network; parallel microwave network carries primarily radio, TV and some telephone channels; automatic system; broadcast stations—5 AM, 360 (mostly repeaters) FM, 880 (mostly repeaters) TV; 5 submarine coaxial cables; satellite earth stations—1 Atlantic Ocean INTELSAT and 1 EUTELSAT

## Defense Forces

**Branches:** Swedish Army, Royal Swedish Navy, Swedish Air Force
**Manpower availability:** males age 15-49 2,146,145; fit for military service 1,874,787; reach military age (19) annually 55,262 (1994 est.)
**Defense expenditures:** exchange rate conversion—$6.7 billion, 3.8% of GDP (FY92/93)

## Geography

**Location:** Nordic State, Northern Europe, bordering the Baltic Sea, between Norway and Finland
**Map references:** Arctic Region, Asia, Europe, Standard Time Zones of the World
**Area:**
*total area:* 449,964 sq km
*land area:* 410,928 sq km
*comparative area:* slightly smaller than California
**Land boundaries:** total 2,205 km, Finland 586 km, Norway 1,619 km
**Coastline:** 3,218 km
**Maritime claims:**
*continental shelf:* 200-m depth or to depth of exploitation
*exclusive fishing zone:* 200 nm
*territorial sea:* 12 nm
**International disputes:** none
**Climate:** temperate in south with cold, cloudy winters and cool, partly cloudy summers; subarctic in north
**Terrain:** mostly flat or gently rolling lowlands; mountains in west
**Natural resources:** zinc, iron ore, lead, copper, silver, timber, uranium, hydropower potential
**Land use:**
*arable land:* 7%
*permanent crops:* 0%
*meadows and pastures:* 2%
*forest and woodland:* 64%
*other:* 27%
**Irrigated land:** 1,120 sq km (1989 est.)
**Environment:**
*current issues:* acid rain damaging soils and lakes; pollution of the North Sea and the Baltic Sea
*natural hazards:* ice floes in the surrounding waters, especially in the Gulf of Bothnia, can interfere with navigation
*international agreements:* party to—Air Pollution, Air Pollution-Nitrogen Oxides, Air Pollution-Sulphur, Air Pollution-Volatile Organic Compounds, Antarctic-Environmental Protocol, Antarctic Treaty, Biodiversity, Climate Change, Endangered Species, Environmental Modification, Hazardous Wastes, Marine Dumping, Nuclear Test Ban, Ozone Layer Protection, Ship Pollution, Tropical Timber, Wetlands, Whaling; signed, but not ratified—Law of the Sea
**Note:** strategic location along Danish Straits linking Baltic and North Seas

## People

**Population:** 8,778,461 (July 1994 est.)
**Population growth rate:** 0.52% (1994 est.)
**Birth rate:** 13.5 births/1,000 population (1994 est.)
**Death rate:** 10.9 deaths/1,000 population (1994 est.)
**Net migration rate:** 2.62 migrant(s)/1,000 population (1994 est.)
**Infant mortality rate:** 5.7 deaths/1,000 live births (1994 est.)
**Life expectancy at birth:**
*total population:* 78.25 years
*male:* 75.47 years
*female:* 81.2 years (1994 est.)
**Total fertility rate:** 2 children born/woman (1994 est.)
**Nationality:**
*noun:* Swede(s)
*adjective:* Swedish
**Ethnic divisions:** white, Lapp (Sami), foreign born or first-generation immigrants 12% (Finns, Yugoslavs, Danes, Norwegians, Greeks, Turks)
**Religions:** Evangelical Lutheran 94%, Roman Catholic 1.5%, Pentecostal 1%, other 3.5% (1987)
**Languages:** Swedish
*note:* small Lapp- and Finnish-speaking minorities; immigrants speak native languages
**Literacy:** age 15 and over can read and write (1979 est.)
*total population:* 99%
*male:* NA%
*female:* NA%
**Labor force:** 4.552 million (84% unionized, 1992)
*by occupation:* community, social and personal services 38.3%, mining and

manufacturing 21.2%, commerce, hotels, and restaurants 14.1%, banking, insurance 9.0%, communications 7.2%, construction 7.0%, agriculture, fishing, and forestry 3.2% (1991)

## Government

**Names:**
*conventional long form:* Kingdom of Sweden
*conventional short form:* Sweden
*local long form:* Konungariket Sverige
*local short form:* Sverige
**Digraph:** SW
**Type:** constitutional monarchy
**Capital:** Stockholm
**Administrative divisions:** 24 provinces (lan, singular and plural); Alvsborgs Lan, Blekinge Lan, Gavleborgs Lan, Goteborgs och Bohus Lan, Gotlands Lan, Hallands Lan, Jamtlands Lan, Jonkopings Lan, Kalmar Lan, Kopparbergs Lan, Kristianstads Lan, Kronobergs Lan, Malmohus Lan, Norrbottens Lan, Orebro Lan, Ostergotlands Lan, Skaraborgs Lan, Sodermanlands Lan, Stockholms Lan, Uppsala Lan, Varmlands Lan, Vasterbottens Lan, Vasternorrlands Lan, Vastmanlands Lan
**Independence:** 6 June 1809 (constitutional monarchy established)
**National holiday:** Day of the Swedish Flag, 6 June
**Constitution:** 1 January 1975
**Legal system:** civil law system influenced by customary law; accepts compulsory ICJ jurisdiction, with reservations
**Suffrage:** 18 years of age; universal
**Executive branch:**
*chief of state:* King CARL XVI GUSTAF (since 19 September 1973); Heir Apparent Princess VICTORIA Ingrid Alice Desiree, daughter of the King (born 14 July 1977)
*head of government:* Prime Minister Carl BILDT (since 3 October 1991); Deputy Prime Minister Bengt WESTERBERG (since NA)
*cabinet:* Cabinet; appointed by the prime minister
**Legislative branch:** unicameral
*parliament (Riksdag):* elections last held 15 September 1991 (next to be held NA September 1994); results—Social Democratic

Party 37.6%, Moderate Party (conservative) 21.9%, Liberal People's Party 9.1%, Center Party 8.5%, Christian Democrats 7.1%, New Democracy 6.7%, Left Party (Communist) 4.5%, Green Party 3.4%, other 1.2%; seats— (349 total) Social Democratic 138, Moderate Party (conservative) 80, Liberal People's Party 33, Center Party 31, Christian Democrats 26, New Democracy 25, Left Party (Communist) 16; note—the Green Party has no seats in the Riksdag because it received less than the required 4% of the vote
**Judicial branch:** Supreme Court (Hogsta Domstolen)
**Political parties and leaders:** ruling four-party coalition consists of Moderate Party (conservative), Carl BILDT; Liberal People's Party, Bengt WESTERBERG; Center Party, Olof JOHANSSON; and the Christian Democratic Party, Alf SVENSSON; Social Democratic Party, Ingvar CARLSSON; New Democracy Party, Harriet COLLIANDER; Left Party (VP; Communist), Gudrun SCHYMAN; Communist Workers' Party, Rolf HAGEL; Green Party, no formal leader
**Member of:** AfDB, AG (observer), AsDB, Australian Group, BIS, CBSS, CCC, CE, CERN, COCOM (cooperating), CSCE, EBRD, ECE, EFTA, ESA, FAO, G-6, G-8, G-9, G-10, GATT, IADB, IAEA, IBRD, ICAO, ICC, ICFTU, IDA, IEA, IFAD, IFC, ILO, IMF, IMO, INMARSAT, INTERPOL, INTELSAT, IOC, IOM, ISO, ITU, LORCS, MTRC, NAM (guest), NC, NEA, NIB, NSG, OECD, ONUSAL, PCA, UN, UNAVEM II, UNCTAD, UNESCO, UNFICYP, UNHCR, UNIDO, UNIFIL, UNIKOM, UNMOGIP, UNOMIG, UNOMOZ, UNOSOM, UNPROFOR, UNTAC, UNTSO, UPU, WFTU, WHO, WIPO, WMO, ZC
**Diplomatic representation in US:**
*chief of mission:* Ambassador Carl Henrik LILJEGREN
*chancery:* Suites 1200 and 715, 600 New Hampshire Avenue NW, Washington, DC 20037
*telephone:* (202) 944-5600
*FAX:* (202) 342-1319
*consulate(s) general:* Los Angeles and New York

**US diplomatic representation:**
*chief of mission:* Ambassador Thomas
SIEBERT
*embassy:* Strandvagen 101, S-115 89
Stockholm
*mailing address:* use embassy street address
*telephone:* [46] (8) 783-5300
*FAX:* [46] (8) 661-1964
**Flag:** blue with a yellow cross that extends to
the edges of the flag; the vertical part of the
cross is shifted to the hoist side in the style of
the Dannebrog (Danish flag)

**U.S. Government Contacts:**

**U.S. Trade Desk**: (202) 482-4414

**American Embassy Commercial Section**
Strandvagen 101
c/o U.S. Department of State (Stockholm)
Washington, DC 20521-5750
Tel: 46-8-783-5346
Fax: 46-8-660-9181

**Sweden Government Contacts:**

**Embassy of Sweden Commercial Section**
600 New Hampshire Avenue, N.W.
Washington, DC 20037
Tel: (202) 944-5600

**Swedish Trade Council**
150 North Michigan Ave., Suite 1200
Chicago, IL 60601-7594
Tel: 1-800-SWEDEN4
Fax: (312) 346-0683

**Chambers of Commerce &
Organizations:**

**American Chamber of Commerce in Sweden**
Box 5512
114 85 Stockholm, Sweden
Tel: (46) 8 666 11 00
Fax: (48) 8 662 8884

**Travel:**

**International Airlines to Country:**
American, Continental

**International Hotels in Country:**
Stockholm:
Continental, Tel: 468/244020, Fax:
468/113695
Diplomat, Tel: 468/663-5800, Fax: 468/783-
6634
Lady Hamilton, Tel: 468/234680, Fax:
468/111148.

# SWITZERLAND

100 km

## Economy

**Overview:** Switzerland's economy—one of the most prosperous and stable in the world — is nonetheless undergoing a painful adjustment after both the inflationary boom of the late-1980s and the electorate's rejection of membership in the European Economic Area in 1992. The Swiss finally emerged from a three-year recession in mid-1993 and posted a –0.6% GDP growth for the year. After a three-year struggle with inflation, the Swiss central bank's tight monetary policies have begun to pay off. Inflation slowed to 3.3% in 1993 from about 4% in 1992 and is expected to slow down further to 1.5% in 1994. Unemployment, however, will continue to be a problem over the near term. Swiss unemployment reached 5.1% in 1993 and will likely remain at that level through 1994 before declining in 1995. The voters' rejection of a referendum on membership in the EEA, which was supported by most political, business, and financial leaders has raised doubts that the country can maintain its preeminent prosperity and leadership in commercial banking in the twenty-first century. Despite these problems, Swiss per capita output, general living standards, education and science, health care, and diet remain unsurpassed in Europe. The country has few natural resources except for the scenic natural beauty that has made it a world leader in tourism. Management-labor relations remain generally harmonious.

**National product:** GDP—purchasing power equivalent—$149.1 billion (1993)

**National product real growth rate:** –0.6% (1993)

**National product per capita:** $21,300 (1993)

**Inflation rate (consumer prices):** 3.3% (1993 est.)

**Unemployment rate:** 5.1% (1993 est.)

**Budget:**
*revenues:* $23.7 billion
*expenditures:* $26.9 billion, including capital expenditures of $NA (1993 est.)

**Exports:** $63 billion (f.o.b., 1993)
*commodities:* machinery and equipment, precision instruments, metal products, foodstuffs, textiles and clothing
*partners:* Western Europe 63.1% (EC countries 56%, other 7.1%), US 8.8%, Japan 3.4%

**Imports:** $60.7 billion (c.i.f., 1993)
*commodities:* agricultural products, machinery and transportation equipment, chemicals, textiles, construction materials
*partners:* Western Europe 79.2% (EC countries 72.3%, other 6.9%), US 6.4%

**External debt:** $NA

**Industrial production:** growth rate 0.0% (1993 est.)

**Electricity:**
*capacity:* 17,710,000 kW
*production:* 56 billion kWh
*consumption per capita:* 8,200 kWh (1992)

**Industries:** machinery, chemicals, watches, textiles, precision instruments

**Agriculture:** dairy farming predominates; less than 50% self-sufficient in food; must import fish, refined sugar, fats and oils (other than butter), grains, eggs, fruits, vegetables, meat

159

**Illicit drugs:** money-laundering center
**Economic aid:**
*donor:* ODA and OOF commitments (1970-89), $3.5 billion
**Currency:** 1 Swiss franc, franken, or franco (SwF) = 100 centimes, rappen, or centesimi
**Exchange rates:** Swiss francs, franken, or franchi (SwF) per US$1—1.715 (January 1994), 1.4776 (1993), 1.4062 (1992), 1.4340 (1991), 1.3892 (1990), 1.6359 (1989)
**Fiscal year:** calendar year

## Communications

**Railroads:** 4,418 km total; 3,073 km are government owned and 1,345 km are nongovernment owned; the government network consists of 2,999 km 1.435-meter standard gauge and 74 km 1.000-meter narrow gauge track; 1,432 km double track, 99% electrified; the nongovernment network consists of 510 km 1.435-meter standard gauge, and 835 km 1.000-meter gauge, 100% electrified
**Highways:**
*total:* 71,106 km
*paved:* 71,106 km (including 1,502 km of expressways)
**Inland waterways:** 65 km; Rhine (Basel to Rheinfelden, Schaffhausen to Bodensee); 12 navigable lakes
**Pipelines:** crude oil 314 km, natural gas 1,506 km
**Ports:** Basel (river port)
**Merchant marine:** 23 ships (1,000 GRT or over) totaling 337,455 GRT/592,213 DWT, cargo 4, roll-on/roll-off cargo 2, chemical tanker 5, specialized tanker 1, bulk 10, oil tanker 1
**Airports:**
*total:* 70
*usable:* 69
*with permanent-surface runways:* 42
*with runways over 3,659 m:* 3
*with runways 2,440-3,659 m:* 4
*with runways 1,220-2,439 m:* 18
**Telecommunications:** excellent domestic, international, and broadcast services; 5,890,000 telephones; extensive cable and microwave networks; broadcast stations—7 AM, 265 FM, 18 (1,322 repeaters) TV; communications satellite earth station operating in the INTELSAT (Atlantic Ocean and Indian Ocean) system

## Defense Forces

**Branches:** Army (Air Force is part of the Army), Frontier Guards, Fortification Guards
**Manpower availability:** males age 15-49 1,853,075; fit for military service 1,589,288; reach military age (20) annually 43,005 (1994 est.)
**Defense expenditures:** exchange rate conversion—$3.5 billion, 1.7% of GDP (1993 est.)

## Geography

**Location:** Central Europe, between France and Austria
**Map references:** Europe, Standard Time Zones of the World
**Area:**
*total area:* 41,290 sq km
*land area:* 39,770 sq km
*comparative area:* slightly more than twice the size of New Jersey
**Land boundaries:** total 1,852 km, Austria 164 km, France 573 km, Italy 740 km, Liechtenstein 41 km, Germany 334 km
**Coastline:** 0 km (landlocked)
**Maritime claims:** none; landlocked
**International disputes:** none
**Climate:** temperate, but varies with altitude; cold, cloudy, rainy/snowy winters; cool to warm, cloudy, humid summers with occasional showers
**Terrain:** mostly mountains (Alps in south, Jura in northwest) with a central plateau of rolling hills, plains, and large lakes
**Natural resources:** hydropower potential, timber, salt
**Land use:**
*arable land:* 10%
*permanent crops:* 1%
*meadows and pastures:* 40%
*forest and woodland:* 26%
*other:* 23%

**Irrigated land:** 250 sq km (1989)
**Environment:**
*current issues:* air pollution from vehicle emissions and open air burning; acid rain; water pollution from increased use of agricultural fertilizers; loss of biodiversity
*natural hazards:* subject to avalanches, landslides, flash floods
*international agreements:* party to—Air Pollution, Air Pollution-Nitrogen Oxides, Air Pollution-Sulphur, Air Pollution-Volatile Organic Compounds, Antarctic Treaty, Climate Change, Endangered Species, Environmental Modification, Hazardous Wastes, Marine Dumping, Marine Life Conservation, Nuclear Test Ban, Ozone Layer Protection, Ship Pollution, Tropical Timber, Wetlands, Whaling; signed, but not ratified—Antarctic-Environmental Protocol, Biodiversity, Law of the Sea
**Note:** landlocked; crossroads of northern and southern Europe; along with southeastern France and northern Italy, contains the highest elevations in Europe

---

**People**

**Population:** 7,040,119 (July 1994 est.)
**Population growth rate:** 0.7% (1994 est.)
**Birth rate:** 12.23 births/1,000 population (1994 est.)
**Death rate:** 9.2 deaths/1,000 population (1994 est.)
**Net migration rate:** 3.97 migrant(s)/1,000 population (1994 est.)
**Infant mortality rate:** 6.5 deaths/1,000 live births (1994 est.)
**Life expectancy at birth:**
*total population:* 78.17 years
*male:* 74.8 years
*female:* 81.71 years (1994 est.)
**Total fertility rate:** 1.6 children born/woman (1994 est.)
**Nationality:**
*noun:* Swiss (singular and plural)
*adjective:* Swiss
**Ethnic divisions:**
*total population:* German 65%, French 18%, Italian 10%, Romansch 1%, other 6%

*Swiss nationals:* German 74%, French 20%, Italian 4%, Romansch 1%, other 1%
**Religions:** Roman Catholic 47.6%, Protestant 44.3%, other 8.1% (1980)
**Languages:** German 65%, French 18%, Italian 12%, Romansch 1%, other 4%
*note:* figures for Swiss nationals only—German 74%, French 20%, Italian 4%, Romansch 1%, other 1%
**Literacy:** age 15 and over can read and write (1980 est.)
*total population:* 99%
*male:* NA%
*female:* NA%
**Labor force:** 3.31 million (904,095 foreign workers, mostly Italian)
*by occupation:* services 50%, industry and crafts 33%, government 10%, agriculture and forestry 6%, other 1% (1989)

---

**Government**

**Names:**
*conventional long form:* Swiss Confederation
*conventional short form:* Switzerland
*local long form:* Schweizerische Eidgenossenschaft (German) Confederation Suisse (French) Confederazione Svizzera (Italian)
*local short form:* Schweiz (German) Suisse (French) Svizzera (Italian)
**Digraph:** SZ
**Type:** federal republic
**Capital:** Bern
**Administrative divisions:** 26 cantons (cantons, singular—canton in French; cantoni, singular—cantone in Italian; kantone, singular—kanton in German); Aargau, Ausser-Rhoden, Basel-Landschaft, Basel-Stadt, Bern, Fribourg, Geneve, Glarus, Graubunden, Inner-Rhoden, Jura, Luzern, Neuchatel, Nidwalden, Obwalden, Sankt Gallen, Schaffhausen, Schwyz, Solothurn, Thurgau, Ticino, Uri, Valais, Vaud, Zug, Zurich
**Independence:** 1 August 1291
**National holiday:** Anniversary of the Founding of the Swiss Confederation, 1 August (1291)
**Constitution:** 29 May 1874

**Legal system:** civil law system influenced by customary law; judicial review of legislative acts, except with respect to federal decrees of general obligatory character; accepts compulsory ICJ jurisdiction, with reservations

**Suffrage:** 18 years of age; universal

**Executive branch:**

*chief of state and head of government:* President Otto STICH (1994 calendar year; presidency rotates annually); Vice President Kaspar VILLIGER (term runs concurrently with that of president)

*cabinet:* Federal Council (German— Bundesrat, French—Censeil Federal, Italian— Consiglio Federale); elected by the Federal Assembly from own members

**Legislative branch:** bicameral Federal Assembly (German—Bundesversammlung, French—Assemblee Federale, Italian— Assemblea Federale)

*Council of States:* (German—Standerat, French—Conseil des Etats, Italian—Consiglio degli Stati) elections last held throughout 1991 (next to be held NA 1995); results—percent of vote by party NA; seats—(46 total) FDP 18, CVP 16, SVP 4, SPS 3, LPS 3, LdU 1, Ticino League 1

*National Council:* (German—Nationalrat, French—Conseil National, Italian—Consiglio Nazionale) elections last held 20 October 1991 (next to be held NA October 1995); results— percent of vote by party NA; seats—(200 total) FDP 44, SPS 42, CVP 37, SVP 25, GPS 14, LPS 10, AP 8, LdU 6, SD 5, EVP 3, PdA 2, Ticino League 2, other 2

**Judicial branch:** Federal Supreme Court

**Political parties and leaders:** Free Democratic Party (FDP), Bruno HUNZIKER, president; Social Democratic Party (SPS), Helmut HUBACHER, chairman; Christian Democratic People's Party (CVP), Eva SEGMULLER-WEBER, chairman; Swiss People's Party (SVP), Hans UHLMANN, president; Green Party (GPS), Peter SCHMID, president; Automobile Party (AP), DREYER; Alliance of Independents' Party (LdU), Dr. Franz JAEGER, president; Swiss Democratic Party (SD), NA; Evangelical People's Party (EVP), Max DUNKI, president; Workers' Party (PdA; Communist), Jean SPIELMANN,

general secretary; Ticino League, leader NA; Liberal Party (LPS), Gilbert COUTAU, president

**Member of:** AfDB, AG (observer), AsDB, Australian Group, BIS, CCC, CE, CERN, COCOM (cooperating), CSCE, EBRD, ECE, EFTA, ESA, FAO, G-8, G-10, GATT, IADB, IAEA, IBRD, ICAO, ICC, ICFTU, IDA, IEA, IFAD, IFC, ILO, IMF, IMO, INMARSAT, INTELSAT, INTERPOL, IOC, IOM, ISO, ITU, LORCS, MINURSO, MTRC, NAM (guest), NEA, NSG, OAS (observer), OECD, PCA, UN (observer), UNCTAD, UNESCO, UNHCR, UNIDO, UNOMIG, UNPROFOR, UNTSO, UPU, WCL, WHO, WIPO, WMO, WTO, ZC

**Diplomatic representation in US:**

*chief of mission:* Ambassador Carlo JAGMETTI

*chancery:* 2900 Cathedral Avenue NW, Washington, DC 20008

*telephone:* (202) 745-7900

*FAX:* (202) 387-2564

*consulate(s) general:* Atlanta, Chicago, Houston, Los Angeles, New York, and San Francisco

**US diplomatic representation:**

*chief of mission:* (vacant); Charge d'Affaires Michael C. POLT

*embassy:* Jubilaeumstrasse 93, 3005 Bern

*mailing address:* use embassy street address

*telephone:* [41] (31) 357-7011

*FAX:* [41] (31) 357-7344

*branch office:* Geneva

*consulate(s) general:* Zurich

**Flag:** red square with a bold, equilateral white cross in the center that does not extend to the edges of the flag

---

**U.S. Government Contacts:**

**U.S. Trade Desk**: (202) 482-2920

**American Embassy Commercial Section**
Jubilaeumstrasse 93
3005 Bern, Switzerland
c/o U.S. Department of State (Bern)
Washington, DC 20521-5110
Tel: 41-31-437-341
Fax: 41-31-437336

# The Internationalist

## Switzerland Government Contacts:

**Embassy of Switzerland Commercial Section**
2900 Cathedral Avenue, N.W.
Washington, DC 20008
Tel: (202) 745-7900

**Federal Office for Labor and Industry**
Mattenhofstrasse 5
CH-3003 Bern
Tel: 00 41 31/61 28 71
Fax: 00 41 31/46 41 04

**Canton of Berne**
Dr. Hugo Tschudin
215 River Vale Road
River Vale, NJ 07675
Tel: (201) 666-3456
Fax: (201) 666-8470

**Canton of Geneva**
Development Counsellors International
461 Park Avenue South (31st St.), 12th Fl.
New York, NY 10016
Tel: (212) 725-0707
Fax: (212) 725-2254

**Canton of Neuchatel**
Mr. MIchael R. Oestreicher
Suite 1400
312 Walnut Street
Cincinnati, OH 45202
Tel: (513) 352-6630
Fax: (513) 241-4771

**Canton of Fribourg**
GCR International Inc.
641 Lexington Ave. 27th Floor
New York, NY 10022
Tel: (212) 888-1525
Fax: (212) 888-1751

**Canton of Vaud**
Graydon Associates, INc.
P.O. Box 566
216 Maple Ave
Red Bank, NY 07701
Tel: (908) 741-2690
Fax: (908) 741-4148

## Chambers of Commerce & Organizations:

**Swiss American Chamber of Commerce**
Talacker 41
8001 Zurich, Switzerland
Tel: 41-1-211-2454
Fax: 41-1-211-9572

## Legal Services:

**Benz & Partner**
Dufourstrasse 24
8008 Zurich, Switzerland
Tel: 268 251 17 77
Fax: 268 251 18 38
*Licenses, Franchising, Bankruptcy, Transportation Law, Arbitration and Commercial Litigation.*

**Gambazzi & Berra**
via Dogana Vecchia 2/via Nassa
6900 Lugano, Switzerland
Tel: 268 091 22.70.91
Fax: 268 091 23.68.62
*General and International Practice, Business, Corporate, Banking and Financial Law and Services, Real Estate, Litigation and Arbitration.*

**Wiederkehr Forster & Weber**
Bahnhofstrasse 44
8023 Zurich, Switzerland
Tel: 268 211 13 32
Fax: 268 211 80 68
*General Contracts, Corporate, Banking, Tax, Antitrust and Unfair Competition, Estate Planning, Commercial Litigation, Arbitration.*

## Travel:

**International Airlines to Country:**
American, United

**International Hotels in Country:**
Zurich:
Baur au Lac, Tel: 411/2211650, Fax: 411/2118139
Dolder Grand, Tel: 411/2516231, Fax: 411/2518829
Savoy Baur en Ville, Tel: 411/2115360, Fax: 411/2111467.

# TURKEY

400 km

Black Sea

Mediterranean Sea

## Economy

**Overview:** In early 1994, after an impressive economic performance through most of the 1980s, Turkey faces its most damaging economic crisis in the last 15 years. Sparked by the downgrading in mid-January of Turkey's international credit rating by two US credit rating agencies, the crisis stems from two years of loose fiscal and monetary policies that have exacerbated inflation and allowed the public debt, money supply, and current account deficit to explode. Under Prime Minister CILLER, Ankara has followed seriously flawed policies that have destroyed public confidence in the government's ability to manage the economy. Inflation is now running at an annual rate of 107% and the public sector deficit is equivalent to 16% of GDP. Turkish firms have been hurt by high interest rates and a dramatic drop in consumer demand. Three Turkish banks have folded and the stock market has fallen 48% since the beginning of the year. Economic growth may drop to between 0% and 2% in 1994, compared to 7.3% in 1993. Moreover, the government is facing a severe cash crunch. In March 1994, the treasury came close to defaulting on a loan, and official foreign currency reserves are equal to less than two months' worth of imports. The unprecedented effort by the Kurdistan Workers' Party (PKK) to raise the economic costs of its insurgency against the Turkish state is adding to Turkey's economic problems. Attacks against the tourism industry have cut tourist revenues, which account for about 3% of GDP, while economic activity in southeastern Turkey, where most of the violence occurs, has dropped considerably. To cope with the economic crisis and instill domestic and international investor confidence in the fragile coalition government, CILLER has asked the IMF to endorse a stabilization package she introduced in early April 1994. Negotiations are underway for a standby agreement, which would give Turkey access to $450 million this year and enable her cash-starved government to return to the foreign capital markets.

**National product:** GDP—purchasing power equivalent—$312.4 billion (1993)

**National product real growth rate:** 7.3% (1993)

**National product per capita:** $5,100 (1993)

**Inflation rate (consumer prices):** 65% (1993)

**Unemployment rate:** 12.2% (1993)

**Budget:**
*revenues:* $36.5 billion
*expenditures:* $47.6 billion, including capital expenditures of $5 billion (1994)

**Exports:** $14.9 billion (f.o.b., 1992)
*commodities:* manufactured products 72%, foodstuffs 23%, mining products 4%
*partners:* EC countries 53%, US 6%, Russia 4%, Saudi Arabia 3%

**Imports:** $22.9 billion (c.i.f., 1992)
*commodities:* manufactured products 68%, fuels 17%, foodstuffs 4%
*partners:* EC countries 44%, US 11%, Saudi Arabia 7%, Russia 5%

**External debt:** $59.4 billion (1993)

**Industrial production:** growth rate 4.3% (1992); accounts for 28% of GDP

**Electricity:**
*capacity:* 14,400,000 kW
*production:* 44 billion kWh
*consumption per capita:* 750 kWh (1991)
**Industries:** textiles, food processing, mining (coal, chromite, copper, boron minerals), steel, petroleum, construction, lumber, paper
**Agriculture:** accounts for 16% of GDP and employs about half of working force; products—tobacco, cotton, grain, olives, sugar beets, pulses, citrus fruit, variety of animal products; self-sufficient in food most years
**Illicit drugs:** major transit route for Southwest Asian heroin and hashish to Western Europe and the US via air, land, and sea routes; major Turkish, Iranian, and other international trafficking organizations operate out of Istanbul; laboratories to convert imported morphine base into heroin are in remote regions of Turkey as well as near Istanbul; government maintains strict controls over areas of legal opium poppy cultivation and output of poppy straw concentrate
**Economic aid:**
*recipient:* US commitments, including Ex-Im (FY70-89), $2.3 billion; Western (non-US) countries, ODA and OOF bilateral commitments (1970-89), $10.1 billion; OPEC bilateral aid (1979-89), $665 million; Communist countries (1970-89), $4.5 billion
*note:* aid for Persian Gulf war efforts from coalition allies (1991), $4.1 billion; aid pledged for Turkish Defense Fund, $2.5 billion
**Currency:** 1 Turkish lira (TL) = 100 kurus
**Exchange rates:** Turkish liras (TL) per US$1—15,196.1 (January 1994), 10,983.3 (1993), 6,872.4 (1992), 4,171.8 (1991), 2,608.6 (1990), 2,121.7 (1989)
**Fiscal year:** calendar year

## Communications

**Railroads:** 8,429 km 1.435-meter gauge (including 795 km electrified)
**Highways:**
*total:* 320,611 km
*paved:* 27,000 km (including 138 km of expressways)
*unpaved:* gravel 18,500 km; earth 275,111 km (1988)

**Inland waterways:** about 1,200 km
**Pipelines:** crude oil 1,738 km, petroleum products 2,321 km, natural gas 708 km
**Ports:** Iskenderun, Istanbul, Mersin, Izmir
**Merchant marine:** 390 ships (1,000 GRT or over) totaling 4,664,205 GRT/8,163,379 DWT, short-sea passenger 7, passenger-cargo 1, cargo 195, container 2, roll-on/roll-off cargo 5, refrigerated cargo 2, livestock carrier 1, oil tanker 41, chemical tanker 10, liquefied gas 4, combination ore/oil 12, specialized tanker 2, bulk 103, combination bulk 5
**Airports:**
*total:* 113
*usable:* 105
*with permanent-surface runways:* 69
*with runways over 3,659 m:* 3
*with runways 2,440-3,659 m:* 32
*with runways 1,220-2,439 m:* 27
**Telecommunications:** fair domestic and international systems; trunk radio relay microwave network; limited open wire network; 3,400,000 telephones; broadcast stations—15 AM; 94 FM; 357 TV; 1 satellite ground station operating in the INTELSAT (2 Atlantic Ocean antennas) and EUTELSAT systems; 1 submarine cable

## Defense Forces

**Branches:** Land Forces, Navy (including Naval Air and Naval Infantry), Air Force, Coast Guard, Gendarmerie
**Manpower availability:** males age 15-49 16,112,783; fit for military service 9,828,853; reach military age (20) annually 614,252 (1994 est.)
**Defense expenditures:** exchange rate conversion—$14 billion, 5.6% of GDP (1994)

## Geography

**Location:** Southwestern Asia (that part west of the Bosporus is sometimes included with Europe), bordering the Mediterranean Sea and Black Sea, between Bulgaria and Iran
**Map references:** Africa, Europe, Middle East, Standard Time Zones of the World
**Area:**
*total area:* 780,580 sq km

*land area:* 770,760 sq km
*comparative area:* slightly larger than Texas
**Land boundaries:** total 2,627 km, Armenia
268 km, Azerbaijan 9 km, Bulgaria 240 km,
Georgia 252 km, Greece 206 km, Iran 499 km,
Iraq 331 km, Syria 822 km
**Coastline:** 7,200 km
**Maritime claims:**
*exclusive economic zone:* in Black Sea only—
to the maritime boundary agreed upon with the
former USSR
*territorial sea:* 6 nm in the Aegean Sea,
12 nm in the Black Sea and in the
Mediterranean Sea
**International disputes:** complex maritime
and air (but not territorial) disputes with
Greece in Aegean Sea; Cyprus question; Hatay
question with Syria; ongoing dispute with
downstream riparians (Syria and Iraq) over
water development plans for the Tigris and
Euphrates Rivers
**Climate:** temperate; hot, dry summers with
mild, wet winters; harsher in interior
**Terrain:** mostly mountains; narrow coastal
plain; high central plateau (Anatolia)
**Natural resources:** antimony, coal,
chromium, mercury, copper, borate, sulphur,
iron ore
**Land use:**
*arable land:* 30%
*permanent crops:* 4%
*meadows and pastures:* 12%
*forest and woodland:* 26%
*other:* 28%
**Irrigated land:** 22,200 sq km (1989 est.)
**Environment:**
*current issues:* water pollution from dumping
of chemicals and detergents; air pollution;
deforestation
*natural hazards:* subject to very severe
earthquakes, especially in northern Turkey,
along an arc extending from the Sea of
Marmara to Lake Van
*international agreements:* party to—Air
Pollution, Nuclear Test Ban, Ozone Layer
Protection, Ship Pollution; signed, but not
ratified—Biodiversity, Environmental
Modification, Hazardous Wastes,
**Note:** strategic location controlling the
Turkish Straits (Bosporus, Sea of Marmara,
Dardanelles) that link Black and Aegean Seas

## People

**Population:** 62,153,898 (July 1994 est.)
**Population growth rate:** 2.02% (1994 est.)
**Birth rate:** 25.98 births/1,000 population
(1994 est.)
**Death rate:** 5.8 deaths/1,000 population
(1994 est.)
**Net migration rate:** 0 migrant(s)/1,000
population (1994 est.)
**Infant mortality rate:** 48.8 deaths/1,000 live
births (1994 est.)
**Life expectancy at birth:**
*total population:* 70.94 years
*male:* 68.61 years
*female:* 73.38 years (1994 est.)
**Total fertility rate:** 3.21 children born/
woman (1994 est.)
**Nationality:**
*noun:* Turk(s)
*adjective:* Turkish
**Ethnic divisions:** Turkish 80%, Kurdish 20%
**Religions:** Muslim 99.8% (mostly Sunni),
other 0.2% (Christian and Jews)
**Languages:** Turkish (official), Kurdish,
Arabic
**Literacy:** age 15 and over can read and write
(1990 est.)
*total population:* 81%
*male:* 90%
*female:* 71%
**Labor force:** 20.8 million
*by occupation:* agriculture 48%, services 32%,
industry 20%
*note:* about 1,800,000 Turks work abroad
(1993)

## Government

**Names:**
*conventional long form:* Republic of Turkey
*conventional short form:* Turkey
*local long form:* Turkiye Cumhuriyeti
*local short form:* Turkiye
**Digraph:** TU
**Type:** republican parliamentary democracy
**Capital:** Ankara
**Administrative divisions:** 73 provinces
(iller, singular—il); Adana, Adiyaman, Afyon,
Agri, Aksaray, Amasya, Ankara, Antalya,

Artvin, Aydin, Balikesir, Batman, Bayburt, Bilecik, Bingol, Bitlis, Bolu, Burdur, Bursa, Canakkale, Cankiri, Corum, Denizli, Diyarbakir, Edirne, Elazig, Erzincan, Erzurum, Eskisehir, Gazi Antep, Giresun, Gumushane, Hakkari, Hatay, Icel, Isparta, Istanbul, Izmir, Kahraman Maras, Karaman, Kars, Kastamonu, Kayseri, Kirikkale, Kirklareli, Kirsehir, Kocaeli, Konya, Kutahya, Malatya, Manisa, Mardin, Mugla, Mus, Nevsehir, Nigde, Ordu, Rize, Sakarya, Samsun, Sanli Urfa, Siirt, Sinop, Sirnak, Sivas, Tekirdag, Tokat, Trabzon, Tunceli, Usak, Van, Yozgat, Zonguldak

**Independence:** 29 October 1923 (successor state to the Ottoman Empire)

**National holiday:** Anniversary of the Declaration of the Republic, 29 October (1923)

**Constitution:** 7 November 1982

**Legal system:** derived from various continental legal systems; accepts compulsory ICJ jurisdiction, with reservations

**Suffrage:** 21 years of age; universal

**Executive branch:**

*chief of state:* President Suleyman DEMIREL (since 16 May 1993)

*head of government:* Prime Minister Tansu CILLER (since 5 July 1993)

*National Security Council:* advisory body to the President and the Cabinet

*cabinet:* Council of Ministers; appointed by the president on nomination of the prime minister

**Legislative branch:** unicameral

*Turkish Grand National Assembly:* (Turkiye Buyuk Millet Meclisi) elections last held 20 October 1991 (next to be held NA October 1996); results—DYP 27.03%, ANAP 24.01%, SHP 20.75%, RP 16.88%, DSP 10.75%, SBP 0.44%, independent 0.14%; seats—(450 total) DYP 178, ANAP 115, SHP 86, RP 40, MCP 19, DSP 7, other 5

*note:* seats held by various parties are subject to change due to defections, creation of new parties, and ouster or death of sitting deputies; present seats by party are as follows: DYP 178, ANAP 101, SHP 55, RP 39, CHP 18, MHP 13, DEP 13, BBP 7, DSP 3, YP 3, MP 2, independents 10, vacant 8

**Judicial branch:** Court of Cassation

**Political parties and leaders:** Correct Way Party (DYP), Tansu CILLER; Motherland Party (ANAP), Mesut YILMAZ; Social Democratic Populist Party (SHP), Murat KARAYALCIN; Welfare Party (RP), Necmettin ERBAKAN; Democratic Left Party (DSP), Bulent ECEVIT; Nationalist Action Party (MHP), Alparslan TURKES; Democracy Party (DEP), Hatip DICLE; Socialist Unity Party (SBP), Sadun AREN; New Party (YP), Yusuf Bozkurt OZAL; Republican People's Party (CHP), Deniz BAYKAL; Labor Party (IP), Dogu PERINCEK; National Party (MP), Aykut EDIBALI; Democrat Party (DP), Aydin MENDERES; Grand Unity Party (BBP), Muhsin YAZICIOGLU; Rebirth Party (YDP), Hasan Celal GUZEL; People's Democracy Party (HADEP), Murat BOZLAK; Main Path Party (ANAYOL), Gurcan BASER

**Other political or pressure groups:** Turkish Confederation of Labor (TURK-IS), Bayram MERAL

**Member of:** AsDB, BIS, BSEC, CCC, CE, CERN (observer), COCOM, CSCE, EBRD, ECE, ECO, FAO, GATT, IAEA, IBRD, ICAO, ICC, ICFTU, IDA, IDB, IEA, IFAD, IFC, ILO, IMF, IMO, INMARSAT, INTELSAT, INTERPOL, IOC, IOM (observer), ISO, ITU, LORCS, NACC, NATO, NEA, OECD, OIC, PCA, UN, UNCTAD, UNESCO, UNHCR, UNIDO, UNIKOM, UNOSOM, UNRWA, UPU, WEU (associate), WFTU, WHO, WIPO, WMO, WTO

**Diplomatic representation in US:**

*chief of mission:* Ambassador Nuzhet KANDEMIR

*chancery:* 1714 Massachusetts Avenue NW, Washington, DC 20036

*telephone:* (202) 659-8200

*consulate(s) general:* Chicago, Houston, Los Angeles, and New York

**US diplomatic representation:**

*chief of mission:* Ambassador Richard C. BARKLEY

*embassy:* 110 Ataturk Boulevard, Ankara

*mailing address:* PSC 93, Box 5000, Ankara, or APO AE 09823

*telephone:* [90] (312) 468-6110 through 6128

*FAX:* [90] (312) 467-0019

*consulate(s) general:* Istanbul

*consulate(s):* Adana

**Flag:** red with a vertical white crescent (the closed portion is toward the hoist side) and white five-pointed star centered just outside the crescent opening

## U.S. Government Contacts:

**U.S. Trade Desk**: (202) 482-3945

**American Embassy Commercial Section**
110 Ataturk Boulevard
Ankara, Turkey
APO AE 09822
Tel: 90-4-167-0949
Fax: 90-4-167-1366

**American Consulate General - Istanbul Commercial Section**
104-108 Mesrutiyet Caddesi
Tepebasl
Istanbul, Turkey
APO AE 09827
Tel: 90-1-151-1651
Fax: 90-1-152-2417

## Turkey Government Contacts:

**Embassy of Turkey Commercial Section**
2523 Massachusetts Avenue, N.W.
Washington, DC 20008
Tel: (202) 483-5366

**Turkish International Cooperation Agency (TICA)**
P.O. Box 86 Ahmetler
06428 Ankara/Turkey
Tel: 90 312 417 27 90
Fax: 90 312 417 27 99

**Turkish Ministry of Finance**
(T.C. Maliye Bakanligi)
Ankara
Tel: 90 312 310 38 80 - 419 12 00
Fax: 90 312 310 51 59 - 324 14 26
310 52 23 - 311 83 78 - 425 00 58

**Turkish Ministry of Industry and Commerce**
(T.C. Sanayi ve Ticaret Bakanligi)
Ankara
Tel: 90 312 231 72 80
Fax: 90 312 230 87 04 - 230 81 47
230 87 85 - 230 42 51

## Chambers of Commerce & Organizations:

**Turkish-American Businessmen's Association**
Fahri Gizdem Sokak 22/5
80280 Gayrettepe, Istanbul, Turkey
Tel: (901) 274-2824/288-6212
Fax: (901) 275-9316

## Legal Services:

**White and Case**
1747 Penn. Ave
Suite 500
Washington, DC
Tel: (202) 872-0013
Fax: (202) 872-0210

**Arnold and Porter**
1200 New Hampshire Ave, N.E.
Washington, DC 20036
Tel: (202) 872-6784
Fax: (202) 872-6720

## Consultants:

**PROFIN - Project Development and Financing Consultant Co.**
Cinnah Cad. 100/2 06550
Cankaya Ankara
Turkey
Tel: 90-312-440-23-17
Fax: 90-312-440-23-15

## Travel:

**International Hotels in Country:**
Istanbul:
Ciragan Palace, Tel: 90 212/258-3377, Fax: 90 212/259-6687
Pera Palace, Tel: 90 212/251-4560, Fax: 90 212/251-4089
Hilton, 90 212/231-4646, Fax: 90 212/240-4165.

# UNITED KINGDOM

## Economy

**Overview:** The UK is one of the world's great trading powers and financial centers, and its economy ranks among the four largest in Western Europe. The economy is essentially capitalistic; over the past thirteen years the ruling Tories have greatly reduced public ownership and contained the growth of social welfare programs. Agriculture is intensive, highly mechanized, and efficient by European standards, producing about 60% of food needs with only 1% of the labor force. The UK has large coal, natural gas, and oil reserves, and primary energy production accounts for 12% of GDP, one of the highest shares of any industrial nation. Services, particularly banking, insurance, and business services, account by far for the largest proportion of GDP while industry continues to decline in importance, now employing only 25% of the work force and generating only 21% of GDP. The economy is emerging out of its 3-year recession with only weak recovery in 1993; even so, the economy fared better in 1993 than the economies of most other European countries. Unemployment is hovering around 10% of the labor force. The government in 1992 adopted a pro-growth strategy, cutting interest rates sharply and removing the pound from the European exchange rate mechanism. Excess industrial capacity probably will moderate inflation which for the first time in a decade is below the EC average. The major economic policy question for Britain in the 1990s is the terms on which it participates in the financial and economic integration of Europe.

**National product:** GDP—purchasing power equivalent—$980.2 billion (1993)

**National product real growth rate:** 2.1% (1993)

**National product per capita:** $16,900 (1993)

**Inflation rate (consumer prices):** 2.6% (1993)

**Unemployment rate:** 10.3% (1993)

**Budget:**
*revenues:* $325.5 billion
*expenditures:* $400.9 billion, including capital expenditures of $33 billion (1993 est.)

**Exports:** $190.1 billion (f.o.b., 1993)
*commodities:* manufactured goods, machinery, fuels, chemicals, semifinished goods, transport equipment
*partners:* EC countries 56.7% (Germany 14.0%, France 11.1%, Netherlands 7.9%), US 10.9%

**Imports:** $221.6 billion (c.i.f., 1993)
*commodities:* manufactured goods, machinery, semifinished goods, foodstuffs, consumer goods
*partners:* EC countries 51.7% (Germany 14.9%, France 9.3%, Netherlands 8.4%), US 11.6%

**External debt:** $16.2 billion (June 1992)

**Industrial production:** growth rate 2.2% (1993 est.)

**Electricity:**
*capacity:* 99,000,000 kW
*production:* 317 billion kWh
*consumption per capita:* 5,480 kWh (1992)

**Industries:** production machinery including machine tools, electric power equipment, equipment for the automation of production, railroad equipment, shipbuilding, aircraft, motor vehicles and parts, electronics and communications equipment, metals, chemicals, coal, petroleum, paper and paper products, food processing, textiles, clothing, and other consumer goods

**Agriculture:** accounts for only 1.5% of GDP and 1% of labor force; highly mechanized and efficient farms; wide variety of crops and livestock products produced; about 60% self-sufficient in food and feed needs

**Illicit drugs:** gateway country for Latin American cocaine entering the European market; producer of synthetic drugs; money-laundering center

**Economic aid:** *donor:* ODA and OOF commitments (1992-93), $3.2 billion

**Currency:** 1 British pound (£) = 100 pence

**Exchange rates:** British pounds (£) per US$1—0.6699 (January 1994), 0.6033 (1993). 0.5664 (1992), 0.5652 (1991), 0.5603 (1990), 0.6099 (1989)

**Fiscal year:** 1 April-31 March

## Communications

**Railroads:** UK, 16,914 km total; Great Britain's British Railways (BR) operates 16,584 km 1,435-mm (standard) gauge (including 4,545 km electrified and 12,591 km double or multiple track), several additional small standard-gauge and narrow-gauge lines are privately owned and operated; Northern Ireland Railways (NIR) operates 330 km 1,600-mm gauge (including 190 km double track)

**Highways:**
*total:* 362,982 km (Great Britian 339,483 km; Northern Ireland 23,499 km)
*paved:* 362,390 km (Great Britian 339,483 km, including 2,573 km limited access divided highway; Northern Ireland 22,907 km)
*unpaved:* gravel 592 km (in Northern Ireland)

**Inland waterways:** 2,291 total; British Waterways Board, 606 km; Port Authorities, 706 km; other, 979 km

**Pipelines:** crude oil (almost all insignificant) 933 km, petroleum products 2,993 km, natural gas 12,800 km

**Ports:** London, Liverpool, Felixstowe, Tees and Hartlepool, Dover, Sullom Voe, Southampton

**Merchant marine:** 180 ships (1,000 GRT or over) totaling 3,428,571 GRT/4,297,489 DWT, passenger 7, short-sea passenger 14, cargo 35, container 24, roll-on/roll-off cargo 13, refrigerated cargo 1, oil tanker 59, chemical tanker 2, liquefied gas 5, specialized tanker 1, bulk 17, combination bulk 1, passenger cargo 1

**Airports:**
*total:* 497
*usable:* 388
*with permanent-surface runways:* 251
*with runways over 3,659 m:* 1
*with runways 2,440-3,659 m:* 37
*with runways 1,220-2,439 m:* 133

**Telecommunications:** technologically advanced domestic and international system; 30,200,000 telephones; equal mix of buried cables, microwave and optical-fiber systems; excellent countrywide broadcast systems; broadcast stations—225 AM, 525 (mostly repeaters) FM, 207 (3,210 repeaters) TV; 40 coaxial submarine cables; 5 satellite ground stations operating in INTELSAT (7 Atlantic Ocean and 3 Indian Ocean), INMARSAT, and EUTELSAT systems; at least 8 large international switching centers

## Defense Forces

**Branches:** Army, Royal Navy (including Royal Marines), Royal Air Force

**Manpower availability:** males age 15-49 14,432,081; fit for military service 12,056,828

**Defense expenditures;** exchange rate conversion—$42.5 billion, 3.8% of GDP (FY92/93)

## Geography

**Location:** Western Europe, bordering on the North Atlantic Ocean and the North Sea, between Ireland and France

**Map references:** Europe, Standard Time Zones of the World
**Area:**
*total area:* 244,820 sq km
*land area:* 241,590 sq km
*comparative area:* slightly smaller than Oregon
*note:* includes Rockall and Shetland Islands
**Land boundaries:** total 360 km, Ireland 360 km
**Coastline:** 12,429 km
**Maritime claims:**
*continental shelf:* as defined in continental shelf orders or in accordance with agreed upon boundaries
*exclusive fishing zone:* 200 nm
*territorial sea:* 12 nm
**International disputes:** Northern Ireland question with Ireland; Gibraltar question with Spain; Argentina claims Falkland Islands (Islas Malvinas); Argentina claims South Georgia and the South Sandwich Islands; Mauritius claims island of Diego Garcia in British Indian Ocean Territory; Rockall continental shelf dispute involving Denmark, Iceland, and Ireland (Ireland and the UK have signed a boundary agreement in the Rockall area); territorial claim in Antarctica (British Antarctic Territory)
**Climate:** temperate; moderated by prevailing southwest winds over the North Atlantic Current; more than half of the days are overcast
**Terrain:** mostly rugged hills and low mountains; level to rolling plains in east and southeast
**Natural resources:** coal, petroleum, natural gas, tin, limestone, iron ore, salt, clay, chalk, gypsum, lead, silica
**Land use:**
*arable land:* 29%
*permanent crops:* 0%
*meadows and pastures:* 48%
*forest and woodland:* 9%
*other:* 14%
**Irrigated land:** 1,570 sq km (1989)
**Environment:**
*current issues:* sulfur dioxide emissions from power plants contribute to air pollution; some rivers polluted by agricultural wastes and coastal waters polluted because of large-scale disposal of sewage at sea
*natural hazards:* NA
*international agreements:* party to—Air Pollution, Air Pollution-Nitrogen Oxides, Antarctic Treaty, Climate Change, Endangered Species, Environmental Modification, Hazardous Wastes, Marine Dumping, Marine Life Conservation, Nuclear Test Ban, Ozone Layer Protection, Ship Pollution, Tropical Timber, Wetlands, Whaling; signed, but not ratified—Air Pollution-Volatile Organic Compounds, Antarctic-Environmental Protocol, Biodiversity
**Note:** lies near vital North Atlantic sea lanes; only 35 km from France and now linked by tunnel under the English Channel; because of heavily indented coastline, no location is more than 125 km from tidal waters

---

**People**

**Population:** 58,135,110 (July 1994 est.)
**Population growth rate:** 0.28% (1994 est.)
**Birth rate:** 13.39 births/1,000 population (1994 est.)
**Death rate:** 10.76 deaths/1,000 population (1994 est.)
**Net migration rate:** 0.17 migrant(s)/1,000 population (1994 est.)
**Infant mortality rate:** 7.2 deaths/1,000 live births (1994 est.)
**Life expectancy at birth:**
*total population:* 76.75 years
*male:* 73.94 years
*female:* 79.69 years (1994 est.)
**Total fertility rate:** 1.83 children born/ woman (1994 est.)
**Nationality:**
*noun:* Briton(s), British (collective pl.)
*adjective:* British
**Ethnic divisions:** English 81.5%, Scottish 9.6%, Irish 2.4%, Welsh 1.9%, Ulster 1.8%, West Indian, Indian, Pakistani, and other 2.8%
**Religions:** Anglican 27 million, Roman Catholic 9 million, Muslim 1 million, Presbyterian 800,000, Methodist 760,000, Sikh 400,000, Hindu 350,000, Jewish 300,000 (1991 est.)
*note:* the UK does not include a question on religion in its census

**Languages:** English, Welsh (about 26% of the population of Wales), Scottish form of Gaelic (about 60,000 in Scotland)
**Literacy:** age 15 and over can read and write (1978 est.)
*total population:* 99%
*male:* NA%
*female:* NA%
**Labor force:** 28.048 million
*by occupation:* services 62.8%, manufacturing and construction 25.0%, government 9.1%, energy 1.9%, agriculture 1.2% (June 1992)

## Government

**Names:**
*conventional long form:* United Kingdom of Great Britain and Northern Ireland
*conventional short form:* United Kingdom
**Abbreviation:** UK
**Digraph:** UK
**Type:** constitutional monarchy
**Capital:** London
**Administrative divisions:** 47 counties, 7 metropolitan counties, 26 districts, 9 regions, and 3 islands areas
*England:* 39 counties, 7 metropolitan counties*; Avon, Bedford, Berkshire, Buckingham, Cambridge, Cheshire, Cleveland, Cornwall, Cumbria, Derby, Devon, Dorset, Durham, East Sussex, Essex, Gloucester, Greater London*, Greater Manchester*, Hampshire, Hereford and Worcester, Hertford, Humberside, Isle of Wight, Kent, Lancashire, Leicester, Lincoln, Merseyside*, Norfolk, Northampton, Northumberland, North Yorkshire, Nottingham, Oxford, Shropshire, Somerset, South Yorkshire*, Stafford, Suffolk, Surrey, Tyne and Wear*, Warwick, West Midlands*, West Sussex, West Yorkshire*, Wiltshire
*Northern Ireland:* 26 districts; Antrim, Ards, Armagh, Ballymena, Ballymoney, Banbridge, Belfast, Carrickfergus, Castlereagh, Coleraine, Cookstown, Craigavon, Down, Dungannon, Fermanagh, Larne, Limavady, Lisburn, Londonderry, Magherafelt, Moyle, Newry and Mourne, Newtownabbey, North Down, Omagh, Strabane

*Scotland:* 9 regions, 3 islands areas*; Borders, Central, Dumfries and Galloway, Fife, Grampian, Highland, Lothian, Orkney*, Shetland*, Strathclyde, Tayside, Western Isles*
*Wales:* 8 counties; Clwyd, Dyfed, Gwent, Gwynedd, Mid Glamorgan, Powys, South Glamorgan, West Glamorgan
**Dependent areas:** Anguilla, Bermuda, British Indian Ocean Territory, British Virgin Islands, Cayman Islands, Falkland Islands, Gibraltar, Guernsey, Hong Kong (scheduled to become a Special Administrative Region of China on 1 July 1997), Jersey, Isle of Man, Montserrat, Pitcairn Islands, Saint Helena, South Georgia and the South Sandwich Islands, Turks and Caicos Islands
**Independence:** 1 January 1801 (United Kingdom established)
**National holiday:** Celebration of the Birthday of the Queen (second Saturday in June)
**Constitution:** unwritten; partly statutes, partly common law and practice
**Legal system:** common law tradition with early Roman and modern continental influences; no judicial review of Acts of Parliament; accepts compulsory ICJ jurisdiction, with reservations
**Suffrage:** 18 years of age; universal
**Executive branch:**
*chief of state:* Queen ELIZABETH II (since 6 February 1952); Heir Apparent Prince CHARLES (son of the Queen, born 14 November 1948)
*head of government:* Prime Minister John MAJOR (since 28 November 1990)
*cabinet:* Cabinet of Ministers
**Legislative branch:** bicameral Parliament
*House of Lords:* consists of a 1,200-member body, four-fifths are hereditary peers, 2 archbishops, 24 other senior bishops, serving and retired Lords of Appeal in Ordinary, other life peers, Scottish peers
*House of Commons:* elections last held 9 April 1992 (next to be held by NA April 1997); results—Conservative 41.9%, Labor 34.5%, Liberal Democratic 17.9%, other 5.7%; seats—(651 total) Conservative 336, Labor 271, Liberal Democratic 20, other 24

**Judicial branch:** House of Lords
**Political parties and leaders:** Conservative and Unionist Party, John MAJOR; Labor Party; Liberal Democrats (LD), Jeremy (Paddy) ASHDOWN; Scottish National Party, Alex SALMOND; Welsh National Party (Plaid Cymru), Dafydd Iwan WIGLEY; Ulster Unionist Party (Northern Ireland), James MOLYNEAUX; Democratic Unionist Party (Northern Ireland), Rev. Ian PAISLEY; Ulster Popular Unionist Party (Northern Ireland), Sir James KILFEDDER; Social Democratic and Labor Party (SDLP, Northern Ireland), John HUME; Sinn Fein (Northern Ireland), Gerry ADAMS
**Other political or pressure groups:** Trades Union Congress; Confederation of British Industry; National Farmers' Union; Campaign for Nuclear Disarmament
**Member of:** AfDB, AG (observer), AsDB, Australian Group, BIS, C, CCC, CDB (non-regional), CE, CERN, COCOM, CSCE, EBRD, EC, ECA (associate), ECE, ECLAC, EIB, ESCAP, ESA, FAO, G-5, G-7, G-10, GATT, IADB, IAEA, IBRD, ICAO, ICC, ICFTU, IDA, IEA, IFAD, IFC, ILO, IMF, IMO, INMARSAT, INTELSAT, INTERPOL, IOC, IOM (observer), ISO, ITU, LORCS, MINURSO, MTRC, NACC, NATO, NEA, NSG, OECD, PCA, SPC, UN, UNCTAD, UNFICYP, UNHCR, UNIDO, UNIKOM, UNPROFOR, UNRWA, UN Security Council, UNTAC, UN Trusteeship Council, UPU, WCL, WEU, WHO, WIPO, WMO, ZC
**Diplomatic representation in US:**
*chief of mission:* Ambassador Sir Robin RENWICK
*chancery:* 3100 Massachusetts Avenue NW, Washington, DC 20008
*telephone:* (202) 462-1340
*FAX:* (202) 898-4255
*consulate(s) general:* Atlanta, Boston, Chicago, Cleveland, Houston, Los Angeles, New York, and San Francisco,
*consulate(s):* Dallas, Miami, Nuku'alofa, and Seattle
**US diplomatic representation:**
*chief of mission:* Ambassador-designate Adm. William CROWE
*embassy:* 24/31 Grosvenor Square, London, W.1A1AE

*mailing address:* PSC 801, Box 40, FPO AE 09498-4040
*telephone:* [44] (71) 499-9000
*FAX:* [44] (71) 409-1637
*consulate(s) general:* Belfast and Edinburgh
**Flag:** blue with the red cross of Saint George (patron saint of England) edged in white superimposed on the diagonal red cross of Saint Patrick (patron saint of Ireland) which is superimposed on the diagonal white cross of Saint Andrew (patron saint of Scotland); known as the Union Flag or Union Jack; the design and colors (especially the Blue Ensign) have been the basis for a number of other flags including dependencies, Commonwealth countries, and others

---

**U.S. Government Contacts:**

**U.S. Trade Desk:** (202) 482-3748

**American Embassy Commercial Section**
24/31Grosvenor Square
London W. 1A 1AE, England
Box 40
FPO AE 09498
Tel: 44-71-499-9000
Fax: 44-71-491-4022

---

**United Kingdom Government Contacts:**

**Embassy of Great Britain Commercial Section**
3100 Massachusetts Avenue, N.W.
Washington, DC 20008
Tel: (202) 462-1340

---

**Chambers of Commerce & Organizations:**

**American Chamber of Commerce in the United Kingdom**
75 Brook Street
London W1Y 2EB, England
Tel: 44-71-493-0381
Fax: 44-71-493-2394

**British American Chamber of Commerce**
8 Staple Inn
London, England WC1V7QH
Tel: 071-404-6400

**North American Business Club**
The Old Vicarage
Somerset Square, Nailsea
Bristol BS192DW
Tel: 44-275-8567000

## Legal Services:

**Bristows, Cooke & Carpmael**
10 Lincoln's Inn Fields
London WC2A 3BP, England
Tel: 44-071-242-0462
Fax: 44-071-242-1232
*Intellectual property and technology litigation and licensing, including patents, trade marks, trade secrets, copyright, registered design, design right and unfair competition.*

**Diaz-Bastien & Truan Abogados**
111 Park Street
London W1Y 3FB, England
Tel: 44-71-409-20-18
     44-71-491-33-08
Fax: 44-71-629-29-02
*Commercial, European Community, Import/Export, Intellectual Property, International, Media, Pharmaceutical, Tax-International, Tax-Offshore.*

**Gill Jennings & Every**
Broadgate House
7 Eldon Street
London EC2M, 7LH, England
Tel: 44-071-377-1377
Fax: 44-071-377-1310
*Patent Attorneys and Trademark Agents. Advocacy in the Boards of Appeal and Opposition Divisions of the European Patent Office.*

**Procope & Hornborg**
Burne House
88/89 High Holborn
London WC1V 6LS, England
Tel: 44-71-831-0292
Fax: 44-71-831-9074
*Firm engaged in Finnish and International Law Practice.*

## Travel:

**International Airlines to Country:**
American, Continental, Northwest, TWA, United

**International Hotels in Country:**
London:
Whites, Bayswater, Tel: 4471/262-2711, Fax: 4471/262-2147
Blakes, Chelsea and Kensington, Tel: 4471/370-6701
Claridges, West End, Tel: 4471/629-8860, Fax: 4471/499-2210
Savoy, West End, Tel: 4471/836-4343, Fax: 4471/240-6040.

# ADDENDA

# Abbreviations & Definitions

| | |
|---|---|
| avdp. | avoirdupois |
| c.i.f. | cost, insurance, and freight |
| CY | calendar year |
| DWT | deadweight ton |
| est. | estimate |
| Ex-Im | Export-Import Bank of the United States |
| f.o.b. | free on board |
| FRG | Federal Republic of Germany (West Germany); used for information dated before 3 October 1990 or CY91 |
| FSU | former Soviet Union |
| FY | fiscal year |
| FYROM | The Former Yugoslav Republic of Macedonia |
| GDP | gross domestic product |
| GDR | German Democratic Republic (East Germany); used for information dated before 3 October 1990 or CY91 |
| GNP | gross national product |
| GRT | gross register ton |
| GWP | gross world product |
| km | kilometer |
| kW | kilowatt |
| kWh | kilowatt hour |
| m | meter |
| NA | not available |
| NEGL | negligible |
| nm | nautical mile |
| NZ | New Zealand |
| ODA | official development assistance |
| OOF | other official flows |
| PDRY | People's Democratic Republic of Yemen [Yemen (Aden) or South Yemen]; used for information dated before 22 May 1990 or CY91 |
| sq km | square kilometer |
| sq mi | square mile |
| UAE | United Arab Emirates |
| UK | United Kingdom |
| US | United States |
| USSR | Union of Soviet Socialist Republics (Soviet Union); used for information dated before 25 December 1991 |
| YAR | Yemen Arab Republic [Yemen (Sanaa) or North Yemen]; used for information dated before 22 May 1990 or CY91 |

**Administrative divisions:** The numbers, designatory terms, and first-order administrative divisions are generally those approved by the US Board on Geographic Names (BGN). Changes that have been reported but not yet acted on by BGN are noted.

**Area:** Total area is the sum of all land and water areas delimited by international boundaries and/or coastlines. Land area is the aggregate of all surfaces delimited by international boundaries and/or coastlines, excluding inland water bodies (lakes, reservoirs, rivers). Comparative areas are based on total area equivalents. Most entities are compared with the entire US or one of the 50 states. The smaller entities are compared with Washington, DC (178 sq km, 69 sq mi) or The Mall in Washington, DC (0.59 sq km, 0.23 sq mi, 146 acres).

**Birth rate:** The average annual number of births during a year per 1,000 population at midyear; also known as crude birth rate.

**Dates of information:** In general, information available as of 1 January 1994 was used in the preparation of this edition. Population figures are estimates for 1 July 1994, with population growth rates estimated for calendar year 1994. Major political events have been updated through May 1994.

**Death rate:** The average annual number of deaths during a year per 1,000 population at midyear; also known as crude death rate.

**Digraphs:** The digraph is a two-letter "country code" that precisely identifies every entity without overlap, duplication, or omission. AF, for example, is the digraph for Afghanistan. It is a standardized geopolitical data element promulgated in the *Federal Information Processing Standards Publication* (FIPS) 10-3 by the National Institute of Standards and Technology (US Department of Commerce) and maintained by the Office of the Geographer (US Department of State). The digraph is used to eliminate confusion and incompatibility in the collection, processing, and dissemination of area-specific data and is particularly useful for interchanging data between databases.

**Diplomatic representation:** The US Government has diplomatic relations with 183 nations, including 177 of the 184 UN members (excluded UN members are Bhutan, Cuba, Iran, Iraq, North Korea, Vietnam, and former Yugoslavia). In addition, the US has diplomatic relations with 6 nations that are not in the UN—Holy See, Kiribati, Nauru, Switzerland, Tonga, and Tuvalu.

**Economic aid:** This entry refers to bilateral commitments of official development assistance (ODA) and other official flows (OOF). ODA is defined as financial assistance which is concessional in character, has the main objective to promote economic development and welfare of LDCs. and contains a grant element of at least 25%. OOF transactions are also official government assistance, but with a main objective other than development and with a grant element less than 25%. OOF transactions include official export credits (such as Ex-Im Bank credits), official equity and portfolio investment, and debt reorganization by the official sector that does not meet concessional terms. Aid is considered to have been committed when agreements are initialed by the parties involved and constitute a formal declaration of intent.

**Entities:** Some of the nations, dependent areas, areas of special sovereignty, and governments included in this publication are not independent, and others are not officially recognized by the US Government. "Nation" refers to a people politically organized into a sovereign state with a definite territory. "Dependent area" refers to a broad category of political entities that are associated in some way with a nation. Names used for page headings are usually the short-form names as approved by the US Board on Geographic Names. There are 266 entities in *The World Factbook* that may be categorized as follows:

NATIONS

183 UN members (excluding both the Socialist Federal Republic of Yugoslavia and the Federal Republic of Yugoslavia; membership status in the UN is still to be determined)

7 nations that are not members of the UN—Holy See, Kiribati, Nauru, Serbia and Montenegro, Switzerland, Tonga, Tuvalu

OTHER

1 Taiwan

DEPENDENT AREAS

6 Australia—Ashmore and Cartier Islands, Christmas Island, Cocos (Keeling) Islands, Coral Sea Islands, Heard Island and McDonald Islands, Norfolk Island

2 Denmark—Faroe Islands, Greenland

16 France—Bassas da India, Clipperton Island, Europa Island, French Guiana, French Polynesia, French Southern and Antarctic Lands, Glorioso Islands, Guadeloupe, Juan de Nova Island, Martinique, Mayotte, New Caledonia, Reunion, Saint Pierre and Miquelon, Tromelin Island, Wallis and Futuna

2 Netherlands—Aruba, Netherlands Antilles

3 New Zealand—Cook Islands, Niue, Tokelau

3 Norway—Bouvet Island, Jan Mayen, Svalbard

1 Portugal—Macau

16 United Kingdom—Anguilla, Bermuda, British Indian Ocean Territory, British Virgin Islands, Cayman Islands, Falkland Islands, Gibraltar, Guernsey, Hong Kong, Jersey, Isle of Man, Montserrat, Pitcairn Islands, Saint Helena, South Georgia and the South Sandwich Islands, Turks and Caicos Islands

15 United States—American Samoa, Baker Island, Guam, Howland Island, Jarvis Island, Johnston Atoll, Kingman Reef, Midway

Islands, Navassa Island, Northern Mariana Islands, Trust Territory of the Pacific Islands (Palau), Palmyra Atoll, Puerto Rico, Virgin Islands, Wake Island

MISCELLANEOUS

6    Antarctica, Gaza Strip, Paracel Islands, Spratly Islands, West Bank, Western Sahara

OTHER ENTITIES

4    oceans—Arctic Ocean, Atlantic Ocean, Indian Ocean, Pacific Ocean

1    World
--
266 total

**Exchange rate:** The value of a nation's monetary unit at a given date or over a given period of time, as expressed in units of local currency per US dollar and as determined by international market forces or official fiat.

**Gross domestic product (GDP):** The value of all final goods and services produced within a nation in a given year.

**Gross national product (GNP):** The value of all final goods and services produced within a nation in a given year, plus income earned abroad, minus income earned by foreigners from domestic production.

**Gross world product (GWP):** The aggregate value of all goods and services produced worldwide in a given year.

**GNP/GDP methodology:** In the "Economy" section, GNP/GDP dollar estimates for the great majority of countries are derived from *purchasing power parity* (PPP) calculations rather than from conversions at official currency exchange rates. The PPP method normally involves the use of international dollar price weights, which are applied to the quantities of goods and services produced in a given economy. In addition to the lack of reliable data from the majority of countries, the statistician faces a major difficulty in specifying, identifying, and allowing for the quality of goods and services. The division of a GNP/GDP estimate in local currency by the corresponding PPP estimate in dollars gives *the PPP conversion rate*. On average, one thousand dollars will buy the same market basket of goods in the US as one thousand dollars—converted to the local currency at the PPP conversion rate—will buy in the other country. Whereas PPP estimates for OECD countries are quite reliable, PPP estimates for developing countries are often rough approximations. The latter estimates are based on extrapolation of numbers published by the UN International Comparison Program and by Professors Robert Summers and Alan Heston of the University of Pennsylvania and their colleagues. Because currency exchange rates depend on a variety of international and domestic financial forces that often have little relation to domestic output, use of these rates is less satisfactory for calculating GNP/GDP than the PPP method. In developing countries with weak currencies the exchange rate estimate of GNP/GDP in dollars is typically one-fourth to one-half the

PPP estimate. Furthermore, exchange rates may suddenly go up or down by 10% or more because of market forces or official fiat whereas real output has remained unchanged. On 12 January 1994, for example, the 14 countries of the African Financial Community (whose currencies are tied to the French franc) devalued their currencies by 50%. This move, of course, did not cut the real output of these countries by half. One additional caution: the proportion of, say, defense expenditures as a percent of GNP/GDP in local currency accounts may differ substantially from the proportion when GNP/GDP accounts are expressed in PPP terms, as, for example, when an observer estimates the dollar level of Russian or Japanese military expenditures.

**Growth rate (population):** The annual percent change in the population, resulting from a surplus (or deficit) of births over deaths and the balance of migrants entering and leaving a country. The rate may be positive or negative.

**Illicit drugs:** There are five categories of illicit drugs—narcotics, stimulants, depressants (sedatives), hallucinogens, and cannabis. These categories include many drugs legally produced and prescribed by doctors as well as those illegally produced and sold outside medical channels.

Cannabis (Cannabis sativa) is the common hemp plant, which provides hallucinogens with some sedative properties, and includes marijuana (pot, Acapulco gold, grass, reefer), tetrahydrocannabinol (THC, Marinol), hashish (hash), and hashish oil (hash oil).

Coca (Erythroxylon coca) is a bush, and the leaves contain the stimulant cocaine. Coca is not to be confused with cocoa, which comes from cacao seeds and is used in making chocolate, cocoa, and cocoa butter.

Cocaine is a stimulant derived from the leaves of the coca bush.

Depressants (sedatives) are drugs that reduce tension and anxiety and include chloral hydrate, barbiturates (Amytal, Nembutal, Seconal, phenobarbital), benzodiazepines (Librium, Valium), methaqualone (Quaalude), glutethimide (Doriden), and others (Equanil, Placidyl, Valmid).

Drugs are any chemical substances that effect a physical, mental, emotional, or behavioral change in an individual.

Drug abuse is the use of any licit or illicit chemical substance that results in physical, mental, emotional, or behavioral impairment in an individual.

Hallucinogens are drugs that affect sensation, thinking, self-awareness, and emotion. Hallucinogens include LSD (acid, microdot), mescaline and peyote (mexc, buttons, cactus), amphetamine variants (PMA, STP, DOB), phencyclidine (PCP, angel dust, hog), phencyclidine analogues (PCE, PCPy, TCP), and others (psilocybin, psilocyn).

Hashish is the resinous exudate of the cannabis or hemp plant (Cannabis sativa).

Heroin is a semisynthetic derivative of morphine.

Mandrax is a synthetic chemical depressant, the same as, or similar to, Quaalude.

Marijuana is the dried leaves of the cannabis or hemp plant (Cannabis sativa).

Narcotics are drugs that relieve pain, often induce sleep, and refer to opium, opium derivatives, and synthetic substitutes. Natural narcotics include opium (paregoric, parepectolin), morphine (MS-Contin, Roxanol), codeine (Tylenol with codeine, Empirin with codeine, Robitussan AC), and thebaine. Semisynthetic narcotics include heroin (horse, smack), and hydromorphone (Dilaudid). Synthetic narcotics include meperidine or Pethidine (Demerol, Mepergan), methadone (Dolophine, Methadose), and others (Darvon, Lomotil).

Opium is the milky exudate of the incised, unripe seedpod of the opium poppy.

Opium poppy (Papaver somniferum) is the source for many natural and semisynthetic narcotics.

Poppy straw concentrate is the alkaloid derived from the mature dried opium poppy.

Qat (kat, khat) is a stimulant from the buds or leaves of catha edulis that is chewed or drunk as tea.

Stimulants are drugs that relieve mild depression, increase energy and activity, and include cocaine (coke, snow, crack), amphetamines (Desoxyn, Dexedrine), phenmetrazine (Preludin), methylphenidate (Ritalin), and others (Cylert, Sanorex, Tenuate).

**Infant mortality rate:** The number of deaths to infants under one year old in a given year per 1,000 live births occurring in the same year.

**International disputes:** This category includes a wide variety of situations that range from traditional bilateral boundary disputes to unilateral claims of one sort or another. Information regarding disputes over international boundaries and maritime boundaries has been reviewed by the Department of State. References to other situations involving borders or frontiers may also be included, such as resource disputes, geopolitical questions, or irredentist issues. However, inclusion does not necessarily constitute official acceptance or recognition by the US Government.

**Irrigated land:** The figure refers to the land area that is artificially supplied with water.

**Land use:** Human use of the land surface is categorized as *arable land*—land cultivated for crops that are replanted after each harvest (wheat, maize, rice); *permanent crops*—land cultivated for crops that are not replanted after each harvest (citrus, coffee, rubber); *meadows and pastures*—land permanently used for herbaceous forage crops; *forest and woodland*—under dense or open stands of trees; and *other*—any land type not specifically mentioned above (urban areas, roads, desert).

**Leaders:** The chief of state is the titular leader of the country who represents the state at official and ceremonial functions but is not involved with the day-to-day activities of the government. The head of government is the administrative leader who manages the day-to-day activities of the government. In the UK, the monarch is the chief of state, and the Prime Minister is the head of government. In the US, the President is both the chief of state and the head of government.

**Life expectancy at birth:** The average number of years to be lived by a group of people all born in the same year, if mortality at each age remains constant in the future.

**Literacy:** There are no universal definitions and standards of literacy. Unless otherwise noted, all rates are based on the most common definition—the ability to read and write at a specified age. Detailing the standards that individual countries use to assess the ability to read and write is beyond the scope of this publication.

**Maritime claims:** The proximity of neighboring states may prevent some national claims from being extended the full distance.

**Merchant marine:** All ships engaged in the carriage of goods. All commercial vessels (as opposed to all nonmilitary ships), which excludes tugs, fishing vessels, offshore oil rigs, etc.; also, a grouping of merchant ships by nationality or register.

Captive register—A register of ships maintained by a territory, possession, or colony primarily or exclusively for the use of ships owned in the parent country; also referred to as an offshore register, the offshore equivalent of an internal register. Ships on a captive register will fly the same flag as the parent country, or a local variant of it, but will be subject to the maritime laws and taxation rules of the offshore territory. Although the nature of a captive register makes it especially desirable for ships owned in the parent country, just as in the internal register, the ships may also be owned abroad. The captive register then acts as a flag of convenience register, except that it is not the register of an independent state.

Flag of convenience register—A national register offering registration to a merchant ship not owned in the flag state. The major flags of convenience (FOC) attract ships to their register by virtue of low fees, low or nonexistent taxation of profits, and liberal manning requirements. True FOC registers are characterized by having relatively few of the ships registered actually owned in the flag state. Thus, while virtually any flag can be used for ships under a given set of circumstances, an FOC register is one where the majority of the merchant fleet is owned abroad. It is also referred to as an open register.

Flag state—The nation in which a ship is registered and which holds legal jurisdiction over operation of the ship, whether at home or abroad. Differences in flag state maritime legislation determine how a ship is manned and taxed and whether a foreign-owned ship may be placed on the register.

Internal register—A register of ships maintained as a subset of a national register. Ships on the internal register fly the national flag and have that nationality but are subject to a separate set of maritime rules from those on the main national register. These differences usually include lower taxation of profits, manning by foreign nationals, and, usually, ownership outside the flag state (when it functions as an FOC register). The Norwegian International Ship Register and Danish International Ship

Register are the most notable examples of an internal register. Both have been instrumental in stemming flight from the national flag to flags of convenience and in attracting foreign owned ships to the Norwegian and Danish flags.

Merchant ship—A vessel that carries goods against payment of freight; commonly used to denote any nonmilitary ship but accurately restricted to commercial vessels only.

Register—The record of a ship's ownership and nationality as listed with the maritime authorities of a country; also, the compendium of such individual ships' registrations. Registration of a ship provides it with a nationality and makes it subject to the laws of the country in which registered (the flag state) regardless of the nationality of the ship's ultimate owner.

**Money figures:** All money figures are expressed in contemporaneous US dollars unless otherwise indicated.

**National product:** The total output of goods and services in a country in a given year. See Gross domestic product (GDP), Gross national product (GNP), and GNP/GDP methodology.

**Net migration rate:** The balance between the number of persons entering and leaving a country during the year per 1,000 persons (based on midyear population). An excess of persons entering the country is referred to as net immigration (3.56 migrants/1,000 population); an excess of persons leaving the country as net emigration (-9.26 migrants/1,000 population).

**Population:** Figures are estimates from the Bureau of the Census based on statistics from population censuses, vital statistics registration systems, or sample surveys pertaining to the recent past, and on assumptions about future trends. Starting with the 1993 Factbook, demographic estimates for some countries (mostly African) have taken into account the effects of the growing incidence of AIDS infections; in 1993 these countries were Burkina, Burundi, Central African Republic, Congo, Cote d'Ivoire, Haiti, Kenya, Malawi, Rwanda, Tanzania, Uganda, Zaire, Zambia, Zimbabwe, Thailand, and Brazil.

**Total fertility rate:** The average number of children that would be born per woman if all women lived to the end of their childbearing years and bore children according to a given fertility rate at each age.

**Years:** All year references are for the calendar year (CY) unless indicated as fiscal year (FY).

# International Organizations Abbreviations

| | |
|---|---|
| ABEDA | Arab Bank for Economic Development in Africa |
| ACC | Arab Cooperation Council |
| ACCT | Agence de Cooperation Culturelle et Technique; see Agency for Cultural and Technical Cooperation |
| ACP | African, Caribbean, and Pacific Countries |
| AfDB | African Development Bank |
| AFESD | Arab Fund for Economic and Social Development |
| AG | Andean Group |
| AL | Arab League |
| ALADI | Asociacion Latinoamericana de Integracion; see Latin American Integration Association (LAIA) |
| AMF | Arab Monetary Fund |
| AMU | Arab Maghreb Union |
| ANZUS | Australia-New Zealand-United States Security Treaty |
| APEC | Asia Pacific Economic Cooperation |
| AsDB | Asian Development Bank |
| ASEAN | Association of Southeast Asian Nations |
| BAD | Banque Africaine de Developpement; see African Development Bank (AfDB) |
| BADEA | Banque Arabe de Developpement Economique en Afrique; see Arab Bank for Economic Development in Africa (ABEDA) |
| BCIE | Banco Centroamericano de Integracion Economico; see Central American Bank for Economic Integration (BCIE) |
| BDEAC | Banque de Developppment des Etats de l'Afrique Centrale; see Central African States Development Bank (BDEAC) |
| Benelux | Benelux Economic Union |
| BID | Banco Interamericano de Desarrollo; see Inter-American Development Bank (IADB) |
| BIS | Bank for International Settlements |
| BOAD | Banque Ouest-Africaine de Developpement; see West African Development Bank (WADB) |
| BSEC | Black Sea Economic Cooperation Zone |
| C | Commonwealth |
| CACM | Central American Common Market |
| CAEU | Council of Arab Economic Unity |

| | |
|---|---|
| CARICOM | Caribbean Community and Common Market |
| CBSS | Council of the Baltic Sea States |
| CCC | Customs Cooperation Council |
| CDB | Caribbean Development Bank |
| CE | Council of Europe |
| CEAO | Communaute Economique de l'Afrique de l'Ouest; see West African Economic Community (CEAO) |
| CEEAC | Communaute Economique des Etats de l'Afrique Centrale; see Economic Community of Central African States (CEEAC) |
| CEI | Central European Initiative |
| CEMA | Council for Mutual Economic Assistance; also known as CMEA or Comecon; abolished 1 January 1991 |
| CEPGL | Communaute Economique des Pays des Grands Lacs; see Economic Community of the Great Lakes Countries (CEPGL) |
| CERN | Conseil Europeen pour la Recherche Nucleaire; see European Organization for Nuclear Research (CERN) |
| CG | Contadora Group |
| CIS | Commonwealth of Independent States |
| CMEA | Council for Mutual Economic Assistance (CEMA); also known as Comecon; abolished 1 January 1991 |
| COCOM | Coordinating Committee on Export Controls |
| Comecon | Council for Mutual Economic Assistance (CEMA); also known as CMEA; abolished 1 January 1991 |
| CP | Colombo Plan |
| CSCE | Conference on Security and Cooperation in Europe |
| DC | developed country |
| EADB | East African Development Bank |
| EBRD | European Bank for Reconstruction and Development |
| EC | European Community; see European Union (EU) |
| ECA | Economic Commission for Africa |
| ECAFE | Economic Commission for Asia and the Far East; see Economic and Social Commission for Asia and the Pacific (ESCAP) |
| ECE | Economic Commission for Europe |
| ECLA | Economic Commission for Latin America; see Economic Commission for Latin America and the Caribbean (ECLAC) |
| ECLAC | Economic Commission for Latin America and the Caribbean |
| ECO | Economic Cooperation Organization |
| ECOSOC | Economic and Social Council |
| ECOWAS | Economic Community of West African States |

| | |
|---|---|
| ECSC | European Coal and Steel Community |
| ECWA | Economic Commission for Western Asia; see Economic and Social Commission for Western Asia (ESCWA) |
| EEC | European Economic Community |
| EFTA | European Free Trade Association |
| EIB | European Investment Bank |
| Entente | Council of the Entente |
| ESA | European Space Agency |
| ESCAP | Economic and Social Commission for Asia and the Pacific |
| ESCWA | Economic and Social Commission for Western Asia |
| EU | European Union |
| Euratom | European Atomic Energy Community |
| FAO | Food and Agriculture Organization |
| FLS | Front Line States |
| FZ | Franc Zone |
| G-2 | Group of 2 |
| G-3 | Group of 3 |
| G-5 | Group of 5 |
| G-6 | Group of 6 (not to be confused with the Big Six) |
| G-7 | Group of 7 |
| G-8 | Group of 8 |
| G-9 | Group of 9 |
| G-10 | Group of 10 |
| G-11 | Group of 11 |
| G-15 | Group of 15 |
| G-19 | Group of 19 |
| G-24 | Group of 24 |
| G-30 | Group of 30 |
| G-33 | Group of 33 |
| G-77 | Group of 77 |
| GATT | General Agreement on Tariffs and Trade |
| GCC | Gulf Cooperation Council |
| Habitat | Commission on Human Settlements |
| IADB | Inter-American Development Bank |
| IAEA | International Atomic Energy Agency |
| IBEC | International Bank for Economic Cooperation |

| | |
|---|---|
| IBRD | International Bank for Reconstruction and Development |
| ICAO | International Civil Aviation Organization |
| ICC | International Chamber of Commerce |
| ICEM | Intergovernmental Committee for European Migration; see International Organization for Migration (IOM) |
| ICFTU | International Confederation of Free Trade Unions |
| ICJ | International Court of Justice |
| ICM | Intergovernmental Committee for Migration; see International Organization for Migration (IOM) |
| ICRC | International Committee of the Red Cross |
| IDA | International Development Association |
| IDB | Islamic Development Bank |
| IEA | International Energy Agency |
| IFAD | International Fund for Agricultural Development |
| IFC | International Finance Corporation |
| IFCTU | International Federation of Christian Trade Unions |
| IGADD | Inter-Governmental Authority on Drought and Development |
| IIB | International Investment Bank |
| ILO | International Labor Organization |
| IMCO | Intergovernmental Maritime Consultative Organization; see International Maritime Organization (IMO) |
| IMF | International Monetary Fund |
| IMO | International Maritime Organization |
| INMARSAT | International Maritime Satellite Organization |
| INTELSAT | International Telecommunications Satellite Organization |
| INTERPOL | International Criminal Police Organization |
| IOC | International Olympic Committee |
| IOM | International Organization for Migration |
| ISO | International Organization for Standardization |
| ITU | International Telecommunication Union |
| LAES | Latin American Economic System |
| LAIA | Latin American Integration Association |
| LAS | League of Arab States; see Arab League (AL) |
| LDC | less developed country |
| LLDC | least developed country |
| LORCS | League of Red Cross and Red Crescent Societies |

| | |
|---|---|
| MERCOSUR | Mercado Comun del Cono Sur; see Southern Cone Common Market |
| MINURSO | United Nations Mission for the Referendum in Western Sahara |
| MTCR | Missile Technology Control Regime |
| NACC | North Atlantic Cooperation Council |
| NAM | Nonaligned Movement |
| NATO | North Atlantic Treaty Organization |
| NC | Nordic Council |
| NEA | Nuclear Energy Agency |
| NIB | Nordic Investment Bank |
| NIC | newly industrializing country; see newly industrializing economy (NIE) |
| NIE | newly industrializing economy |
| NSG | Nuclear Suppliers Group |
| OAPEC | Organization of Arab Petroleum Exporting Countries |
| OAS | Organization of American States |
| OAU | Organization of African Unity |
| OECD | Organization for Economic Cooperation and Development |
| OECS | Organization of Eastern Caribbean States |
| OIC | Organization of the Islamic Conference |
| ONUSAL | United Nations Observer Mission in El Salvador |
| OPANAL | Organismo para la Proscripcion de las Armas Nucleares en la America Latina y el Caribe; see Agency for the Prohibition of Nuclear Weapons in Latin America and the Caribbean |
| OPEC | Organization of Petroleum Exporting Countries |
| PCA | Permanent Court of Arbitration |
| RG | Rio Group |
| SAARC | South Asian Association for Regional Cooperation |
| SACU | Southern African Customs Union |
| SADC | Southern African Development Community |
| SADCC | Southern African Development Coordination Conference |
| SELA | Sistema Economico Latinoamericana; see Latin American Economic System (LAES) |
| SPARTECA | South Pacific Regional Trade and Economic Cooperation Agreement |
| SPC | South Pacific Commission |
| SPF | South Pacific Forum |
| UDEAC | Union Douaniere et Economique de l'Afrique Centrale; see Central African Customs and Economic Union (UDEAC) |

| | |
|---|---|
| UN | United Nations |
| UNAVEM II | United Nations Angola Verification Mission |
| UNCTAD | United Nations Conference on Trade and Development |
| UNDOF | United Nations Disengagement Observer Force |
| UNDP | United Nations Development Program |
| UNEP | United Nations Environment Program |
| UNESCO | United Nations Educational, Scientific, and Cultural Organization |
| UNFICYP | United Nations Force in Cyprus |
| UNFPA | United Nations Fund for Population Activities; see UN Population Fund (UNFPA) |
| UNHCR | United Nations Office of the High Commissioner for Refugees |
| UNICEF | United Nations Children's Fund |
| UNIDO | United Nations Industrial Development Organization |
| UNIFIL | United Nations Interim Force in Lebanon |
| UNIKOM | United Nations Iraq-Kuwait Observation Mission |
| UNMOGIP | United Nations Military Observer Group in India and Pakistan |
| UNOMIG | United Nations Observer Mission in Georgia |
| UNOMOZ | United Nations Operation in Mozambique |
| UNOMUR | United Nations Observer Mission Uganda-Rwanda |
| UNOSOM | United Nations Operation in Somalia |
| UNPROFOR | United Nations Protection Force |
| UNRWA | United Nations Relief and Works Agency for Palestine Refugees |
| UNTAC | United Nations Transitional Authority in Cambodia |
| UNTSO | United Nations Truce Supervision Organization |
| UPU | Universal Postal Union |
| WADB | West African Development Bank |
| WCL | World Confederation of Labor |
| WEU | Western European Union |
| WFC | World Food Council |
| WFP | World Food Program |
| WFTU | World Federation of Trade Unions |
| WHO | World Health Organization |
| WIPO | World Intellectual Property Organization |
| WMO | World Meteorological Organization |
| WP | Warsaw Pact (members met 1 July 1991 to dissolve the alliance) |
| WTO | World Tourism Organization |
| ZC | Zangger Committee |

# International Metric Equivalents

| Unit | Metric Equivalent |
|------|-------------------|
| acre | 0.404 685 64 hectares |
| acre | 4,046,856 4 meters$^2$ |
| acre | 0.004 046 856 4 kilometers$^2$ |
| are | 100 meters$^2$ |
| barrel (petroleum, US) | 158.987 29 liters |
| (proof spirits, US) | 151.416 47 liters |
| (beer, US) | 117.347 77 liters |
| bushel | 35.239 07 liters |
| cable | 219.456 meters |
| chain (surveyor's) | 20.116 8 meters |
| cord (wood) | 3.624 556 meters$^3$ |
| cup | 0.236 588 2 liters |
| degrees, celsius | (water boils at 100° degrees C, freezes at 0° C) |
| degrees, fahrenheit | subtract 32 and divide by 1.8 to obtain °C |
| dram, avoirdupois | 1.771 845 2 grams |
| dram, troy | 3.887 934 6 grams |
| dram, liquid (US) | 3.696 69 milliliters |
| fathom | 1.828 8 meters |
| foot | 30.48 centimeters |
| foot | 0.304 8 meters |
| foot | 0.000 304 8 kilometers |
| foot$^2$ | 929.030 4 centimeters$^2$ |
| foot | 2 0.092 903 04 meters$^2$ |
| foot$^3$ | 28.316 846 592 liters |
| foot$^3$ | 0.028 316 847 meters$^3$ |
| furlong | 201.168 meters |
| gallon, liquid (US) | 3.785 411 784 liters |
| gill (US) | 118.294 118 milliliters |
| grain | 64.798 91 milligrams |
| gram | 1,000 milligrams |
| hand (height of horse) | 10.16 centimeters |

| | |
|---|---|
| hectare | 10,000 meters$^2$ |
| hundredweight, long | 50.802 345 kilograms |
| hundredweight, short | 45.359 237 kilograms |
| inch | 2.54 centimeters |
| inch$^2$ | 6.451 6 centimeters$^2$ |
| inch$^3$ | 16.387 064 centimeters$^3$ |
| inch$^3$ | 16.387 064 milliliters |
| inch$^3$ | 16.387 064 milliliters |
| kilogram | 0.001 tons, metric |
| kilometer | 1,000 meters |
| kilometer$^2$ | 100 hectares |
| kilometer$^2$ | 1,000,000 meters$^2$ |
| knot (1 nautical mi/hr) | 1.852 kilometers/hour |
| league, nautical | 5.559 552 kilometers |
| league, statute | 4.828.032 kilometers |
| link (surveyor's) | 20.116 8 centimeters |
| liter | 0.001 meters$^3$ |
| liter | 0.1 dekaliter |
| liter | 1,000 milliliters |
| meter | 100 centimeters |
| meter$^2$ | 10,000 centimeters$^2$ |
| meter$^3$ | 1,000 liters |
| micron | 0.000 001 meter |
| mil | 0.025 4 millimeters |
| mile, nautical | 1.852 kilometers |
| mile$^2$, nautical | 3.429 904 kilometers$^2$ |
| mile, statute | 1.609 344 kilometers |
| mile$^2$, statute | 258.998 811 hectares |
| mile$^2$, statute | 2.589 988 11 kilometers$^2$ |
| minim (US) | 0.061 611 52 milliliters |
| ounce, avoirdupois | 28.349 523 125 grams |
| ounce, liquid (US) | 29.573 53 milliliters |
| ounce, troy | 31.103 476 8 grams |
| pace | 76.2 centimeters |
| peck | 8.809 767 5 liters |
| pennyweight | 1.555 173 84 grams |
| pint, dry (US) | 0.550 610 47 liters |

| | |
|---|---|
| pint, liquid (US) | 0.473 176 473 liters |
| point (typographical) | 0.351 459 8 millimeters |
| pound, avoirdupois | 453.592 37 grams |
| pound, troy | 373.241 721 6 grams |
| quart, dry (US) | 1.101 221 liters |
| quart, liquid (US) | 0.946 352 946 liters |
| quintal | 100 kilograms |
| rod | 5.029 2 meters |
| scruple | 1.295 978 2 grams |
| section (US) | 2.589 988 1 kilometers$^2$ |
| span | 22.86 centimeters |
| stere | 1 meter$^3$ |
| tablespoon | 14.786 76 milliliters |
| teaspoon | 4.928 922 milliliters |
| ton, long or deadweight | 1,016.046 909 kilograms |
| ton, metric | 1,000 kilograms |
| ton, metric | 1,000 kilograms |
| ton, register | 2.831 684 7 meters$^3$ |
| ton, short | 907.184 74 kilograms |
| township (US) | 93.239 572 kilometers$^2$ |
| yard | 0.914 4 meter$^1$ |
| yard$^2$ | 0.836 127 36 meters$^2$ |
| yard$^3$ | 0.764 554 86 meters$^3$ |
| yard$^3$ | 764.554 857 984 liters |

# Export Resources

## Department of Commerce

The scope of services provided by the Department of Commerce to exporters is vast, but it is often overlooked by many companies. Most of the information and programs of interest to U.S. exporters are concentrated in the department's International Trade Administration (ITA), of which the subdivision called the U.S. and Foreign Commercial Service (US&FCS) maintains a network of international trade specialists in the United States and commercial officers in foreign cities to help American companies do business abroad. By contacting the nearest Department of Commerce district office, the U.S. exporter can tap into all assistance programs available from ITA and all trade information gathered by U.S. embassies and consulates worldwide. Addresses and phone numbers for all district offices, listed by state, are given in appendix III. The following sections detail the kinds of assistance offered.

### Export assistance available in the United States

#### Department of Commerce District Offices

Sixty-eight Department of Commerce district and branch offices in cities throughout the United States and Puerto Rico provide information and professional export counseling to business people. Each district office is headed by a director and supported by trade specialists and other staff. Branch offices usually consist of one trade specialist. These professionals can counsel companies on the steps involved in exporting, help them assess the export potential of their products, target markets, and locate and check out potential overseas partners. In fact, because Commerce has a worldwide network of international business experts, district offices can answer almost any question exporters are likely to ask – or put them in touch with someone who can.

Each district office can offer information about

• international trade opportunities abroad,

• foreign markets for U.S. products and services,

• services to locate and evaluate overseas buyers and representatives,

• financial aid to exporters,

• international trade exhibitions,

• export documentation requirements,

• foreign economic statistics,

• U.S. export licensing and foreign nation import requirements, and

• export seminars and conferences.

Most district offices also maintain business libraries containing Commerce's latest reports as well as other publications of interest to U.S. exporters. Important data bases, such as the NTDB, are also available through many district offices that provide trade leads, foreign business contacts, in-depth country market research, export-import trade statistics, and other valuable information.

#### District Export Councils

Besides the immediate services of its district offices, the Department of Commerce gives the exporter direct contact with seasoned exporters experienced in all phases of export trade. The district offices work closely with 51 district export councils (DECs) comprising nearly 1,800 business and trade experts who volunteer to help U.S. firms develop solid export strategies.

These DECs assist in many of the workshops and seminars on exporting arranged by the district offices (see below) or sponsor their own. DEC members may also provide direct, personal counseling to less experienced exporters, suggesting marketing strategies, trade contacts, and ways to maximize success in overseas markets.

Assistance from DECs may be obtained through the Department of Commerce district offices with which they are affiliated.

#### Export Seminars and Educational Programming

In addition to individual counseling sessions, an effective method of informing local business communities of the various aspects of international trade is through the conference and seminar program. Each year, Commerce district offices conduct approximately 5,000 conferences, seminars, and workshops on topics such as export documentation and licensing procedures, country-specific market opportunities, export trading companies, and U.S. trade promotion and trade policy initiatives. The seminars are usually held in conjunction with DECs, local chambers of commerce, state agencies, and world trade clubs. For information on scheduled seminars across the country, or for educational programming assistance, contact the nearest district office.

#### Assistance Available From Department of Commerce Specialists in Washington, D.C.

Among the most valuable resources available to U.S. exporters are the hundreds of trade specialists, expert in various areas of international business, that the Department of Commerce has assembled in its Washington headquarters.

*Country counseling.* Every country in the world is assigned a *country desk officer*. These desk officers (see appendix II for a list), in Commerce's International Economic Policy (IEP) area, look at the needs of an individual U.S. firm wishing to sell in a particular country, taking into account that country's overall economy, trade policies, political situation, and other relevant factors. Each desk officer collects up-to-date information on the country's trade regulations, tariffs and value-added taxes, business practices, economic and political developments, trade data and trends, market size and growth, and so on. Desk officers also participate in preparing Commerce's country-specific market research reports, such as *Foreign Economic Trends* and *Overseas Business Reports* (see appendix V), available from the U.S. Government Printing Office and through the NTDB. The value of IEP's market data may be gauged from the fact that this agency develops much of the country-specific background for negotiating positions of the U.S. trade representative.

***Product and service sector counseling.*** Complementing IEP's country desks are the *industry desk officers* of Commerce's Trade Development area. They are grouped in units (with telephone numbers):

- Aerospace, 202-377-2835.
- Automotive Affairs and Consumer Goods, 202-377-0823.
- Basic Industries, 202-377-0614.
- Capital Goods and International Construction, 202-377-5023.
- Science and Electronics, 202-377-3548.
- Services, 202-377-5261.
- Textiles and Apparel, 202-377-3737.

The industry desk officers (see appendix II for a list) participate in preparing reports on the competitive strength of selected U.S. industries in domestic and international markets for the publication *U.S. Industrial Outlook* (available from the U.S. Government Printing Office). They also promote exports for their industry sectors through marketing seminars, trade missions and trade fairs, foreign buyer groups, business counseling, and information on market opportunities.

***Export counseling and international market analysis.*** The Market Analysis Division provides U.S. firms with assistance in market research efforts and export counseling on market research. Many of the research reports described in this chapter are planned and prepared by the Office of Product Development and Distribution, Market Analysis Division (202-377-5037).

***Major projects.*** For major projects abroad, the International Construction unit works with American planning, engineering, and construction firms to win bid contracts. The Major Projects Reference Room in Commerce's Washington headquarters keeps detailed project documents on multilateral development bank and U.S. foreign assistance projects. Companies able to bid on major overseas projects can reach the Major Projects Reference Room on 202-377-4876.

The Office of Telecommunications (202-377-4466) has major projects information exclusively for that sector.

***Other assistance.*** Rounding out the Trade Development area is a unit that cuts across industry sector issues. Trade Information and Analysis gathers, analyzes, and disseminates trade and investment data for use in trade promotion and policy formulation. It also includes specialists in technical areas of international trade finance,

such as countertrade and barter, foreign sales corporations, export financing, and the activities of multilateral development banks. For more information, contact the nearest Department of Commerce district office.

## Export marketing information and assistance available overseas

### US&FCS Overseas Posts

Much of the information about trends and actual trade leads in foreign countries is gathered on site by the US&FCS. About half of approximately 186 US&FCS American officers working in 67 countries (with 127 offices) have been hired from the private sector, many with international trade experience. All understand firsthand the problems encountered by U.S. companies in their efforts to trade abroad. U.S.-based regional directors for the US&FCS can be contacted at the following telephone numbers:

- Africa, Near East and South Asia, 202-377-4836.
- East Asia and Pacific, 202-377-8422.
- Europe, 202-377-1599.
- Western Hemisphere, 202-377-2736.
- Fax (Europe and Western Hemisphere), 202-377-3159.
- Fax (all others), 202-377-5179.

In addition, a valued asset of the US&FCS is a group of about 525 foreign nationals, usually natives of the foreign country, who are employed in the U.S. embassy or consulate and bring with them a wealth of personal understanding of local market conditions and business practices. The US&FCS staff overseas provides a range of services to help companies sell abroad: background information on foreign companies, agency-finding services, market research, business counseling, assistance in making appointments with key buyers and government officials, and representations on behalf of companies adversely affected by trade barriers. (Some of the more important services are described fully in chapter 7.)

U.S. exporters usually tap into these services by contacting the Department of Commerce district office in their state. While exporters are strongly urged to contact their district office *before* going overseas, U.S. business travelers abroad can also contact U.S. embassies and consulates directly for help during their trips. District offices can provide business travel facilitation assistance before departure by arranging advance appointments with embassy personnel, market briefings, and other assistance in cities to be visited.

US&FCS posts also cooperate with overseas representatives of individual states. Almost all 50 states have such representation in overseas markets, and their efforts are closely coordinated with the resources of the US&FCS.

## Other Commerce export services

Besides ITA, a number of other Department of Commerce agencies offer export services.

### Export Administration

The under secretary for export administration is responsible for U.S. export controls (see chapter 11). Assistance in complying with export controls can be obtained directly from local district offices or from the Exporter Counseling Division within the Bureau of Export Administration (BXA) Office of Export Licensing in Washington, DC (202-377-4811). BXA also has four field offices that specialize in counseling on export controls and regulations: the Western Regional Office (714-660-0144), the Northern California Branch Office (408-748-7450), the Portland Branch Office (503-326-5159), and the Eastern Regional Office (603-834-6300).

### Trade Adjustment Assistance

Trade Adjustment Assistance, part of Commerce's Economic Development Administration, helps firms that have been adversely affected by imported products to adjust to international competition. Companies eligible for trade adjustment assistance may receive technical consulting to upgrade operations such as product engineering, marketing, information systems, export promotion, and energy management. The federal government may assume up to 75 percent of the cost of these services. For more information call 202-377-3373.

### Travel and Tourism

The U.S. Travel and Tourism Administration (USTTA) promotes U.S. export earnings through trade in tourism. USTTA stimulates foreign demand, helps to remove barriers, increases the number of small and medium-sized travel businesses participating in the export market, provides timely data, and forms marketing partnerships with private industry and with state and local governments.

To maintain its programs in international markets, USTTA has offices in Toronto, Montreal, Vancouver, Mexico City, Tokyo, London, Paris, Amsterdam, Milan, Frankfurt, Sydney, and (serving South America) Miami.

Travel development activities in countries without direct USTTA representation are carried out under the direction of USTTA regional directors, who cooperate with Visit USA committees composed of representatives from the U.S. and foreign travel industry in those countries, and also with the US&FCS. For more information, U.S. destinations and suppliers of tourism services interested in the overseas promotion of travel to the United States should call 202-377-4003.

### Foreign Requirements for U.S. Products and Services

For information about foreign standards and certification systems, write National Center for Standards and Certificates Information, National Institute for Standards and Technology (NIST), Administration Building, A629, Gaithersburg, MD 20899; telephone 301-975-4040, 4038, or 4036. NIST maintains a General Agreement on Tariffs and Trade (GATT) hotline (301-975-4041) with a recording that reports on the latest notifications of proposed foreign regulations that may affect trade. Exporters can also get information from the nongovernmental American National Standards Institute (212-354-3300).

### Minority Business Development Agency (MBDA)

The MBDA identifies minority business enterprises (MBEs) in selected industries to increase their awareness of their relative size and product advantages and to aggressively take them through the advanced stages of market development.

Through an interagency agreement with the ITA, MBDA provides information on market and product needs worldwide. MBDA and ITA coordinate MBE participation in Matchmaker and other trade delegations.

MBDA provides counseling through the Minority Business Development Center network to help MBEs prepare international marketing plans and promotional materials and to identify financial resources.

For general export information, the field organizations of both MBDA and ITA provide information kits and information on local seminars. Contact Minority Business Development Agency, Office of Program Development, U.S. Department of Commerce, Washington, DC 20230; telephone 202-377-3237.

### Foreign Metric Regulations

The Office of Metric Programs (202-377-0944) provides exporters with guidance and assistance on matters relating to U.S. transition to the metric system. It can also give referrals to metric contacts in state governments.

### Fishery Products Exports

The National Oceanic and Atmospheric Administration (NOAA) assists seafood exporters by facilitating access to foreign markets. NOAA's National Marine Fisheries Service provides inspection services for fishery exports and issues official U.S. government certification attesting to the findings. Contact Office of Trade and Industry Services, National Marine Fisheries Service, Room 6490, 1335 East-West Highway, Silver Spring, MD 20910. Telephone numbers are as follows: Trade Matters, 301-427-2379 or 2383; Export Inspection, 301-427-2355; and Fisheries Promotion, 301-427-2379.

### Bureau of the Census

The Bureau of the Census is the primary source of trade statistics that break down the quantity and dollar value of U.S. exports and imports by commodity (product) and country. Commerce district offices can help retrieve Census export statistics for exporters who want to identify potential export markets for their products. Firms interested in more extensive statistical data can contact the Bureau of the Census at 301-763-5140.

Census can also provide authoritative guidance on questions concerning shippers' export declarations (see chapter 12). Call 301-763-5310.

## Department of State

The Department of State has a diverse staff capable of providing U.S. exporters with trade contacts. These staff members include bureau commercial coordinators, country desk officers, policy officers in the functional bureaus (such as the Bureau of Economic and Business

Affairs), and all U.S. embassies and consular posts abroad. While the Department of Commerce's US&FCS is present in 67 countries, the Department of State provides commercial services in 84 embassies and numerous consular posts. Their addresses and telephone numbers are published in the directory titled *Key Officers of Foreign Service Posts*, available from the U.S. Government Printing Office (202-783-3238).

The ambassador takes the lead in promoting U.S. trade and investment interests in every U.S. embassy. All members of U.S. diplomatic missions abroad have the following continuing obligations:

- To ascertain the views of the American business sector on foreign policy issues that affect its interests, in order to ensure that those views are fully considered in the development of policy.

- To seek to ensure that the ground rules for conducting international trade are fair and nondiscriminatory.

- To be responsive when U.S. firms seek assistance, providing them with professional advice and analysis as well as assistance in making and developing contacts abroad.

- To vigorously encourage and promote the export of U.S. goods, services, and agricultural commodities and represent the interests of U.S. business to foreign governments where appropriate.

- To assist U.S. business in settling investment disputes with foreign governments amicably and, in cases of expropriation or similar action, to obtain prompt, adequate, and effective compensation.

## Bureau of Economic and Business Affairs

The Bureau of Economic and Business Affairs has primary responsibility within the Department of State for (1) formulating and implementing policies regarding foreign economic matters, trade promotion, and business services of an international nature and (2) coordinating regional economic policy with other bureaus. The bureau is divided functionally as follows: Planning and Economic Analysis Staff; Office of Commercial, Legislative, and Public Affairs; Trade and Commercial Affairs (including textiles and food policy); International Finance and Development (including investment and business practices); Transportation (including aviation and maritime affairs); International Energy and Resources Policy; and International Trade Controls. For more information, contact Commercial Coordinator, Bureau of Economic and Business Affairs; telephone 202-647-1942.

## Regional bureaus

Regional bureaus, each under the direction of an assistant secretary of state, are responsible for U.S. foreign affairs activities in specific major regions of the world. Bureau commercial coordinators can be reached on the following telephone numbers:

- Bureau of African Affairs, 202-647-3503.
- Bureau of East Asian and Pacific Affairs, 202-647-2006.
- Bureau of Near Eastern and South Asian Affairs, 202-647-4835.

- Bureau of European and Canadian Affairs, 202-647-2395.
- Bureau of International Communications and Information Policy, 202-647-5832.

Country desk officers maintain day-to-day contact with overseas diplomatic posts and provide country-specific economic and political analysis and commercial counseling to U.S. business.

## Cooperation between state and commerce

The Departments of State and Commerce provide many services to U.S. business jointly. Firms interested in establishing a market for their products or expanding sales abroad should first seek assistance from their nearest Department of Commerce district office, which can tap into the worldwide network of State and Commerce officials serving in U.S. missions abroad and in Washington.

# Small Business Administration

Through its 107 field offices in cities throughout the United States (see appendix III for addresses and telephone numbers), the U.S. Small Business Administration (SBA) provides counseling to potential and current small business exporters. These no-cost services include the following:

- *Legal advice.* Through an arrangement with the Federal Bar Association (FBA), exporters may receive initial export legal assistance. Under this program, qualified attorneys from the International Law Council of the FBA, working through SBA field offices, provide free initial consultations to small companies on the legal aspects of exporting.

- *Export training.* SBA field offices cosponsor export training programs with the Department of Commerce, other federal agencies, and various private sector international trade organizations. These programs are conducted by experienced international traders.

- *Small Business Institute and small business development centers.* Through the Small Business Institute, advanced business students from more than 500 colleges and universities provide in-depth, long-term counseling under faculty supervision to small businesses. Additional export counseling and assistance are offered through small business development centers, which are located in some colleges and universities. Students in these two programs provide technical help by developing an export marketing feasibility study and analysis for their client firms.

- *Export counseling.* Export counseling services are also furnished to potential and current small business exporters by executives and professional consultants. Members of the Service Corps of Retired Executives, with practical experience in international trade, help small firms evaluate their export potential and strengthen their domestic operations by identifying financial, managerial, or technical problems. These advisers also can help small firms develop and implement basic export marketing plans, which show where and how to sell goods abroad.

For information on any of the programs funded by SBA, contact the nearest SBA field office (see appendix III).

## Department of Agriculture

The U.S. Department of Agriculture (USDA) export promotion efforts are centered in the Foreign Agricultural Service (FAS), whose marketing programs are discussed in chapter 7. However, other USDA agencies also offer services to U.S. exporters of agricultural products: the Economic Research Service, the Office of Transportation, the Animal and Plant Health Inspection Service, the Food Safety and Inspection Service, and the Federal Grain Inspection Service. A wide variety of other valuable programs is offered, such as promotion of U.S. farm products in foreign markets; services of commodity and marketing specialists in Washington, D.C.; trade fair exhibits; publications and information services; and financing programs. For more information on programs contact the director of the High-Value Product Services Division, Foreign Agricultural Service, U.S. Department of Agriculture, Washington, DC 20250; telephone 202-447-6343.

## State governments

State economic development agencies, departments of commerce, and other departments of state governments often provide valuable assistance to exporters. State export development programs are growing rapidly. In many areas, county and city economic development agencies also have export assistance programs. The aid offered by these groups typically includes the following:

- *Export education* – helping exporters analyze export potential and orienting them to export techniques and strategies. This help may take the form of group seminars or individual counseling sessions.

- *Trade missions* – organizing trips abroad enabling exporters to call on potential foreign customers. (For more information on trade missions, see chapter 7.)

- *Trade shows* – organizing and sponsoring exhibitions of state-produced goods and services in overseas markets.

Appendix III lists the agencies in each state responsible for export assistance to local firms. Also included are the names of other government and private organizations, with their telephone numbers and addresses. Readers interested in the role played by state development agencies in promoting and supporting exports may also wish to contact the National Association of State Development Agencies, 444 North Capitol Street, Suite 611, Washington, DC 20001; telephone 202-624-5411.

To determine if a particular county or city has local export assistance programs, contact the appropriate economic development agency. Appendix III includes contact information for several major cities.

## Commercial banks

More than 300 U.S. banks have international banking departments with specialists familiar with specific foreign countries and various types of commodities and transactions. These large banks, located in major U.S. cities, maintain correspondent relationships with smaller banks throughout the country. Larger banks also maintain correspondent relationships with banks in most foreign countries or operate their own overseas branches, providing a direct channel to foreign customers.

International banking specialists are generally well informed about export matters, even in areas that fall outside the usual limits of international banking. If they are unable to provide direct guidance or assistance, they may be able to refer inquirers to other specialists who can. Banks frequently provide consultation and guidance free of charge to their clients, since they derive income primarily from loans to the exporter and from fees for special services. Many banks also have publications available to help exporters. These materials often cover particular countries and their business practices and can be a valuable tool for initial familiarization with foreign industry. Finally, large banks frequently conduct seminars and workshops on letters of credit, documentary collections, and other banking subjects of concern to exporters.

Among the many services a commercial bank may perform for its clients are the following:

- Exchange of currencies.

- Assistance in financing exports.

- Collection of foreign invoices, drafts, letters of credit, and other foreign receivables.

- Transfer of funds to other countries.

- Letters of introduction and letters of credit for travelers.

- Credit information on potential representatives or buyers overseas.

- Credit assistance to the exporter's foreign buyers.

## Export intermediaries

Export intermediaries are of many different types, ranging from giant international companies, many foreign owned, to highly specialized, small operations. They provide a multitude of services, such as performing market research, appointing overseas distributors or commission representatives, exhibiting a client's products at international trade shows, advertising, shipping, and arranging documentation. In short, the intermediary can often take full responsibility for the export end of the business, relieving the manufacturer of all the details except filling orders.

Intermediaries may work simultaneously for a number of exporters on the basis of commissions, salary, or retainer plus commission. Some take title to the goods they handle, buying and selling in their own right. Products of a trading company's clients are often related, although the items usually are noncompetitive. One advantage of using an intermediary is that it can immediately make available marketing resources that a smaller firm would need years to develop on its own. Many export intermediaries also finance sales and extend credit, facilitating prompt payment to the exporter. For more information on using export intermediaries see chapter 4.

## World trade centers and international trade clubs

Local or regional world trade centers and international trade clubs are composed of area business people who represent firms engaged in international trade and shipping, banks, forwarders, customs brokers, government agencies, and other service organizations involved in world trade. These organizations conduct educational programs on international business and organize promotional events to stimulate interest in world trade. Some 80 world trade centers or affiliated associations are located in major trading cities throughout the world.

By participating in a local association, a company can receive valuable and timely advice on world markets and opportunities from business people who are already knowledgeable on virtually any facet of international business. Another important advantage of membership in a local world trade club is the availability of benefits – such as services, discounts, and contacts – in affiliated clubs from foreign countries.

## Chambers of commerce and trade associations

Many local chambers of commerce and major trade associations in the United States provide sophisticated and extensive services for members interested in exporting. Among these services are the following:

- Conducting export seminars, workshops, and round-tables.
- Providing certificates of origin.
- Developing trade promotion programs, including overseas missions, mailings, and event planning.
- Organizing U.S. pavilions in foreign trade shows.
- Providing contacts with foreign companies and distributors.
- Relaying export sales leads and other opportunities to members.
- Organizing transportation routings and shipment consolidations.
- Hosting visiting trade missions from other countries.
- Conducting international activities at domestic trade shows.

In addition, some industry associations can supply detailed information on market demand for products in selected countries or refer members to export management companies. Most trade associations play an active role in lobbying for U.S. trade policies beneficial to their industries. Industry trade associations typically collect and maintain files on international trade news and trends affecting manufacturers. Often they publish articles and newsletters that include government research.

## American chambers of commerce abroad

A valuable and reliable source of market information in any foreign country is the local chapter of the American chamber of commerce. These organizations are knowledgeable about local trade opportunities, actual and potential competition, periods of maximum trade activity, and similar considerations.

American chambers of commerce abroad usually handle inquiries from any U.S. business. Detailed service, however, is ordinarily provided free of charge only for members of affiliated organizations. Some chambers have a set schedule of charges for services rendered to nonmembers. For contact information on American chambers in major foreign markets, see appendix IV.

## International trade consultants and other advisers

International trade consultants can advise and assist a manufacturer on all aspects of foreign marketing. Trade consultants do not normally deal specifically with one product, although they may advise on product adaptation to a foreign market. They research domestic and foreign regulations and also assess commercial and political risk. They conduct foreign market research and establish contacts with foreign government agencies and other necessary resources, such as advertising companies, product service facilities, and local attorneys.

These consultants can locate and qualify foreign joint venture partners as well as conduct feasibility studies for the sale of manufacturing rights, the location and construction of manufacturing facilities, and the establishment of foreign trade branches. After sales agreements are completed, trade consultants can also ensure that follow-through is smooth and that any problems that arise are dealt with effectively.

Trade consultants usually specialize by subject matter and by global area or country. For example, firms may specialize in high-technology exports to the Far East. Their consultants can advise on which agents or distributors are likely to be successful, what kinds of promotion are needed, who the competitors are, and how to deal with them. They are also knowledgeable about foreign government regulations, contract laws, and taxation. Some firms may be more specialized than others; for example, some may be thoroughly knowledgeable on legal aspects and taxation and less knowledgeable on marketing strategies.

Many large accounting firms, law firms, and specialized marketing firms provide international trade consulting services. When selecting a consulting firm, the exporter should pay particular attention to the experience and knowledge of the consultant who is in charge of its project. To find an appropriate firm, advice should be sought from other exporters and some of the other resources listed in this chapter, such as the Department of Commerce district office or local chamber of commerce.

Consultants are of greatest value to a firm that knows exactly what it wants. For this reason, and because private consultants are expensive, it pays to take full advantage of publicly funded sources of advice before hiring a consultant.

## Notes